THE
SUSTAINABILITY
PROJECT

MY JOURNEY FROM TOXIC AND
THROWAWAY TO CLEAN AND GREEN

CARLY TIZZANO

For more information, email carly@carlytizzano.com.

Paperback ISBN: 979-8-9873647-0-3
eBook ISBN: 979-8-9873647-1-0
Library of Congress Control Number: 2022922639

To Mom, Dad, and Mrs. Pope —
Thank you for teaching me how to write and use punctuation,
and for giving me the confidence to write this book.

TABLE OF CONTENTS

INTRODUCTION:
A GIRL LIVING IN A THROWAWAY WORLD

I am a serial murderer. I have killed the environment one small step, one insignificant choice, one mylar-coated birthday balloon, at a time. I have been a plastic-using, environmentally ignorant, consumption machine. I have gone through countless shampoo bottles, Starbucks cups, and squeeze pouches of applesauce. I have tossed out straws, plastic bags, and toothbrushes. I have spent many unnecessary hours in the shower, walked blindly past litter, and driven miles out of the way to get my favorite queso.

I never would have predicted that I would write a book about saving the planet. But here we are.

My journey began two years ago. I was reading *How to Give Up Plastic: A Conscious Guide to Changing the World, One Plastic Bottle at a Time* by Will McCallum, a book I had checked out of the library on a whim. In the book, there is a story about a picture that had gone viral. I'd never seen the picture, but the book's description of rescue workers pulling a plastic straw painfully out of the nose of an innocent sea turtle turned my world upside down.

This was happening in the world? It had to stop!

Of course, on some level, I had known that this kind of harm was happening in the world around me. I knew that plastic floated in the oceans and that landfills were growing larger every day. Up until that moment, however, I hadn't made it a personal mission. I had always believed that other people would make the changes. My mistake.

And now here I am, trying to change that.

Shortly after finishing *How to Give Up Plastic*, I decided that my "word" for the following year, my focus and goal, would be "sustainability." I wanted to figure out how to ensure that my habits, purchases, and lifestyle were in line with living on the earth sustainably. Instead of focusing solely on environmental concerns or ethical ones, I settled on "sustainability" because it is very future-focused. The choices we make today and continue to make tomorrow will produce benefits for us all.

And so, on January 1st, I embarked on the goal of learning more, being gentler on the earth by reducing my waste, and reducing my support of destructive industries. It was a year-long path, one I want to help you to traverse, too. I hope this book will help guide your journey and save you from some of the pitfalls and potholes that I stumbled into along the way.

I am far from perfect even now as I write this book. But the more people I talk to, the more I have realized that most people know that they need to make different choices — they know that many of the choices they are currently making are damaging the earth. But many people have no idea where to start. I understand that. I didn't either.

As I began to live out my sustainability project, there were times I felt paralyzed by indecision and overwhelmed by statistics and information. But I was convinced even more that this book had to be written.

My writing style was influenced by two other books in this genre. *The Happiness Project* by Gretchen Rubin and *The Wellness Project* by Phoebe Lapine both inspired readers with the idea that we can pursue lofty life changes through measured steps of marginal improvement. Changing your life, without changing your life.

These books, and my sustainability project, are "projects" designed to be undertaken during a calendar year. As a New Year's Resolution coach, I know how much change can be made between January 1st and December 31st, so it is no surprise that my project would follow the same pattern. I also understand the power of living in alignment with our personal values. As I planned my own sustainability project, I knew that the coming year would be the perfect way to transform my life while also demonstrating that transformational power to my community and my clients.

And while the main focus of this book is environmental sustainability, that topic touches on other major social issues — world hunger, animal activism, racism, classism, and countless others. This is a beautiful reminder that our actions in this one area can spill over into so many others and vice versa. For example, environmental issues don't affect everyone proportionally.

Statistics show that the wealthiest 10% of the population is responsible for 50% of global emissions. The wealthiest 20% contribute 70% — like the Pareto principle, but not in a good way.

People of color in the US are three times more likely to die from pollution-related diseases, ranging from lung cancer to heart disease to stroke, and they are 1.5 times more likely to be exposed to pollutants in general. They are 79% more likely to live in neighborhoods with toxic industrial pollution and are exposed to 38% higher levels of nitrogen dioxide, which inflames the lungs and can lead to an increased risk of respiratory problems.

These issues don't have easy answers or easy solutions but the statistics do not relieve us of our individual responsibility to the environment we share. We must all work to be informed and take actions that will better care for our planet and our neighbors. Both are infinitely important and being able to make a difference that impacts both is extraordinary.

Government and big businesses play a massive role in sustainability, or rather the lack thereof, in the world today. When both refuse to take the necessary steps towards sustainability, that action, or some part of it, falls to the consumers. Whether they don't listen to us or whether we aren't speaking loudly enough (with our words or our wallets) is a different question, and one I don't intend to delve into in this book. Research indicates that 100 companies are responsible for 71% of global emissions. But that doesn't mean our actions as individuals aren't important. I urge you to fight for legislation that supports sustainable practices, reach out to brands you love (or brands you hate) to revolutionize their practices and increase transparency and sustainability, fight with your words, dollars, and actions. We definitely have a role to play in ensuring that sustainability advances are made on these levels.

In this book, I focus on what we, as consumers and individuals, can do to affect sustainable change — in our habits, practices, and purchases. I'm not discounting the importance of institutional change, and there have been other great books written on that topic, but the actions I wanted to focus on in my sustainability project were my own.

I want to encourage you to make changes in your life. But the effects of these changes will stretch far beyond yourself, into the lives of others, and to the world as a whole. As a wise person once said, we aren't inheriting this world from our forebears, we are borrowing it from our grandchildren.

There is no wrong way to build a sustainable life — except to ignore that you probably need to do it. It is comfortable to think that our actions make little difference. But that is simply not true. And through this book, I hope to inspire you to pursue important, if small, actions.

I share a lot about how our lifestyle, actions, and purchases can impact the planet. But it's not just a long list of items you need to buy, or things to check off, to live a "sustainable" life.

You can still live a sustainable life and use plastic straws sometimes. You can live a sustainable life and eat meat every day. You can live a sustainable life and drive a Suburban — growing up with four siblings, I know some people need to.

When plastic was invented only a few decades ago, it was considered a marvel. But as the decades passed, people began to see the impact it has and will have on the environment in the future.

I want to give you a direction and a starting point. My suggestions will not be perfect. I hope that you will join me in doing what we can, with what we have, with what we know in this current time.

Some people will disagree with me, and that's okay. If they are living a 100% environmentally conscious and sustainable life, I am happy for them and support them in their efforts, 100%. But I think that you can be sustainable, and still dry your clothes in your dryer, and not on a clothesline. Just like you can be healthy and still eat cake. But it is important to understand that you can't likely eat cake, cookies, chicken alfredo, soda, onion rings, chocolate bars, donuts, and fried chicken and still be the healthiest version of yourself — unless you indulge in extreme moderation.

My goal is to help increase your awareness of the choices you make as you progress in your sustainability journey and not to let having a big car, a big family, or a big pile of laundry make you believe that you can't make a big impact.

As I began my journey towards living a more sustainable life, I read numerous articles about the things we do because we think we are helping the earth but actually may not be, or at least not as much as we think. These articles, while well-intentioned, often do much more harm than good. I hope to bring clarity to some of these ideas.

Be aware that you may meet opposition from unexpected places. While you are enjoying the "high" from making incremental changes to improve the environment, you may meet others who will try to convince you that you're doing it wrong. This phenomenon is called "whataboutism." You share about your progress, and someone will say "well, what about…" This often arises with conversations about fast fashion, what milk to drink, reusable grocery bags, and other topics. Whataboutisms may be well-intended but are rarely helpful. They don't initiate action, drive discussion, or further the cause in any way. More often they lead to confusion and hesitation, which stalls or maybe even halts our progress in the direction we want to go.

Sustainability isn't all or nothing. It isn't black and white. It isn't either-or. As long as we are alive, there are some things that we do and participate in that aren't sustainable. Even when we die, how and where we are buried can have drastic environmental consequences (don't worry, we'll talk about that too). I share the facts so you can understand the impact of whatever choices you make, and I will encourage you to experiment, try, shift, and change. But what you do is ultimately up to you. And questioning the journey of others, or peppering them with whataboutisms, is unlikely to move any of us towards sustainability.

While I focus primarily on environmental sustainability in this book, I also reference being financially responsible and sustainable as well. Whatever your financial status, you can support sustainability — through your lifestyle and through the purchases you make.

Sustainability isn't about having money to buy new eco-friendly things or starting to compost in the backyard. It isn't even about dedicating yourself to clearing roadside litter. It is about simplicity, ease, and figuring out what works for you. It's using less and using what we have. This book was written to meet you where you're at right now; to increase your awareness; give you the tools to consciously make decisions on how to live a sustainable life; and to encourage you to move forward, in the right direction, one step at a time, one month at a time.

The point of this book isn't to convince you that saving our planet and taking sustainable action is important. I hope that if you are reading this, you already believe that wholeheartedly. I am so glad to have you along on this journey with me. You may not know what you should be doing (even though you probably know there is a lot you could be doing), and you may be overwhelmed by the research, statistics, information, and projections.

That's why I'm here. I'm going to walk you through my journey, starting with the same overwhelm, through curiosity, and into conscious, intentional, imperfect action. The first step is hard, but you've already taken it. You're here. And don't worry, we'll walk through the rest together.

As I began the journey of researching and writing this book, I felt alone. And I can't tell you the number of times that I slammed down my phone or shut my laptop and sat feeling sad, lost, and overwhelmed.

The social campaigns are endless. The steps that could be taken are infinite. The options and possibilities and upsides and downsides are innumerable.

I've laughed when I found something amazing or read something hopeful. And I've cried when I read about plastic in the oceans or when I saw pictures of animals in cages with beauty products smeared across their faces.

I had to take action.

The only question that remains is what action to take.

And that, I soon realized, was a very, very tough question.

CHAPTER 1

JANUARY: STARTING STRONG

I knew I was about to undertake my sustainability project. It was planned, I was ready.

They say the longest journey starts with a single step, and for me, that step was a paragraph in a book about a turtle and a straw. From that small beginning, my journey toward sustainability began.

Those who, like me, live in the Pacific Northwest know that in January you have very little hope of seeing summer or the sun ever again. But despite the dismal weather and being continually cold, I was ready to start my sustainability journey — or so I thought.

I wanted to know what the recycling numbers mean on the bottom of my soap and shampoo bottles. I knew I wanted to upgrade to reusable products and find nontoxic cleaners and makeup to benefit my home and my skin. I was prepared to walk more, drive less, and bring my reusable grocery bags to the store.

I set a general goal to spend the new year embarked on this sustainability project and to make sure that my actions were aligned with this overall focus for the year. But I didn't realize how much of a project it would turn out to be. I planned out February through December broadly, but January was still a blank slate so I decided to spend the cold dark month of January developing a base level of knowledge and understanding about sustainability and the other factors that play a role in the well-being of our planet.

Looking back now, I wonder what I was thinking! I am a very Type A person. I'm a 1 on the Enneagram. I'm a life coach and own a professional organizing company. I started a blog years ago just for fun. I don't do things without a plan, and I certainly don't set out on a year-long adventure without double-checking my direction, filling my water bottle, and packing a bag full of snacks.

But thankfully, my lack of planning on this occasion is, I think, what put me exactly where I needed to be.

Early in the year, I stumbled across Instagram's discovery tab (and I confess that since I have spent excessive amounts of time there). I enjoy immersing myself in the amazing content posted by millions of people I will never know.

That's where I came across a photo of a man standing in front of a garbage can inside a well-known coffee retailer. The photo showed the man with his arm going into the side of the can that read "trash" but his hand could be seen coming out the top of the other side of the can that read "recycling." Despite the appearance, everything was actually ending up in the trash. This eye-opening photo revealed a sad truth: even though it may appear that a business is taking responsible steps towards caring for the planet, the reality may be very different.

That photo sent me down an Instagram rabbit hole (it doesn't take much). I soon found myself looking at dozens of sustainability posts and other things under #greenwashing.

I couldn't get that image out of my head.

Things escalated when I saw a post about how long it takes for certain things to break down in the environment. Mylar balloons, for example, which my family buys to celebrate birthdays and graduations and every event in between, never break down. Never. Ever. They last forever.

A few days later, I was sharing with my friend, Heidi, about my sustainability project. I told her about my discovery and my newfound fear of a future filled with deflated foil balloons. In my nightmare, the balloons blow aimlessly along roads like tumbleweeds, float across oceans like seaweed, and are compressed together like bricks to construct buildings and bridges. A WALL-E-style world, composed entirely of deflated Mylar balloons.

"Wow," Heidi said, with a small smile, seemingly unsure of what to say about the dystopian future I had described.

I couldn't stop. "Now, I know it is an unlikely reality — especially since we will run out of helium long before that could ever happen. Not too long from now, actually, so it is unlikely our children will ever have foil balloons, or balloons of any kind — not that I would buy them, knowing what I know now."

Heidi laughed, and we moved on to discussing less dramatic aspects of my project. We agreed that while many things around us seemed to be speeding up, at the same time, many things appeared to be winding down. I felt desperate to know what I could do to protect the earth, while still enjoying things like birthday parties (sans balloons).

GREENWASHING

Even before starting my project, I had tried to choose the green option whenever possible. I wanted to live in line with the values I was developing and picking up laundry detergent with a tree on the label or that read "green" was an easy switch.

But as I began my research, I quickly discovered (and also already understood at some level) that sustainability is much than label (or trash can) deep. I had fallen into the greenwashing trap, and it was time to fight my way out.

The Journal of Consumer Research recently shared about the "greenconsumption effect." This is when a person uses a sustainable or "green" product and feels good about themselves and their choices. They often have a 'warm glow feeling,' that they don't get when using a conventional counterpart.

Greenwashing happens when a company attempts to label a product with deceptive jargon about its environmental friendliness without being fully transparent, or without making any real changes to lessen its impact on the environment. As more consumers (like me and you) desire to make more sustainable choices and purchases, the issue of greenwashing becomes very important. When companies project the mirage of environmental concern without taking actions to back it up, it can be hard for consumers to make the right choices or to even know what those choices might be.

Unfortunately, greenwashing is a prevalent practice. In 2010, 4,744 "green" products from the US and Canada were surveyed and 95% were found guilty of greenwashing.

Although greenwashing is technically monitored under the Green Guides of the Federal Trade Commission, companies aren't always held accountable, since vague statements and failure to disclose information are rarely prosecuted. Determining whether a product has been greenwashed or whether a company is actually working to protect the environment, and whether we should or should not purchase a particular product, are difficult decisions that consumers are left to make.

Greenwashing normally takes place on the surface level, such as on the product label, whereas the evidence to support these claims, everything from how items are sourced, produced, shipped, and distributed, can be harder to identify. To make this identification easier, the environmental marketing agency, TerraChoice, has developed a list of the "seven sins of greenwashing: hidden trade-off, no proof, vagueness, worshiping false labels, irrelevance, lesser of two evils, and fibbing."[1]

While a few companies are enacting positive changes to protect the environment, too many others prefer to just appear to be taking action. As with the food industry, terms like "healthy," "clean," "organic," or "all-natural," sound pleasing, and might make you reach for a product, but these words don't necessarily speak the truth about what is inside the package.

Even if a product lives up to its packaging and is actually "eco-friendly," it may not be sustainable. Ethics and social justice issues also play a role in determining sustainability, and without evidentiary backup, this is just another example of greenwashing. We'll explore this further later.

Companies producing everything from food to detergent to shampoo utilize greenwashing in an attempt to increase sales and improve public perception. They may use ubiquitous or vague terms that sound great but mean nothing. "Natural," "eco-friendly," "non-toxic," "chemical-free," "biodegradable," "socially responsible," "green," "bioplastic," and even "sustainable," are commonly used without real substantiation.

Because greenwashing continues to happen, for now, it is up to us to try to decipher whether a claim is true or simply greenwashing. To do this, we start with the label. We need to make sure the company can back up its claims with specific data or research. Look for certifications on the product label — such as Fair Trade Certified, Certified B Corporation, or Food Justice Certified. Some certifications not only mean that the product or corporation is taking steps to ensure minimal environmental harm, but also that workers are treated fairly, and products are produced sustainably. Some brands will also indicate the carbon footprint of the item on the packaging, which is another practical way to substantiate the environmental impact of the product rather than a simple label proclaiming it as "green."

As with certifications, we can also look for products or companies with third-party assessments or awards such as Fairtrade, the EPA's Safer Choice, GreenSeal, OEKO-TEX standard, and the Global Organic Textile Standard.

It is worth noting that while some smaller brands cannot afford to get certified, they may be a viable sustainable option, especially if they are local to you.

If the product label doesn't give you the answers you are looking for, you can determine whether greenwashing is occurring by researching the company's website and presence. The first thing to look for is whether they actually discuss their sustainability efforts. If it isn't discussed at all, that's a red flag. If a company does share their environmental goals, look for specificity of steps and a timeline — moving towards something that is statistically insignificant or vague isn't likely to have a big impact. Truly transparent companies will share facts, statistics, reports, and explanations.

It is also worth considering whether the company you are researching is working to reduce their emissions or whether they are merely planning to purchase offsets (we will discuss offsetting more in Chapter 4). Companies that are truly striving to benefit the environment may go so far as to invest in climate-safe technology or lobby for environmental policies.[2]

Expect and seek transparency, and hopefully, that is what you will find.

It's easy to grab the product that looks more environmentally friendly — paper over plastic, or recycled-looking cardboard over the fresher, newer-looking alternative. And although these packaging options are something to look for and are likely the better choice over a plastic-wrapped alternative, the packaging doesn't inherently mean anything about the product itself. And even when the product is really and truly "green" it is often up to us to close the loop and make sure it stays that way — by repairing, reusing, or recycling.

Remember that even the brand with the certifications and the recycled and recyclable packaging isn't perfect. The things that we consume, and the way they are produced, inherently have an impact on the planet.[3] We can do our best to be educated as to what that impact is, and take the necessary steps, or make the necessary purchases, to minimize the impact when and where we can.

The Good Housekeeping Institute conducted a survey that found that just 2% of respondents aren't concerned about making "green" choices in their homes.[4] Hopefully, as time goes on, more and more companies will listen to the 98% of people who want to purchase clean, green products, and take the actions necessary to label their products and provide the evidence to back up their claims.

Don't be fooled by the word "green" or the sprout image on the package, unless you know that the sustainability claims are more than surface deep.

THE REALITY OF RECYCLING

I've certainly been guilty of tossing a dirty container into the trash, instead of taking the time and effort to clean it or to find out if it was recyclable. I knew I wasn't alone, but I had no idea that over 80% of the items that are sent to landfills could have been recycled instead. Many of these items will take hundreds or thousands of years to break down in the landfill.

On a scale from solution to pollution, I was a walking red plastic Solo cup. But I was a Solo cup in solidarity with the majority of the population.

Actually, I've been committed to recycling for as long as I can remember. I placed the can with the blue lid alongside the green can at the curb on trash day. But although I considered myself a "recycler," I never paid a lot of attention to the numbers on the bottom of the recyclable containers. If I could see the arrows, into the recycling can it went. I've since learned that while the arrows are a general indicator of recyclability, the number inside the arrows is actually more important.

Growing up, I remember seeing posters portraying what could and could not go into the recycling can, but I never understood how the chart correlated with the numbers. So, when I decided to start my sustainability project, I knew I needed to make sure I had all the information necessary to take purposeful action. I needed to figure out what those numbers meant.

I quickly learned that these numbers indicate different types of recyclables. These are just general guidelines about what can be recycled, so it's important to check the local or county guidelines to ensure that the items you are putting out on the street to be recycled actually can be. The variations on what can be accepted in a given area often result from the capacity and capabilities of each recycling center.[5, 6]

One type of recyclable that we've all had significant contact with is labeled with the number 1, which identifies products made from polyethylene terephthalate (PETE). PETE is one of the most easily recyclable materials and is often found in soda or water bottles. When recycled, it can be made into another bottle, or into polyester fibers for carpet or fleece clothing. It should be mentioned here that PETE-containers release endocrine-disrupting chemicals over time, so a product made out of PETE should only be used once, not refilled and used again and again. A major step we can take to reduce number 1 recyclables is to take a reusable cup or water bottle with us when we're on the go. After all, washing and reusing are the best options when possible.

Recyclables labeled with the number 2 are products made with high-density polyethylene (HDPE), which is often used for containers that contain bleach, detergent, milk, or hair care products. These containers can also be easily recycled once they have been cleaned. These materials can be remade into bags or other bottles, or into products as diverse as decks and frisbees. It is worth noting that some of the additives in HDPE have never been tested for public safety. Thankfully, new alternatives are being created which have a lower environmental footprint, in terms of how the products and their containers are produced. I will be sharing more about some of these companies and products in the coming chapters.

Number 3 recyclables, made of polyvinyl chloride (PVC), are familiar. This material is found in, of course, PVC pipes, but can also be found in furniture, shower curtains, clothing, toys, and packaging. Unfortunately, PVC is very difficult to recycle and is not accepted by most curbside recycling programs. PVC is the most toxic kind of plastic, leaching carcinogens and phthalates, and has been linked to cancer, organ toxicity, reproductive problems, and other significant health issues. This isn't a material that I want to come into frequent contact with, much less see used for things as innocent as toys. If you are faced with the decision to purchase a product that would conventionally be made with PVC, I urge you to consider whether there is an alternative. While it may be harder to find a shower curtain without some amount of PVC, you can probably find children's toys without it.

Number 4 recyclables, while less dangerous to public health, have a worrying environmental impact. Low-density polyethylene (LDPE) is used in grocery and sandwich bags, laminates, six-pack rings, plastic wrap, and playground slides. Most of the time, these items can be recycled to become more of the same products. While they don't necessarily pose a chemical concern to our health, these products break down very slowly if they are discarded and not recycled. Unfortunately, like number 3 recyclables, number 4 recyclables are not widely accepted by most curbside recycling programs. However, more and more communities are working to be able to accept and process them, and some stores will take back their plastic bags. Fortunately, there are many ways to reduce our use of these items in general or substitute them with more sustainable options, which we will discuss in-depth later in this book. And although we may largely be able to switch to alternatives, as someone who grew up using playgrounds with metal slides, I think future generations will appreciate it if we stick with LDPE for playground equipment.

Number 5 recyclables consist of polypropylene (PP) and can be found in products like packaging, clothing, carpets, stationery, rope, diapers, dairy containers, and medicine bottles. Polypropylene has never been tested for public safety, although it is used in products that have close contact with our bodies. As with number 4 recyclables, many communities are working to accept polypropylene in their curbside recycling programs. When properly recycled, polypropylene can be used to make many things including battery cables, brooms, ice scrapers, bicycle racks, rakes, and my favorite, signal lights. Aside from dairy containers, many of these items are never recycled, although they certainly could be. There aren't many clear-cut alternatives to number 5 recyclables, so it's best to avoid these products wherever possible and recycle them when we can't.

Number 6 recyclables are made from polystyrene (PS), which is commonly known as Styrofoam. We find this material in everything from packing peanuts, fast food containers, and meat trays, to DVD cases and insulation. Unfortunately, despite its low weight, it is bulky and extremely difficult to recycle. Polystyrene leaches toxic chemicals for its entire lifespan. Many curbside recycling programs do not accept number 6 items, but those that do, turn the polystyrene into more of the same. This is a material we should replace with more sustainable alternatives. For example, we could use glass, ceramic, or metal cups instead of Styrofoam ones, and shredded newspaper could replace packing peanuts.

Finally, number 7 recyclables are everything else, including combinations of the materials identified above. They are unpredictable to deal with so most curbside recycling programs won't accept them. Examples of number 7 recyclables are nylon, DVDs, sunglasses, phone cases, and even some bulletproof materials. The good news is that if you find yourself with a lot of one type of number 7 recyclables, such as DVDs, there may be companies or organizations that will accept and process these items. Some of the materials in the number 7 category contain hormone-disrupting chemicals that can cause infertility and other serious health issues. Whenever possible, it is ideal to avoid number 7 recyclables or opt for longer-lasting, higher-quality items that you'll be able to use longer.

I found it challenging to keep all of these numbers, categories, and materials straight! I looked online to see if anyone had written a catchy song to help me remember the important things — alas, one has yet to be created. Maybe I will write one in the future for all of us who find ourselves hesitating over the recycling can.

To recap, most curbside recycling programs will accept recyclables identified with the numbers 1 and 2. For items labeled 3-7, it is best to check with your county or other local municipality. They may accept additional categories of recyclables and it is worth checking to make sure you know which ones those are. Ultimately, if you find yourself confused or overwhelmed or just forget what is what, that is okay. I have been there, too. The key is for each of us to take responsibility and make time to check before tossing an item in the trash can. Any small step that we take makes a difference!

Whenever possible, choose and reuse metal and glass materials. If you take plastic, or some other "recyclable," please dispose of it properly.

In the United States, a recent survey found that while 94% of people support recycling, and 74% say it is a priority, the average recycling rate is still only 34.7%.[7] This leaves almost two-thirds of potential recyclables heading to landfills, contributing to greenhouse gas emissions, in incinerators, or floating in the oceans as litter. The sad truth is that the average piece of litter will be found within 16 feet of a rubbish bin. Good intentions are certainly important, but only good intentions followed by purposeful action will make a difference.

The average American generates over 4 pounds of trash each day for the landfill. Between take-out dinners, shampoo bottles, convenience coffees, and daily Amazon deliveries, I can see how this is quite possible. Ideally, we can reduce that number by at least the items that can and should end up in the recycling can.

Once I understood the recycling fundamentals, I knew it was time to take the extra step and research for myself what recycling looks like in my county and its environmental impact. As I researched, I was shocked to find out where these materials ultimately end up and how they get there. The journey to my recycling can is just the beginning.

All of the recycling for my county and the surrounding area is transported to Tacoma, a city just outside of Seattle, to be sorted. From there, it is put into bales and sold to domestic and international buyers. If the bale is clean and uncontaminated, the processors are willing to pay a higher price. This leads to a rebate on the county's garbage and recycling bills. However, if the bale is contaminated or cannot be sold, the processors will want to be paid to take it. If it is not sold, the bale will have to be re-sorted and decontaminated.

Even before my sustainability project, I had heard that if someone neglected to thoroughly clean a container before tossing it into the recycling can, it could contaminate an entire load of otherwise clean recyclables. Ever since I have put extra effort into making sure that the items I recycle won't contaminate everything else, which, if you've ever tried to clean out a peanut butter jar, you know is quite an effort.

Unfortunately, the long journey for my county's recyclables does not end in Tacoma. The plastic containers (bottles, jugs, and dairy tubs) are taken to a "secondary" facility in Canada to be sorted again. From there, the plastics are sold to manufacturers all over the world. While I'm very excited that recyclables are given a second life, the many steps, the distance traveled, and the energy required is almost overwhelming. To make matters worse, when the price of oil is low, manufacturers are less likely to use recycled plastics and more likely to use virgin plastics.

But wait, there's more. Some of the paper recycling, food boxes, and cartons are able to be sold to other parts of the state. But the rest ends up in places like India, Malaysia, or other countries in that region — a long way for paper to travel just to have a second life![8]

The outlook for metal cans is better. They can be recycled repeatedly and will be back on the shelves within a couple of months! I wonder if I've ever bought a can that was made from a can I've bought before. Tin cans used in my county are processed right here in Seattle. Aluminum cans must travel further and are often recycled in the southeastern part of the United States. While that seems like a great distance, it's not nearly as far away as Asia!

Aluminum, according to some reports, is the most valuable material in your recycling can. It's commonly found in beverage and food cans for both man and animals, in baking trays, and of course, in aluminum foil. Sadly, Americans throw away about $1 billion worth of aluminum each year! The demand for aluminum continues to grow and when it is recycled, it saves 90% of the energy that would be used to produce new metals. If you throw away an aluminum can, instead of recycling it, the energy wasted is equivalent to filling the can halfway with gasoline and dumping it on the ground. On the other hand, if that same can is recycled, the energy saved is enough to power a 100-watt light bulb for almost a whole day, power your TV or computer for 2-3 hours, or play a full album on your iPhone. Fortunately, aluminum is a highly recycled material and about 75% of all aluminum processed in the US is still in use. That's great, but we still have a way to go, because every three months in the US, we throw away enough aluminum to rebuild our entire commercial air fleet.

Glass is another infinitely recyclable material. These recyclables don't have a clear journey but are usually purchased by a buyer. I found it interesting to learn that the glass is crushed in processing and "is sometimes purchased to serve as an 'alternative daily cover,' which is a material placed over the surface of an active landfill to control pests, fires, odors, and blowing litter." When you consider all the work we do to keep recyclables out of the landfill, it seems painfully ironic that some of these materials end up there on purpose, even if it is to serve an albeit important one.[9]

About 10 million metric tons of glass are disposed of in the US each year, but of the 33% that is sent for recycling, only about 40% of it will actually be recycled. Most of it will be thrown away. The US throws away enough glass each week to fill a 1,350-foot building. In contrast, some European countries, like Germany and Switzerland, have a glass recycling rate closer to 90%. Improper cleaning, cross-contamination, or misplacement into the wrong recycling bin results in a lower rate in the US and other countries. Consumer education and regulations to increase recycling rates could help raise the US and overall world rates to ensure that this infinitely recyclable material has the chance to be so.

As I clicked away from the county website, I realized with frustration that although I knew that the recycling centers weren't "just around the corner," I had never stopped to consider that they might actually be "around the world."[10]

THE PLASTIC PROBLEM

While learning about recycling is important, I felt that I needed a deeper understanding of the problem, so I spent some time getting familiar with one of the biggest banes of the sustainable world — plastic.

The first iteration of what we now call "plastic" was created in 1907. As the science surrounding plastic developed, the uses for this material grew. More new plastics emerged in the 1930s and by the 1940s, plastic was being used by the US military during World War II. As a result, plastic production almost quadrupled, from 213 million pounds at the start of the war, to 818 million pounds by 1945. When the war ended, the production of plastic continued to expand.

New York hosted the first National Plastics Exposition at the end of that decade, and thousands of consumers, who were weary of strife and scarcity, came to see how new plastic products could lead to an era of abundance. When the Chairman of the National Plastics Exposition announced, "Nothing can stop plastics," the excitement was real and palpable. In retrospect, however, we can see how prophetic he was.

In 1955, *Life* magazine released a story titled "Throwaway Living," which featured an image of a family throwing dozens of common disposable items into the air while smiling broadly. The article begins, "the objects flying through the air in this picture would take 40 hours to clean — except that no housewife need bother. They are all meant to be thrown away after use."[11] None of the ideas expressed here have aged well. The feature goes on to list the items pictured, ranging from vases to water wings to ashtrays — all meant to be thrown away after use. Just a few decades ago, this was considered to be the height of luxury; to be able to dispose of things once they had fulfilled their purpose. Convenience was king. In many ways, we share this attitude today. Unfortunately, the idea that things can be thrown "away" reveals little about where the "away" is, and how much disposability it can accommodate.

Since the 1950s and the *Life* magazine feature, 10 billion pounds of plastic have been produced. And production shows no indication of slowing, as half of the plastic ever made has been made in just over the last decade. In 2018, 400 million tons were produced and production is projected to quadruple by 2050. As we've learned, some of this plastic gets recycled, but the majority of it ends up in landfills, ditches, oceans, and incinerators, and too much of it is in the environment breaking down into microplastics (we'll get to that shortly).

The explosion of plastic and its appearance in countless items we buy and use today was encouraged by advertisements like "Throwaway Living." As the use of plastic grew in those early years, our knowledge of its impact has grown in the more recent ones. Many people consider plastic to be the most scorned material of our day. In fact, American novelist Norman Mailer went so far as to refer to plastic as "a malign force of the universe… the social equivalent of cancer."

The recycling rate for plastics currently hovers around 14%. That fact, and the fact that only 30% of the plastics that have been made are still in use today, means that innumerable plastic items have been tossed into landfills, dropped along roadways, or left floating in rivers, lakes and oceans. Many of these items will take about 450 years to break down.

People began to wake up to the plastic problem a few decades ago when it was just a fraction of the problem it is today. To compare, the world produced 50 million tons of plastic in 1977, and in 2015 it produced 322 million tons. And we know that most of the plastic produced from 1977 to the present still exists. Yet we continue to produce hundreds of millions of tons of new plastic on top of the thousands of millions already in existence. The plastic and the plastic problem will continue to grow, cumulatively, every single year.

The amount of plastics produced each year weighs about the same as all of humanity. And that's how much humanity actually weighs now, not humanity at its goal weight. That's a lot of plastic that will break down, pile up, and wash onto our shores.

Did you know that the equivalent of 5 grocery bags of plastic waste for every foot of coastline currently ends up in the ocean each year? And if we continue on our current trajectory, the amount of global plastic waste is predicted to triple.[12]

Um, yikes.

If plastic pollution isn't slowed or stopped, by 2050 it will outweigh all of the fish in the ocean combined. Trust me, those sharks down there weigh a lot.

Speaking of sharks, I have long been terrified by the simple fact of their existence. They are a consistent theme in my worst nightmares (so much so that I even check backyard swimming pools before jumping in!). The fact that sharks rarely kill humans has never helped. The number of reported deaths by sharks per year varies wildly, somewhere between 0 and 6 people per year, on average. However, the number of sharks killed by humans is pretty consistent — about 100 million sharks per year. Or about 11,500 sharks an hour. Turns out, we are the real predators. And although the vast majority of those sharks are killed by things other than pollution, it is definitely one of the factors. A research team from the University of Exeter determined that hundreds of sharks die after getting tangled in drifting "ghost nets" and other plastic waste.

The sad reality of how man's lifestyle impacts marine life does not end with sharks. 54% of marine animals will become entangled in plastic in some form and 100 million will die from plastic pollution each year. Above the water, a million seabirds will die as a result of plastic pollution and it's estimated that 99% of seabird species will have some form of plastic in their stomachs by 2050.[13]

The plastic dumped in the oceans every year is equivalent to a full garbage truck of plastic being emptied into the ocean every minute of every day, all year. And even if you live far away from the ocean, about 80% of the plastic in the ocean comes from land and only about 20% actually comes from boats and the people on them.

The plastic pollution in the ocean is so prevalent that an average of 46,000 pieces of plastic are floating per square mile of the ocean's surface. If you've ever seen a picture of the earth from space, you know that surface is pretty vast. And the problem doesn't end at the surface. The book *How to Give Up Plastic* landed a second staggering blow other than that sent me down the path to my sustainability project when it discussed this topic. It reported that Greenpeace ships, which have been testing for ocean plastics since the 1990s, have been finding ever-increasing amounts of plastic. In fact, "from the frozen Arctic tundra to the deepest trenches in the ocean, scientists have found plastics almost everywhere in the world…"

MICROPLASTICS

Plastic isn't the only problem. It is also the tiny microplastics that plastic breaks down into. Microplastics are pieces of plastic measuring less than 5 millimeters and many can only be seen under a microscope. Recently researchers have even begun talking about nanoplastics — fragments of plastic smaller than 1,000 nanometers. There is no way to eliminate these particles and they will continue to break down into smaller and smaller pieces over time.

As the research by Greenpeace indicates, the problem is widespread. Research done in 2019 found a substantial amount of microplastic in the snow in the Arctic. And the effect of microplastics doesn't fall solely on the environment.

The average American adult unknowingly consumes about 110,000 particles of microplastic each year, the size of a credit card every week. I definitely didn't count the 52 credit cards I would be unintentionally consuming this year in my health plan, and I don't think that it's in line with any recommended diets. The amount we consume isn't surprising when you realize that microplastics have been found in beer, salt, seafood, sugar, alcohol, and honey. They also end up on food that was stored in plastic packaging and result in our ingesting the microplastics along with the food.

Not only are microplastics in our food, but 81% of the world's tap water is also contaminated. Since plastics are generally made from petrochemicals, they easily leech into our water and, from there, enter the food chain. If you drink solely tap water, you may only receive about 4,000 plastic particles from the water you drink. However, if you drink primarily bottled water, you will consume closer to 90,000 plastic particles each year.[14]

We even inhale them like dust.

The effect of these microplastics in our body remains to be seen and certainly varies depending on the type of plastic we ingest. However, as Pete Myers, Ph.D., and chief scientist at Environmental Health Sciences has pointed out, "there cannot be no effect." Like smog in the atmosphere, microplastics are undeniably there, and the long-term consequences to our bodies and our health are unlikely to be positive.

The microplastic problem is the perfect example of how the plastic issue not only affects the planet globally but also affects us individually. We all suffer from the impact of plastic pollution.

Water treatment plants may be able to filter out about 99% of microplastics, but of the 8 million tons of plastic that make it into the ocean each year, they account for approximately one-fifth. They affect marine microorganisms by altering their feeding behavior, reproduction, and larval development, which, through the food chain, can impact the health of the whole marine ecosystem. If microorganisms are consuming plastic instead of the nutrients that they need, the deficiency will multiply up the food chain.

And it does. At least two-thirds of the world's fish currently suffer from ingesting plastic in some form. But it doesn't stop there. People will eat those fish or possibly even the bigger fish that ate them.

It is staggering to think of the change plastic has brought on the world in a little over 100 years. While this can be very disheartening, it serves as an important reminder of the great positive change we can make over the course of the next 100 years. Taking intentional action with the goal of making a difference is certainly more work than passively consuming, but at this point, we have few other options.

Humanity has lived without plastic before, and not that long ago. There was a time in our recent past when disposable was not the default and throw-away was not an option. While plastics, and our demand for them, will never completely disappear, we can take a lesson from history, and work to diminish the negative, while maximizing the good, and using what we have learned to create a plan for the future.

SOFT PLASTIC ISN'T A SOLUTION

Plastic bags and plastic film, which is wrapped around products you buy online, cannot just be tossed in the recycle bin. At least, not in most places. But once again, be sure to check your local recycling requirements.

Most plastic bags — like those you get from the grocery store (although hopefully, you won't continue to use those when you have finished reading this book) or bread bags can be recycled, but not through curbside recycling. Most soft or filmy plastics like candy wrappers, the film from the top of a microwave lunch, or cellophane from a baked good cannot be recycled. They are trash.

If you live in a place that doesn't accept plastic film in curbside recycling, that's okay. But it is still important to take the extra step to learn how and where to recycle it — and then take the necessary additional step to follow through. You may know of a local drop-off location for plastic film. If not, you can visit plasticfilmrecycling.org to find a location. Although walking into the local Walmart with a plastic bag full of other plastic bags may feel awkward at first, it will eventually become second nature. And you will appreciate having use of the space under the sink that currently houses an accumulation of plastic bags.

Additionally, please don't toss soft plastics into the recycling can if you know they aren't accepted. This is "wishcycling," which can clog up the recycling machinery at your local processing plant and cause other, potentially larger, issues.

WISHCYCLING

When you toss something into the recycle can, more out of a hope that it will be recycled rather than knowing that it will, you are wishcycling. This practice is also known as aspirational recycling. While innocent on the surface, wishcycling can be dangerous and detrimental. An entire load of recyclable materials may end up in the landfill because of one misplaced item.

Unfortunately, this is a pretty prevalent problem. The National Waste & Recycling Association reports that contamination rates are around 25 percent. Recycling centers can sort recyclables from non-recyclables, but this extra work leaves them with trash to deal with.

Contaminants could be the plastic film mentioned above, paper coffee cups, pretty much any items that aren't cleaned properly, or even perfectly good recyclables disposed of in a plastic bag.

This is important! Don't put your recyclables inside a trash/plastic bag. Or at least, don't try to recycle them that way. Recycling numbers exist to help determine what should be put in your recycling can — and what shouldn't. Always do a quick search to determine which numbers and other materials are accepted in your neighborhood recycling program.

If you aren't sure if something should go into the recycling can, check. Lots of materials can be recycled, but not through curbside recycling. Tossing these items in the can would definitely be wishcycling. Instead, search your local area for programs or places that accept these items for recycling. And if you can't find a way to recycle them, unfortunately, it is probably best to toss them into the trash can. They will probably end up in a landfill but won't take a load of recyclable material with them.

The more often you come across something to dispose of, the more sure you will become of how to properly dispose of it. And that is also the perfect opportunity to consider reducing your use of that recurring product, item, or material, if possible.

THE CYCLE

Before we dive into the rest of the year, and all the things that I learned and did throughout my sustainability project, I wanted to take a minute to share about the "cycle." Once a product has been manufactured and sold, I think of it as having joined the cycle of all the other products that exist. We currently live in what is, for the most part, a linear economy. Things are produced, sold, consumed, and then disposed of. Some research suggests that 99% of the items people buy are disposed of within 6 months of purchasing them, and the material is not recovered for reuse.

On the other end of the spectrum is the idealized circular economy which focuses on recovering materials that have reached the end of their current use and preventing excess waste and preserving energy by keeping items in use for as long as is feasible. There are different theories as to how to make this practicable, and theories as to how to enact the different components — energy preservation and management, materials recycling, and so on. On the whole, to transition from the more linear economy that we have now, to more of a circular economy, we need to focus on designing, developing, and distributing products with longevity that can be easily repaired or remanufactured.[15]

This is important because a lot of what I have learned about living a more sustainable life comes back to making sure that you are adding as few new things into the cycle (linear or not) as possible, or even as few components as possible. When you use or buy something that has already been used and produced, and thus is already part of the cycle, nothing new is being added.

So many things are bought, used, and disposed of, with no second life or continuing purpose. Thanks to recycling, some materials can be reused or remade into new (or sometimes the same) things. However, when we can make the cycle even more circular and reuse, repair, resell, and recycle, the cycle becomes tighter and fewer things spin out of it into the landfill.

I struggled with this idea at first, because I thought of all the large and small stores across the country, full of products. It was difficult to think that purchasing shampoo in a bar instead of a bottle (fewer waste components produced) could make a difference. After all, someone else would come along behind me and buy the shampoo in the bottle. But I realized that when I don't buy the shampoo in the bottle, and you don't buy the shampoo in the bottle, and maybe a few other people who read this book do the same, we are making a difference! We are also sending a message with our money that we want to purchase environmentally friendly products.

Even if you feel as though you are the only one reaching for the sustainable option, paying more for it, and you don't fully know what impact your choice will have, that is absolutely not a reason not to take action. It will make a difference. It will have an impact! It is one less bottle in the cycle and, ultimately, one less bottle in a landfill.

RECYCLING AS A LONG-TERM ANSWER

Unfortunately, recycling is not the long-term solution that we've been led to believe it is. Many businesses involved in the plastic industry have invested lots of money to make us believe that recycling is the answer — or at least a big part of the answer. And as long as we believe it is, there will be no reason to look at or address the real issue — the continued production and consumption of plastic. Plastic is less recyclable than we've been led to believe, and recycling as a whole is not a sustainable solution. Yes, we need to recycle the things that can be recycled, and we need to make sure that those items are clean so they can be processed properly. But unfortunately, managing the problem is not enough to achieve true sustainability or efficiency in the long run.

As we now know, only 9% of recyclable material is recycled. The other 91% ends up in an incinerator, landfill, or the environment. And much of what is recycled is too contaminated to be properly processed. In early 2018, China stopped accepting all recycled materials with a contamination rate of 0.5% or higher. Unfortunately, even the best processing facilities in the United States have a contamination level of approximately 4%.

Terracycle is a company dedicated to collecting hard to recycle items and recycling them. They receive shipments of everything from electronics to latex paint, which are weighed and sorted into different material types (plastic, metal alloys, fibers, etc.). From there, the materials are shredded, melted down, and combined with other additives to become usable, raw components which can then cycle back into the supply chain to become new products.

Even then, recycling isn't a circular process. Yes, it takes used materials and transforms them so they can be used and maybe one day remade again — if we're lucky. But to make that possible, a lot of additional energy, water, chemicals, and effort are required. And most of the time, even the most recyclable items are downcycled into lower quality products that may not be able to be recycled the next time around and will end up in a landfill.

It is important that we recycle, but it is more important that we reduce our need to recycle.

Recycling won't solve the environmental issues that we are facing or stop the overall net negative effect of our consumerism. Recycling won't solve the problem. It won't even reverse the problem. But I do believe that it is a part — maybe a small part, but still a part — of the solution.

Given that global recycling numbers hover around 14%, I have to imagine there would be something powerful in our ability to recycle the other 86%. Recycling reduces pollution, keeps things out of landfills, and reduces the need for new raw materials in the production of products.

Many people and organizations have suggested other solutions to this growing problem, everything from stopping production of all items that can't be completely recycled, to forcing companies to take back all pieces, components, and items that can't be recycled and making them responsible for the waste, to any number of other alternative and creative solutions. What will happen with these suggestions and their potential effectiveness remains to be seen, but I remain focused on what we can do today as consumers in the world that exists currently. And part of that involves recycling.

CO2

Along with plastic, one of the topics that comes up again and again in environmental discussions is carbon emissions. Although I had a cursory familiarity with the topic (thank you, 7th-grade earth science), I knew I needed to understand a bit more about the impact of CO_2 on the environment before embarking on the rest of my project.

Carbon dioxide is such a large part of the discussion because it is the most common and prevalent greenhouse gas in the atmosphere. It is also considered to be the "baseline" greenhouse gas, and all other greenhouse gases are measured against it.

Whether we are discussing CO_2 or any other greenhouse gas, two major factors need to be considered — their lifetime and warming potential. The lifetime of a greenhouse gas is how long it will stay in the atmosphere, most likely having a negative impact on the environment. The warming potential, on the other hand, has to do with how much heat the gas can trap.

When it comes to CO_2, the emissions being generated today are causing increases in concentrations of the gas that will last for thousands of years. In an attempt to help offset this, carbon taxes are assigned based on the amount of CO_2 entering the atmosphere during a given activity.

Although carbon emissions are an increasing problem in need of many overlapping solutions, there are things that we can do as consumers to affect and impact the emissions that result from our daily lives. It would be impossible to completely eliminate our footprint, but we can work to reduce it.

EARTH OVERSHOOT DAY

Each year, an Earth Overshoot Day is determined using a calendar year to graphically illustrate the date in the year in which we will have consumed all of the resources which could sustainably be produced in that year. In 2018, the day was August 1st. Just 3 years later, in 2021, it was June 5th.

We are using so much more than the earth has to supply, yet we live as though we have a spare earth waiting in the wings. But we don't. And it is up to all of us to take care of the one we have.

At this point I determined that I had developed a baseline amount of knowledge and felt ready to begin making some changes in pursuit of my sustainability project. With a heart full of passion and a slight fear of plastic, I took my first step forward.

CHAPTER 2
FEBRUARY: CLEANING

Since I wanted to give my lifestyle a fresh start, I elected to spend February dedicated to learning more about sustainable cleaning, to ensure that my actions and purchases would also serve to create a cleaner world.

CLEANING PRODUCTS

To determine which products I should use to clean my home, I looked to one of the top resources on deciphering what is least toxic and most beneficial to the environment — the Environmental Working Group, EWG.

If you've ever wandered through the cleaning aisles at your local Walmart or Target, you know that the number of product options appears endless. To simplify my research, I narrowed my focus to general cleaning products such as paper towels, dishwashing liquid, laundry soap, and the issues that determine the sustainability factors for these products.

My search for the most sustainable product in each of these categories, which foreshadowed much of what I would face in the months to come, was nearly impossible. Those items that were best for the environment, i.e. those that didn't use plastic in the product or as part of the packaging, were often given mediocre reviews by the EWG. And other, more sustainable, products were often given no review at all — likely because they tend to be made by smaller companies that haven't crossed the EWG review desk yet.

I was faced with a difficult choice — should I choose the sustainable option and take the risk of a potentially toxic and unreviewed product?

Or should I choose one that may be less ethically produced or sustainably sourced, but is given high praise by the EWG and so is less likely to slowly poison me as I use it?

The more I researched, the more overwhelmed I became. It was frustrating to see that there was so little information available to bridge the gap.

Even those products that I have always used, and which I would've assumed were healthy (if not sustainable) before starting my project, weren't rated very highly.

I spent countless hours during the February chill with my laptop, either sitting on my couch or bundled up in the cleaning aisles, researching product after product.

The debate over "clean versus green" swirled endlessly through my head. The project felt like it was off to a rocky start, but I was determined to persist.

GENERAL CLEANERS

My first big break occurred when I came across a relatively recent start-up, Blueland. I fell in love with their concept. The company sells reusable glass spray bottles to hold their cleaning products. You simply fill the bottles with water and add a soap tablet. Once the tablet has dissolved — you are ready to clean! I felt that I was making forward progress at last.

Although I loved the idea of this, it took a bit longer for me to fall in love with the bottles. The company offers spray bottles in a variety of bold colors for its multi-surface, glass, and bathroom cleaners. I personally prefer a monochromatic, neutral color scheme, so I was a bit hesitant about the blue and yellow bottles (but definitely on board with the pink one!). I admit that it was stupid and shallow for me to consider how the bottles under my sink would look, but these would be the bottles I was going to use every day for the rest of my life! Or at least they should be. That is largely the point, after all.

Although not all of the Blueland products have been reviewed by the EWG, the bathroom cleaning tablets were given a "B" rating — which is considered to be in the "green" zone. The EWG rates cleaning products on a scale from A to F, with the A+ level equivalent ranking being products that are considered "EWG verified." Companies that are EWG verified have met the strictest standards for health and transparency. On the other end of the spectrum, "F" products have poor ingredient disclosure or potentially significant health or environmental hazards.

Since the Blueland cleaner was a "B," I felt it would be a safe option for me. Blueland's other products contain only ingredients on the EPA Safer Chemical Ingredients List. They don't use any ingredients rated by EWG as "unacceptable" or which are listed on the Prop 65 Banned Ingredients List. So even though some of Blueland's products have not been individually reviewed, I decided they would be a safe and sustainable option for me.

And so, I took the plunge and made my first purchase.

When I received the Blueland bottles and tablets in the mail, I was very impressed with the packaging (recyclable) and the product (actually very attractive). My satisfaction continued when I used the products. The bathroom and multi-purpose sprays worked very well. I was slightly less satisfied with the glass cleaner, but, ultimately, I determined that it does what it needs to do, even if a bit more scrubbing is required on my part.

Through my research, I came across several other refillable options for soaps and cleaners. Refillable containers are a sustainable choice since they require much less product packaging to be produced and disposed of.

Purchasing concentrated cleaners, like the one from Branch Basics, can become the base for every cleaning product you need. Although this concentrate isn't verified by the EWG, it too has a "B" ranking. If you don't want to go the concentrate route, there are other products that offer refills in bags or cartons, most of which can be composted or recycled.

I have decided that the Blueland method works best for me. The tablets are small and don't take up much space, which is ideal in my apartment. They are also packaged in compostable paper, and only cost about $2 each.

There is no one right or best option when it comes to sustainable cleaning products, just find the ones that are the best fit for you and your home.

The truth is that you can make just about any household cleaner, soap, detergent, or deodorizer from castile soap, vinegar, and water. There are lots of formulas online to help you to make your own cleaning products at home.

While this is a great option, I knew that it wouldn't fit well into my lifestyle, so I opted to purchase sustainable and non-toxic cleaning products instead.

Whatever choice you make, I'm grateful that we can make individualized decisions that will collectively benefit the environment and ourselves.

PAPER TOWELS

I admit that paper towels have pretty much been my go-to when it comes to cleaning up. When I was growing up, my family used cleansing wipes and I always hated them. I knew they killed germs, but I also felt that they were killing brain cells, too, with their overpowering smell and the tingling feeling that lingered on my hands for hours.

Today, I steer clear of them, whenever possible. I know they are useful; even vital in some professions, and that might be a reason I am neither a nurse nor a kindergarten teacher.

Instead of using the wipes, I preferred to use paper towels with some kind of spray cleaner. Paper towels are easy to use, tend to be readily available, and have no off-putting odor. But I knew that for my sustainability project, I would need to let some things go, and paper towels were at the top of my list.

Although I was loath to part with them, sustainability had a higher value for me than convenience. And I know that nothing in the future of the world will be convenient if we don't look to maximize sustainability now.

I wasn't so much worried about the environmental impact of paper towels after they are used, since they can (and should) be composted. But I was concerned by the energy and resources needed to create them in the first place.

Approximately 13 billion pounds of paper towels are used each year (the equivalent of 40 pounds or 80 rolls) per person. That's one roll for each person every four and a half days. To produce these rolls requires 110 million trees and 130 billion gallons of water. I'm not sure I can fully comprehend these numbers. Of course, there is also a lot of energy used, and emissions generated, by the harvesting, processing, and transporting of this paper product around the world. And once a paper towel roll has made its way into your home, after it is used up those sheets will likely end up in a landfill — resulting in more energy use and emissions.

Currently, it is estimated that over 254 million tons of paper towels and toilet paper are used and disposed of every year. The Paperless Project determined that 544,000 trees could be saved if each US household, about 128.6 million, used just one less paper towel roll each year.

I knew that I wanted to replace this environmental disaster sitting on my kitchen counter with a sustainable option. Thanks to the wonders of Pinterest, I found reusable "paper" towels in the form of "UNpaper Towels" made by Marley's Monsters.

Marley's Monsters is an amazing company in Oregon. The company's mission is to implement creative and effective solutions to reduce our environmental impact. Not only do they make zero-waste products for consumers, but as a company, they walk their talk. The company is dedicated to using only reusable items in the production process, they maximize their designs to cut back on waste, use scraps from the manufacture of some of their products to make others, and donate whatever scraps they can't use to local organizations. And their products ship, plastic-free.

Marley's Monsters is a small company but it's making a big impact. I am excited to support this forward-thinking company and their mission, while pursuing my own goal to reduce waste in my life at the same time.

While it is rare to see a company living out its values as well as Marley's Monsters, it is a delight to buy from companies that are in alignment with your values, goals, and purposes. I am excited to see new companies emerge in the sustainability space and to be able to support them in their mission with my money. But I had to remind myself that although it's wonderful to support such businesses, sustainable living emphasizes not buying things that we don't need or won't use.

When I placed my order for the UNpaper Towels, I chose a set in a dark color since I wanted to be able to reuse them for a long time. The towels can be rolled up together and give the appearance of a normal roll of paper towels.

When the towels arrived, I was both intrigued by the material and surprised at their size. They were a bit shorter than the average paper towel. I washed them, rolled them up, and put them to work. After experimenting with them rolled around my old paper towel holder, I quickly determined that I didn't like the look or functionality of this storage method. I finally settled on folding them and keeping them on hand in a kitchen drawer. They are easy to access and get the job done. Although they don't pick up lint or dirt specks quite as effectively as paper towels, I love being able to use them again and again.

Of course, having reusable towels means they also have to be washed, but I feel happy knowing that the washing machine is a far cry from a landfill.

When some people switch to UNpaper Towels or a similar alternative, they cut paper towels out of their lives completely. And while I wanted to belong to that camp, I wasn't ready to commit 100%. So I have a stash of paper towels that I can get to in the case of a fluid-related emergency.

If you're ready to make the switch, there are lots of options online for reusable paper towel alternatives. Keep in mind that cotton options with a larger weave will absorb liquids best. I recommend that you avoid microfiber towels, if possible, since they shed microplastics when washed.

Of course, you can use whatever dish towels or dishcloths that you have on hand as a sub for paper towels. Some people choose old towels or t-shirts, which can be a great option. Remember, the most sustainable option is always what you already have.

Your needs and values may be different than mine, and that's okay. If you decide to stick with paper towels, or, like me, you want to keep a roll or two on hand, just make sure to compost them after use! This allows them to work for you but puts the raw material back to work for the planet when you're done.

WASHING DISHES

One cleaning task that many people dread is doing the dishes. Since I enjoy cleaning most of the time, dishes aren't a challenge for me, but I decided that I needed to check to make sure I was doing this chore effectively and efficiently.

I wasn't surprised to see that current research favors the use of dishwashers. Newer model dishwashers do a good job of washing the dishes while using as little water as possible — only a couple of gallons for most models.

In contrast, washing the dishes by hand generally uses five times more water than an energy-efficient dishwasher. Even if you don't have a dishwasher known for its efficiency, handwashing still uses three and a half times more water than a regular dishwasher — about 23 gallons, compared to 12 gallons for older dishwashers, and 2.5 gallons for the newer, more efficient ones. Dishwashers made after 2013 are the most efficient and use just 5 gallons per load.[16]

Running the dishwasher with a small load requires the same energy and water as running a full dishwasher. In the future, dishwashers may be able to alter their performance based on the size of the load. Until then, if you have only a dish or two to wash, the benefits of handwashing outweigh running a nearly empty dishwasher.

My research told me that I should choose to use an eco-setting, shorter cycle, or lower temperature, too, if possible. As a result, when I run my dishwasher, I use the short 1-hour cycle to preserve energy and water usage. I also resist the urge to use the drying settings, which does result in drips all across my kitchen when I unload, but also saves additional energy.[17]

Most of the time, I have just a few dishes in the sink at the end of the day. If I decided to wait until I had a full dishwasher to run a load, I would be out of clean dishes and utensils before long. So, I compromise. If I have just a few dishes, I wash them by hand. If I have made a full meal, done some baking, and know I will be doing so again in the next day or two, I'll place these items in the dishwasher and wait to run it when it's full.

If you opt for handwashing, you can still make sustainable choices by making sure you don't passively let the water run. Instead, use a bowl, cup, or the sink as a whole to keep a basin of soapy water, and rinse everything together at the end of the wash rather than one item at a time.

DISHWASHING SOAP

As with general cleaning sprays, I decided to go with Blueland for my dishwashing needs. I believe in their mission, goals, price point, and product. The dishwashing tablets arrive in compostable packaging. And since they are smaller and lighter than other dishwashing soap alternatives, shipping them has less environmental impact. The tablets are verified by the EWG and are completely plastic-free. They were a little more expensive, but they cleaned well and my overall savings on their other products more than made up for the slightly higher cost per tablet.

Blueland also sells a dishwashing powder. You can sprinkle the powder from a silicone shaker directly onto a sponge which then foams, just like regular dishwashing liquid. No plastic bottle required. Although the product has not been reviewed by the EWG, the soaps, like the laundry tablets, contain no petroleum, parabens, ammonia, phthalates, or artificial dyes or fragrances.

These products are refillable and the soaps and the packaging are Cradle-to-Cradle Certified, which means they have been assessed for environmental and social performance in several sustainability categories, from material health to material reuse, renewable energy and carbon management, and even water stewardship and social fairness.

I also reviewed the dishwasher detergent offered by Dropps, but the product was given a "C" rating by EWG. Since this soap was going to be washing the things I use to eat, I decided to steer clear, but it may be an option for you, depending on what you are looking for.

I really wanted to avoid anything with plastic packaging and toxic ingredients. There are plastic-free, biodegradable, and environmentally friendly dishwasher tablet options, including those offered by If You Care, which have not been reviewed by the EWG. Of course, Blueland is another option and met my requirements.

If you prefer to wash dishes by hand, there is a good option from Meliora. The product is plastic-free and looks like a bar of soap. Other dish soap bars like the one from No Tox Life are aesthetically appealing — in my opinion. I ultimately decided against these options because I didn't want to deal with the process of getting the soap from the bar onto my sponge. But that probably isn't a deal-breaker for most people. Fortunately, there are sustainable options for all of us.

SPONGES

I have had a lifelong love affair with sponges and for some reason could never get into the whole "scrubber brush on the end of a stick" idea. Everyone has different preferences, but I am definitely in the sponge camp. I don't know why I have a strong opinion on this, maybe I just feel I have more control with a sponge in my hand.

I knew, though, that even a small thing like sponges would need to come under review during my sustainability project. No stone unturned, you might say. Or as I was more afraid to articulate, no sponge left standing.

Most of the "sustainable" dish cleaning products I found had long or short wooden handles and short hard bristles.

If you are looking for a cleaning brush like this, there are lots of great options out there. They tend to be sustainable because the handles can be composted once the brush has reached the end of its useful life, and only the bristles need to be thrown away.

So although my initial research confirmed my scrubbing assumptions, I was determined to find something equally as sustainable, but more spongy, and to my liking.

Thankfully, I did find a sustainable sponge alternative! Compostable sponges made with plant cellulose are a great option and feel pretty much like my old sponges. You can also find sponges made from sheep's wool. If you want to try a wool sponge, make sure you buy one from a company that takes good care of the sheep and harvests the wool sustainably. These will last a long time, can be composted once you are done with them, and don't have any bristles to toss in the trash.

LAUNDRY

All of the energy required to grow fibers, turn those fibers into fabric, sew the fabric into clothes (and dye it, if necessary), and transport it to the store or your doorstep, is nowhere near the energy that we will expend by washing our clothes over their lifetime.

Each wash releases about 700,000 microfibers, reduces the lifespan of our clothes by about 2 years, and uses 155 liters of water, enough to keep a woman in Sub-Saharan Africa hydrated for 2 months.

When we consider the high cost of washing clothes after each wear, we will discover that although we want to be clean and smell nice, we can value caring about the earth at least as much as we care about always wearing just washed clothes and make some intentional choices in alignment with those values.

Don't worry, you still get to wear clean underwear.

One of the keys to doing laundry sustainably, like running a dishwasher, is to only do a full load. I grew up in a house full of kids, so it seemed like laundry was constantly being done. Once I moved out on my own, I was shocked at how infrequently I had to do the laundry.

Even when we were little, unless our clothes were visibly dirty, smelled, or had been worn several times, they were put away to be worn again. This lesson served me (and the planet) well then and it still does to this day. Most Americans wash their jeans every 2.3 wears. But if we were to wear them 10 times before tossing them in the laundry basket, we could reduce our water usage by 77%. The same applies to the rest of our clothing.

I'm good at giving things multiple wears. Unless I spill something, or we are talking about underwear, I typically wear my clothes 5-7 times before I put them in the wash. While that's already better than the 2.3 times for average wear for a pair of jeans, I was curious to see if I could do any better.

Upon reflection, I realized that it wasn't normally a stain or a smell that triggered me to throw something in the wash. It was normally just the feeling that I had worn something several times and therefore it must be dirty. Even if it really wasn't.

I decided to be more intentional about how, when, and why clothes ended up in the hamper. Beyond smell, an item usually ended up in the hamper if it had a stain or other visible marks, or if I had lost track of the number of times it had been worn or if it no longer felt clean enough to go back in the drawer with the other clean clothes. There was also just the sense of "it's time" for some of my clothes — and so straight into the hamper they would go.

If your clothes smell, by all means, toss them in the wash. But the lack of a fresh-and-clean smell doesn't necessarily mean that they need to be washed. This is contrary to every detergent commercial that has ever been made. Many of those detergents with the strongest fragrance have arrived there through an abundance of chemicals. When we are expecting our clean clothes to smell fresh, rather than just to be fresh, we end up overwashing them and coating them in chemicals, and continually cleaning clothes that don't actually need to be washed.

And this is where we can see the evidence that it takes six times more energy to wash our clothes than it did to make them.

Right now, I do a load of laundry about every two or three weeks. This is a good balance between washing more often and having more underwear than one person should own. I could probably purchase more underwear and do a full load about once a month, but I really can't justify owning 30 pairs!

Also, contrary to conventional wisdom, I don't do separate loads for light colors, dark colors, towels, and so on. It would take months to accumulate a full load in any of those categories and I would run out of clothes to wear long before I got there! I do try to take care of my clothes, but I haven't found any issues with washing my clothes together.

If I have a new pair of jeans (which I do not buy very often, for reasons I will share in the next chapter), or a bright red top, for example, I will usually wash it individually for the first time to ensure that the colors don't bleed. But after that, I have not had any issue with my items being washed together.

In addition to doing less laundry (if you have kids, this may not be possible) and fuller loads (if you have kids, this part is definitely possible), there are a few other steps you can take to make laundry more efficient.

Many people use the warm or hot water settings on the washing machine, believing that the heat is necessary to get clothes clean. This is not true. Washing clothes in cold water will do the job for most of your laundry and it will save an incredible amount of energy. Only 10% of the energy for washing clothes goes to powering the washing machine — the other 90% is used to heat the water!

I never paid much attention to the temperature settings on my washing machine, but now I wash my clothes in cold water every time. The good news is, I can't tell the difference!

Most of our clothing comes with a tag containing washing instructions. A tag that tells you to "wash in 'warm' or 'hot' water" isn't telling you that your clothes *should* be washed at that temperature, rather it is letting you know that this is the highest temperature you should use. So, for most items, washing with cold water isn't an issue.

Although research shows that many fabrics release a consistent amount of microfibers regardless of how much they have been washed, newer clothes tend to shed more microfibers than older ones, likely because of the increased usage of synthetic materials. So wearing the clothes we have longer, taking care of them, and buying second-hand will not only save you money, but will help the environment, too.

Temperature isn't the only setting worth adjusting. Studies have found that 800,000 more microfibers are released during delicate wash cycles than regular ones.[18]

Washing with a normal, short, cold water cycle with gentle detergents containing no bleach will extend the lifespan of your clothing. The colors will be less likely to bleed and will maintain their vibrancy. Move over, Mr. Clean, we have a new way to keep our whites, white.

Additionally, a cold, short wash cycle will not only reduce your energy and water usage but will also reduce the number of microfibers shed from your clothing. Using fewer chemical detergents, fabric softeners, stain removers, and synthetic dyes will also reduce the pollutants that end up in our water.

There are positive things we can do while drying our clothes as well! It goes without saying that using a clothesline outside is the most energy-saving approach.

In fact, every person who opts for air drying will prevent an estimated 700 pounds of CO_2 from being released every 6 months (which is equivalent to taking a Prius on an 1,800-mile road trip).

Of course, wet clothes can be hung outside or inside to dry. I live in the Pacific Northwest, so the number of days I can dry my clothes outside is very limited. I also have a small apartment without a laundry room. Air drying isn't a great option for me at this point in life. Even so, there are some items of clothing I always air dry and there are days when wet clothes can be seen hanging off every hook and door handle available.

A creative option is to suspend a rope between any two endpoints in your home and use old-fashioned clothespins, just like a character on *Little House on the Prairie*. Or you can opt for a drying rack to place inside or outside. If you have the time and space to dry all of your clothing this way, it is a great way to preserve your clothes and reduce your environmental footprint. But if weather, or time, or simply the fact you would like your dryer to serve a purpose other than merely taking up space, I understand.

I, for one, am not quite ready to live in an underwear jungle, yet.

And if you, like me, aren't completely sold on the transition to an air-dry approach, you can still minimize your energy usage by drying clothes for a longer time at a lower temperature! This can be somewhat of a pain if you're in a hurry, but thankfully, most of us have enough going on in life that we aren't sitting in front of the dryer waiting for it to stop spinning.

Two additional drying tips: First, make sure that you aren't overdrying. The energy wasted to get your clothes from dry to over-dry is not necessary. Second, remember to clean out the lint filter after each use to keep the required drying time to a minimum.[19]

LAUNDRY DETERGENT

Every year, there are over 1 billion laundry jugs used and discarded. Of those, 700 million will end up in a landfill, the ocean, or incinerated, because they were not cleaned and recycled properly. 700 million jugs represent enough plastic to build 5 Statues of Liberty.

The plastic isn't the only problem. Many laundry detergents contain toxic chemicals, palm oil, or other non-biodegradable substances. And the environmental impact doesn't end there. As we've seen, most of the environmental impact from an article of clothing comes from the way it is cleaned, not the actual production of the article itself. We will talk more about the clothing manufacturing process in the next chapter.

As I began my research in the detergent aisle at the local market, I questioned if it was significant whether I purchased laundry soap in liquid or powder form. And what about the pods? I learned that each form has different pluses and minuses and there isn't one with a clear environmental advantage. Instead, a product's sustainability seems to depend largely on its ingredients and packaging.

Plastic pods tend to be the worst option overall since they require a plastic coating which dissolves as the clothes are washed. And that plastic is ultimately sent down the drain. Approximately 11 billion plastic pods are used in washing machines (and dishwashers) every year. The result is that much of the PVA/PVOH plastic is entering the water system. PVA is petroleum-based and one of the most common pollutants found in water. As we saw in our discussion of microplastics, once it reaches the water, plastic can easily work its way up the food chain.

I spent hours combing through the lists of cleaning products on the EWG website without much progress. The products that were ranked the highest predominantly came in plastic packaging; sometimes quite a lot of it. The items that were packaged sustainably were, unfortunately, not ranked highly on the ingredients.

The best answer came, not too surprisingly by this point, on Instagram. There are lots of zero-waste and sustainability influencers on Instagram, but I wasn't always able to find what I was looking for there. But I struck gold when I found a post about Meliora laundry soap. It was highly recommended, came in a reusable canister, and when I checked with the EWG, it had a favorable rating — an A!

Since the Meliora laundry powder received an "A" (actually all but one of their products at this time have an A rating, the rating just below "verified"), it is considered to have good ingredients disclosure as well as few or no health or environmental hazards.

Meliora allows you to order a reusable canister and refills come in recyclable or compostable bags, are plastic-free, and all you have to do is tear off the tin tie. Their laundry soap is vegan and cruelty-free — designations we'll explore more in Chapter 5. I also love that Meliora gives 1% of every sale to environmental causes.

I love the look of the Meliora tins, as well.

During my research, I also came across Earthbreeze, a company that makes laundry detergent sheets that are small, compact, efficient, and come in plastic-free packaging. Because of the reduced size of the product, the carbon footprint of the product is also much smaller. This is another eco-friendly option, but to date, the company and the products haven't been reviewed by the EWG.

Blueland has created the first "naked" laundry tablet which isn't wrapped in PVA/PVOH plastic. The tablets can be stored in a refillable steel tin and the refills come in compostable paper pouches. The container and tablets are also Cradle-to-Cradle Certified. The tablets have not been reviewed by the EWG, but like the dishwashing soap, they don't contain any petroleum, parabens, ammonia, phthalates, or artificial dyes or fragrances — things that we will discuss more in-depth in Chapter 5.

I'm sure that there are other companies out there making zero- or low-waste laundry soap, so these aren't the only options. Hopefully, more eco-friendly detergents will emerge as time goes on. Before making changes to my laundry routine, I made sure to use up all of the laundry detergent supplies I had on hand. But I did take the time to check these products' rankings with the EWG first. Before making a switch, it's best to use up what you have, but it's also worth checking to ensure that those products don't have any toxic or harmful chemicals.

DRYER BALLS

Partially to get a head start on next month's topic — clothing, and partially to make sure I was cleaning my clothes with the long term in mind, I decided to pick up some items that I knew had the potential to increase the longevity of the items in my closet.

First, I decided to experiment with dryer balls — commonly thought of as a more sustainable alternative to dryer sheets. Although I've never been one to use dryer sheets in the first place, I did face a problem that I hoped the dryer balls would solve. The dryer in my apartment takes *forever* to dry my clothes. So, while I had learned that it was more efficient to dry clothes at a lower temperature for a longer period of time, that meant that I could easily spend an entire evening waiting to fold dry clothes. I hoped that the dryer balls would speed up the drying process (even just a little), and maybe leave my clothes fluffier and softer, too.

Dryer balls have somewhat mixed reviews. Approximately half of the people who use them, love them, and the other half don't seem to think they have much effect. The research on that is pretty inconclusive. But I was ready to try anything to increase the longevity of my clothes and decrease the time they spend in the dryer — even by a few minutes.

There are many dryer ball options on the market, and as with most things, you can even make them at home.

The dryer balls that I purchased are wool, not plastic, and when they are worn out, I can compost them! I love that before I put them in the dryer, I can also add a couple of drops of essential oil, so my clothes come out smelling fresh — without chemicals.

On the whole, the jury is still out on dryer balls. They did seem to cut down the overall drying time by a few minutes and I like the way my clothes smell using natural ingredients. Plus, the clothes do seem a bit fluffier (although that may just be a placebo effect). I am also happy because I'm not generating any waste (thank you, compostables!). But, if you have an efficient late-model dryer, you probably don't need to make any dryer ball-related changes to your drying routine.

LINGERIE BAGS

Another product I purchased with the goal of extending the life of my clothes is lingerie bags. I'd heard of these being used to wash socks to keep them from disappearing in the wash and dry cycles, and I also wanted to use them to separate my undergarments from my other clothes. There have been too many times I opened the washer or the dryer to discover that my bra had become hooked to a lacy top or dress.

The benefits of washing clothes in protective bags may not be easy to identify because longevity is hard to see and measure. But I really enjoy having all of my socks come out together, and ultimately, the bags streamlined my sorting and folding process.

DRY CLEANING

I've never heard anyone in the sustainability community support dry cleaning. The process is fraught with environmental hazards and, in the long run, isn't financially sustainable either.

I don't have to show up for work in a pressed suit or uniform every day, but I know there are many people who do. So, while there may always be some items that will need to be dry cleaned, the less we do it, the better for our wallets and the planet.

I have had great success using the "dewrinkle" setting on the dryer. It doesn't take too long, doesn't use too much energy, and does get the wrinkles out of things (as long as you remember to take the items out of the dryer immediately afterward).

Many people also swear by handheld steamers to de-wrinkle their clothes. There are even travel versions. The best part is, you get all of the 'crispness' without any of the chemicals.

Spot cleaning and handwashing can also take us a long way, although I know this won't work for all fabrics or items. Although not ideal, dry cleaning will probably stay with us, but, hopefully, will be used sparingly.

STAIN REMOVAL

Bleach is an extremely toxic substance, but it is something that most mothers would not want to live without.

Fortunately, if you want to avoid this harsh chemical, you can make your own stain remover at home. There are plenty of recipes to be found online. Depending on the kind of stain you are dealing with, rubbing alcohol, hydrogen peroxide, dish soap, vinegar, and water can take you a long way toward stain removal, and these are things that you probably have on hand already. A Google search can tell you the best way to deal with all kinds of stains.

The good news is that removing stains without bleach, whenever possible, will extend the life of the clothes, and as we know, saving is always sustainable.

APPLIANCES

One of the best and most effective ways to make your cleaning routines more sustainable is to select eco-friendly appliances, or at least ones that have eco-friendly features. Since I currently live in an apartment, this is not really an option for me. And if you have functional appliances, the most sustainable choice is definitely to keep using them! But, if you find yourself moving into a new home, building a home, or finally needing to replace an old or broken appliance, it is definitely worth finding the options that will conserve energy and support the environment. Although these choices may not necessarily be easy on your wallet on the front end, there are both long-term financial and environmental benefits to choosing these appliances.

New appliances are coming out all the time, so there is no point in mentioning specific brands or models here. If you are on the hunt, there are helpful resources online that are updated regularly. Through a quick Google search, you can find whatever option will work best for your home and your lifestyle.

When the time comes to replace an appliance, make sure to recycle the old one. It is so easy for us to think about recycling when it comes to the small everyday things, like cans, sheets of paper, yogurt containers, etc. And while those are very important, recycling the big items makes that much bigger of an impact. Luckily, we don't go through refrigerators as often as we do yogurt containers!

If the old appliance still works, it should be sold or donated whenever possible. This will guarantee that our sustainable choices will continue to have an impact for years into the future. Someday, the new appliance can also be recycled and will continue to conserve energy long after it has left your home.

If an appliance is no longer functional, there is likely a service or company in your area that will accept the appliance for recycling, and they may even pick it up. Where I live, the energy company will pay you to recycle your old appliances!

To further convince you of the importance of recycling your old appliances, it has been shown that for every 100,000 refrigerators and freezers that are recycled, 5.5 million pounds of recyclable materials are diverted from ending up in a landfill.

Although my focus on cleaning didn't lead to the big changes I was hoping for, I did feel that I was well on my way and ready to tackle all that lay ahead in March. Little did I know then that the research and potential for sticky situations had barely begun.

CHAPTER 3
MARCH: CLOTHING

Clothing is one of the great universal commodities. Chances are good that you are wearing clothes, right now. And, if you're not, I would ask that you please do so.

Unfortunately, while most of us own hundreds of articles of clothing and use some of them every day, the clothing manufacturing industry is one of the worst offenders when it comes to pollution, emissions, and the use of toxic chemicals; not to mention the exploitation of women and children.

THE NAKED FACTS

The statistics are staggering. Clothing is a $2.5 trillion industry. It is responsible for 8% of the world's carbon emissions. The carbon dioxide produced by the fashion industry each year exceeds all international flights and naval shipping combined. 20% of the world's industrial water pollution is due to the treatment and dyeing of textiles. The production of fiber to make textiles is responsible for 18% of the world's pesticide use and 25% of its insecticide use. Clothing manufacturing requires 24 trillion gallons of water each year; enough to fill 37 million Olympic-sized swimming pools. One-third of the microplastic pollution in the oceans comes from clothing manufacturing.

In North America, 10.5 million pounds of clothing end up in land-fills every year, the equivalent of a garbage truck's worth of clothing, every two minutes. Collectively, this tossed clothing is 30 times heavier than the

Empire State Building. Worse yet, 95% of this clothing could have been upcycled or recycled in some way.[20] Instead, this 30 Empire State Buildings' worth of clothing are slowly breaking down in landfills all around the world, contributing to the creation of methane, a harmful greenhouse gas that we are working so hard in other areas to combat.

Between 1999 and 2014, the world's clothing consumption doubled — to 100 billion garments a year. Sadly, this number is projected to triple by the year 2050, as our insatiable demand for new and better and faster fashion continues to grow. The worst part is that the emissions, pollution, and water use will continue to grow along with this demand.

Although I was staggered by this initial research, I became more determined than ever to begin March strong.

I decided that the first thing to do would be to examine my own closet and shopping habits. As a professional organizer, I am always looking for an excuse to organize and declutter my closet. But this time, however, I wasn't necessarily looking to eliminate clothing, but rather to assess the pieces that I have.

It was much as I had feared. Clothing from Old Navy, H&M, and Forever21 were hung, folded, or stacked. A hodgepodge of brands purchased at TJ Maxx filled in the gaps. And there were just a few pieces from brands like Patagonia that were slightly less shame-producing.

Fast fashion brands, like Old Navy and H&M, are detrimental to both minimalist closets and the environment. Yet I had spent years ignoring that fact in order to wear cheap t-shirts, flimsy sundresses, and ill-fitting, but fashionable, jeans.

But the truth is that spending more money doesn't necessarily mean you are helping the planet more. Expensive brands often use the same suppliers which leads to the same environmental harms. And purchasing more expensive items or from more expensive brands doesn't necessarily mean that the items were produced without exploitation. Many of the premium labels use the same factories as the fast-fashion brands, so the price of the garment doesn't necessarily mean that the laborers were paid a fair wage.

COUNTING THE COST

As someone not too far out of college who has not yet arrived at the financial success that I hope to enjoy in the future, I know the pain and fear that I will have to spend five, ten, or even twenty times more for my clothes in order to buy sustainably. Paying just $3 for a t-shirt can feel irresistible. I know what a good feeling it is to buy what you need without putting a serious dent in the monthly budget, but it's not a good feeling when you stop to consider why and how the t-shirt is only $3. The reality is that when we pay less, we get less in terms of transparency, accountability, and quality.

If we expect companies to take the necessary steps to improve their ethical and environmental standing, then we will have to be willing to pay the cost difference. Many fast fashion companies say that they are providing clothing at a low cost because that is what we, as consumers, want. And, while it may be true that we want low prices, we must ask ourselves: at what real cost?

There are those who say that we should shop based on value, others tell us to shop based on environmental impact, and still others say that we should shop based on the ethical treatment of workers. The list of "shoulds" only grows from there. I think that we can strive for all of the above, support the companies that are doing the same, and conscientiously try to progress upward, in a continuous spiral of sustainable growth.

THE SHEER SCALE

The clothing industry creates 90 billion garments each year, and the average consumer purchases approximately 62 items per year. This is another 'chicken and egg' scenario. Companies produce all of these clothes because we buy them! And on some level, we purchase the clothes because they are there.

I decided to do a personal assessment of the shopping I had done thus far into my sustainability project. As I looked back on the first few months of the year, I calculated I had purchased 7 new articles of clothing. And I was disappointed to realize that none of those items had been purchased from a viewpoint toward sustainability. That hadn't been my focus and I realized that it wasn't the focus of the companies I had patronized.

Additionally, if I had purchased 7 items in the first quarter of the year, I was on track to end the year with a total of 28 new items before the year was over. While that number is less than half of the average, I still wasn't happy — both as a professional organizer and as a sustainability-seeker. I couldn't even begin to imagine what the additional 21 new items would be or where they would go, but I was determined that if I purchased even one new item during the rest of the year, it would be in alignment with my sustainability mission.

My research continued. The 62 items purchased by the average consumer each year cost an average of $19 each. In the past, an individual might have to save for a year to buy a new coat or new pair of shoes. In comparison, today we might have to work an hour or two to afford the "average" price of our next purchase. The average cost of my 7 purchases was about $35. So I wasn't too far from the average in that respect.

But the statistics regarding our clothing purchases don't end there. Of the 62 items purchased, 18 of them will never be worn.

Yikes!

Collectively, that adds up to 1.7 billion pieces of clothing taking up space with the price tags still attached.

I can proudly say that I have worn all of the pieces I purchased this year, but I will confess that I haven't worn every piece of clothing in my closet. I have donated items back to Goodwill bearing the tags from another Goodwill still attached. I'm not proud of that fact, but I am thankful that all the pieces that come to mind were secondhand to begin with.

The solution to this particular problem may be relatively simple — if we aren't going to wear something, we shouldn't buy it.

FABRICS

I've never been someone who could feel a piece of clothing and know what it is made out of. Some people have that gift or understanding, but I am not one of them. Silk, I know. Velvet, I can pick out. Cotton, I can normally guess. Beyond that, your guess is as good as mine — or probably better, actually.

But I do know that choosing the fabrics you purchase is part of curating a sustainable wardrobe. An estimated 20% of industrial water pollution globally is attributed to dyeing and treating textiles. And of the clothing produced, nearly three-fifths will wind up in incinerators or landfills just a few years after they were made. Yet another vicious cycle.

When you are shopping, avoid polyester, rayon, and nylon — all synthetic fabrics which aren't biodegradable, require a vast amount of fossil fuels and water in production, and are often dyed with chemicals that have been found to be toxic and linked to long-term health issues. They are also responsible for the majority of the half-million tons of microfibers that wind up in the ocean each year, more than 50 billion plastic bottles' worth of plastic.

When it comes to microfibers, acrylic is the worst offender, shedding about 728,000 microplastics in each wash. Polyester sheds about 496,000, and fleece about 285,000. Polyester-cotton blend is better but still sheds about 137,000 microplastic particles. Worse yet, these fabrics make up about 60% of our clothes worldwide.

Cashmere is another material that is hard on the environment in which it is produced and acrylic fabric is flammable and often uses polypropylene in production, which supposedly has the same impact as cyanide when inhaled.

Cotton requires a lot of water to grow, and not just because it is typically grown in dry regions — although that certainly plays a role. The Water Footprint Network has found that an average of 1,200 gallons of water go into growing 1 pound of cotton and that number may go up to 2,640 gallons in places like India. While a pair of jeans may only require one or two pounds of cotton for production, that is a lot of water expenditure for just one piece of the process. Cotton is also the crop with the heaviest pesticide use. Organic cotton, while grown without pesticides, requires more water since it takes more plants to produce the same amount of product.

While bamboo products are considered a sustainable option, many bamboo fabrics are considered a form of rayon, and the manufacturing process is intensive and utilizes harmful chemicals. The production of bamboo is more sustainable than alternatives like cotton, but due to the chemicals in the manufacturing process, bamboo is not the most eco-friendly option when it comes to clothing.

Look instead to purchase items made with linen, hemp, silk, or biodegradable fabrics. You can also opt for organic cotton if you are willing to accept the high water cost. If you're looking for something soft, alpaca, wool, and secondhand cashmere are the way to go.[21]

It isn't just the production or even the use of clothes that are the sole contributors to their environmental impact. We also must consider how the end of their life plays into the equation. Organic cotton can biodegrade completely in 1-5 months, so long as it wasn't genetically modified or grown using chemicals. Bamboo takes a bit longer at 4-6 months, and silk may not even start to break down for 4 years. Hemp fibers soften over time, and also biodegrade quite easily. Jute will break down in 1-4 months, whereas wool will take about a year. Depending on how it was tanned, some leather may be biodegradable and will break down in 20-25 years, while synthetic fibers, like polyester and nylon, may take 40 to 2000 years to disintegrate, and aren't technically biodegradable.

THE HUMAN COST

Another impact of the fashion industry that we have yet to fully explore is the impact on the people that it employs — the vast majority of whom are women and children. The industry isn't just a leader in terms of pollution, it is also the largest employer of child and slave labor.

A survey of 219 clothing brands reveals that just 12% can show that they are making strides toward paying garment workers a living wage. The sad reality is that fewer than 2% of the women working in the garment industry make a living wage, and in Bangladesh, most clothing industry laborers earn just 14% — 25% of what they need to live, equating to as little as $1 a day.

Being underpaid is only the beginning of the story. A survey of garment workers in Bangladesh and India found that 60% have been verbally or physically abused at work. 60% of workers from Dhaka, Bangladesh report that they regularly work an illegal number of overtime hours. In Guangdong, China, the young women who work in the garment industry often put in 150 hours of overtime per month. More than half have no labor contract and 90% have no access to health insurance. In India, a survey of home-workers in the garment industry found that of the 1,452 people interviewed, 99.2% were working under forced labor conditions.

While you may be feeling that the problem is too large for us to make any impact, we can take positive action. First, we can wear what we have and properly dispose of our clothes when we are done with them. Buying less and buying better still make a difference. And we can buy from companies that provide for their people. Unfortunately, the list of such companies is not nearly as long as it should be.

Even though no single brand does all of this perfectly, I want to support the ones who are making positive changes and are publicly committed to moving in the right direction (and are actually doing so).

Fashion Revolution is an organization committed to creating additional safety, transparency, and accountability in the fashion industry through educating people, conducting research, collaborating with companies, and advocating for their mission. Fashion Revolution also provides an annual review of many of the world's largest fashion brands and retailers through their Fashion Transparency Index. They are quick to point out, however, that transparency does not equal sustainability. Brands may disclose a great deal of information about their policies and practices but that doesn't equate to taking sustainable or ethical actions. And while transparency doesn't necessarily precipitate action, it is a first step towards accountability.

Although there was a 3% average increase in transparency according to the Fashion Transparency Index 2020, not a single brand scored above 80% on the index. The entire report is fascinating, although it covers much more than I can share here. It concludes by encouraging consumers to ask brands #WhoMadeMyClothes, either by tagging them on social media or writing to them directly. They also urge us to write to government lawmakers, asking them to require companies and brands to be legally responsible for the impact that they have on the environment and people alike.[22]

So, while it is fascinating to read about which brands are willing to be open about their practices and in which areas, it is still hard to know what to take from that to transfer into additional action. We can tag brands and write to our senators, but what happens when we need new underwear or want to find a basic black t-shirt?

As I researched, I found myself writing "good info — but what do we do?" over and over again in my notes. Unfortunately, there is no easy answer, but our action steps lie in buying less, buying better, shopping less, sharing more, researching responsibly, spending sustainably, and acting collectively. And so, those are some of the things we will talk about next.

WEAR WHAT YOU HAVE

The first and best way to maximize our closets' sustainability is also one of the simplest — wear what you have. It's been suggested that by extending the active life of a garment from one year to just two years, you will have made a significant contribution to the reduction of the overall carbon, water, and waste footprint of the garment.

Aside from the carbon and waste impacts, it can take up to 700 gallons of water to make one cotton t-shirt and 1,800 gallons of water to make a pair of jeans. With statistics like that, it is clear why one of the most sustainable choices you can make is to maximize the clothes that you have and simply wear your clothes! This includes (especially) any fast fashion items that you have in your closet. It can be tempting to toss these items or pass them along — especially once you know about their social and environmental impact. But the choice has already been made. You own these clothes. They are in your closet. Instead of passing them down the chain to end up who knows where, we can make the most of what we have now.

Wearing a piece of clothing 50 times instead of 5 (the average for fast fashion pieces), reduces emissions by 400% percent per year for each item. The fashion industry has promoted the false idea that it is bad to re-wear clothing. The truth is that it's much more likely that no one will notice, or at least no one will care. Today's consumer purchases 60% more clothing items than consumers did in 2000, and thanks to Pinterest, Instagram, and influencers, this is easy to believe.

But consider that some of the most fashionable people in the world actually do re-wear their clothing (think Kate Middleton and Emma Watson). If they can wear the same outfit on a red carpet or an international stage, we can show up to work in the same pantsuit or to the gym in the same top.

As a professional organizer, I want you to have a closet full of clothes that you love and that serve your lifestyle, but the key is knowing that no matter what is in your closet, keeping it is an eco-friendly choice.

When you need something new, invest in pieces that you know you will like, fit your body, and that also fit your style. And consider using services like Rent the Runway and Nuuly which allow you to wear new(ish) clothes without buying them. And if you decide purposefully not to keep certain items of clothing because they no longer reflect your lifestyle or your style — be sure to take note of that so you can apply what you have learned to shopping trips (in person or online) in the future.

It is our collective responsibility to acquire our clothes sustainably, care for them minimally, and dispose of them properly, by donating or recycling. The average person in North America discarded 81 pounds of clothing last year, and 95% of it could have been donated or recycled. I'm confident that I didn't throw away 81 pounds of clothing last year, but I can think of a few hole-y socks and t-shirts that I tossed in the trash because I didn't know what else I could do with them.

I know now, and after what I'm about to share with you, you will too.

CLOTHING DISPOSAL AND DONATION

Less than 1% of clothing is properly recycled each year. Thankfully, since we consume so much clothing to begin with, that means a large number of pieces are being recycled properly! Unfortunately, there is a very high likelihood that most of the remaining 99% will end up in a landfill.

In the future, clothes that you have that are in like-new or very good condition are great candidates to take to a swap, donate, or gift to a friend.

Clothes that are torn (and can't be repaired) or stained are ready to be recycled.

There are a few companies and brands that have stepped up to help ensure that their clothing reaches an appropriate final resting place.

Some brands, like Patagonia, will take back their items to be properly recycled or resold. Other retailers will accept items from any brand for recycling. The North Face and H&M will accept any piece of clothing from any brand to recycle. The North Face also accepts footwear and H&M even accepts things like underwear and single socks. American Eagle Outfitters will take jeans from any brand to be recycled. Look for clothes recycling bins in these stores. You may even receive a discount coupon in return for recycling your unwanted items. And don't forget to time your dropoff with another reason, so you aren't making a special trip.

Many Goodwill locations offer textile recycling for items of clothing that have reached the end of their usefulness. But it is worth checking before you go to drop off your items, and it may be helpful to label the items for textile recycling separately, to help with the sorting process.

Nike will accept any brand of athletic shoes for recycling. The shoes are ground down and then used to make sport courts, fields, and tracks. Gently used shoes can also be donated to Soles4Souls, which accepts donations at any of their drop-off locations. They also offer free shipping through Zappos for Good. Items that are dropped off at The North Face stores are sent to Soles4Souls. They strive to create sustainable jobs and help to provide relief by distributing the donated shoes and clothing.

The Bra Recyclers recycle, reuse or repurpose used bras. They have a few drop-off locations or items can be mailed to them.

Terracycle Fabrics offers a Clothing Zero Waste Box. You can purchase a box, fill it with unwanted articles of clothing, and return the box to them for recycling. These boxes can be on the expensive side, but they will accept most textiles — from bathmats to awnings to scrunchies. If you need help disposing of other unwanted items, Terracycle also offers boxes for used coffee pods, art supplies, athletic balls, automotive parts, garden gnomes, hair, oatmeal packets, and almost everything else.

In addition to these national (and international) resources, there may be a textile recycling program local to where you live. If you don't have an H&M nearby and don't want to have to ship your items, as Internet search may help you find a perfect resource closer to home.

Donation Town is an online service that helps consumers find local donation pick-up services. Those that I found near me were willing to pick up all kinds of donations — not just clothes! Secondary Materials and Recycled Textiles (SMART) and Council for Textile Recycling are other online platforms that can help to locate textile recycling programs near you.

The major takeaway is that we don't have to toss those items that have seen better days. Even our unmatched socks can find a new home and potentially a second life.

Recycled clothing is often used to make home insulation, pillow stuffing, and car seat stuffing. Sometimes the recycled fibers can even be used to make "new" fabric. Although this isn't super glamorous, it keeps the clothing out of the landfills, and in some cases, puts it back on the rack.

If there are pieces you own that you no longer need or want, I encourage you to donate them. But when you do, take the time to consider why you are passing these things on so that you can keep yourself from buying something like that again in the future.

SWAPPING

I know many people in the sustainability community who recommend having clothing swaps with friends or in their community. This has never been an idea that I have loved, but I wanted to be sure to include it just in case it was something you wanted to try!

I don't have friends who wear a similar size or even wear pieces close enough to my style to do something like this. I could put together a community swap, but I've always assumed that if someone nearby has a piece that I love in my size, I will eventually find it in a local thrift store. The bonus is that what I spend will go to the charity the thrift store supports.

I do know many people though who love the sense of community created by a clothing swap, whether it is among a group of friends or the public.

A swap can be a great way to share what you know about sustainable fashion and refresh your closet in a very ethical and environmentally supportive way.

All you need are a few pieces you are ready to part with, a place to hold your swap, and some way of spreading the news! Whether you advertise by texting friends, posting on Facebook, putting up flyers, or getting other local organizations involved, you can rest in the knowledge that you are supporting your values and spreading the sustainability mission. You can also use a service like HauteTrader to swap clothing.

Although we are focusing on clothing in this chapter, the idea of hosting a "swap" certainly doesn't have to be limited to the clothes in your closet! You can host a swap for children's clothing, toys, electronics, small appliances (or big ones too, I guess), books, and just about anything else! The point is to extend the life of things that are not ready to end up in a landfill! And often these are items that may or may not have been properly recycled otherwise.

Swaps can also happen without the fanfare. If your friend is expecting a boy after having only girls, maybe you could swap some of your baby boy clothes for something her girls are done with. A swap with just one other person will save both of you time, effort, and money.

In middle school, I swapped a sweater for a friend's iDog. I used that iDog to rock out to my iPod shuffle for longer than I would care to admit. It was also the closest I ever got to owning a real dog. Although I didn't appreciate the sustainability aspect of the swap at the time, in hindsight, I appreciate my childhood thriftiness and the small impact it may have had.

Swaps don't have to be two-way. You can gift something you no longer use with a friend. She will extend the item's useful life, and you'll receive her utmost appreciation and the personal satisfaction of taking sustainable action.

You can also utilize groups like Buy Nothing on Facebook, or post free items on Craigslist. As a professional organizer, I encourage people not to try to sell items they want to get rid of, unless they are of really high value. Selling takes a lot of time and effort when what you really want is to get that item that is no longer serving you out of your home.

MENDING

An easy sustainable change to implement right off the bat is to make any small clothing repairs yourself. If you have a loose button or a ripped seam, instead of tossing or donating the item, spend a few minutes making the repair.

Although it's reported that 7 out of 10 adults don't know how to sew on a button, if you fall into that category, a quick YouTube or Google search should give you the information you need for assistance with sewing on buttons and every other kind of repair. Martha Stewart and iFixit also have resources. And if you resist the idea, or if you have a slightly bigger project on your hands, don't hesitate to find a talented friend or a local seamstress and enlist their help.

Not only will you be supporting your local economy, a sustainable choice on its own, but you are making a good decision on behalf of the local landfill or donation center.

Thankfully, this was one area I already had a pretty good handle on. I took sewing classes when I was growing up so I can make simple repairs on my own. I can also help some of my less sewing-inclined friends with their repairs.

As I was putting on a skirt recently, I remembered that I had long ago sewn up a small hole along the waistband. The recollection led me to once again review everything else hanging in my closet. I quickly realized that about 10% of the clothes I own have been mended, sewn, or fixed up in some way. This was a nice reminder that I have done some positive things for the planet even before starting my sustainability project. And it motivated me to continue to take similar actions — especially when I discovered another hole in that same skirt later that day.

You may suspect that I am very hard on my clothes. A lot of the things in my closet are from fast fashion stores and, sadly, most of the pieces were just not designed to last a lifetime. And although they probably won't, I do try to take care of them and maintain them in the most sustainable way possible. I'm definitely not perfect, but I try to maximize the longevity of all the clothes in my closet, even if their lifespans were designed to be very different.

Some brands, like Patagonia, offer to repair their items to ensure their lasting quality and ongoing use. I have a Patagonia jacket that I love, but I recently noticed a small hole by the zipper. I was able to easily repair the hole myself, but if you have a larger repair on your hands, you can turn to the experts! This is just another reason to look for, and seek out, brands that are committed to sustainability and the longevity of their products.

Mending our clothes and doing any necessary repairs helps to ensure that our clothes will have the longest lifespan possible and won't end up in a landfill in the near future (or hopefully ever). It should be our goal to make sure that we can wear and care for the clothes we already own and love and avoid more environmental waste or human suffering.

THRIFTING AND RENTING

Another great way to make the most out of clothes that have already been made is to utilize thrifting and renting. Buying a previously owned item cuts the carbon, waste, and water footprint of the item by 82%.

I have to be honest. Although I grew up utilizing thrift stores and garage sales, once I started making my own money, I avoided them almost completely. I found it strange to wear used clothing and I've always hated the smell of most secondhand stores. Much less bringing that smell home with me.

When I started this project, I knew I'd need to get back into the habit of thrifting. And so, as I thought about clothes that I needed to add to my wardrobe, I decided to compromise.

I turned to online sites like ThreadUp which offers a way to search for what I need without having to sort through racks. I can search for specific brands that I like and that I want to support. Plus, I can do it from the comfort of my home, without the smells.

There is a slightly smaller chance that I will find exactly what I am look-ing for on ThreadUp than there would be if I simply typed my search into Google. But I'm okay with that. Part of my goal is to buy only what I need

— and when I don't find what I need, I'm okay with that, too. And when I do find it, I have the double win of getting it at a discount and knowing that I am giving a new (used) piece the love it needs and the wear it deserves.

In truth, ThreadUp has an inventory that is larger than any actual thrift store in existence. A general search for a green sweater in my size could easily turn up 250 pages of results. I certainly don't have time for that. My attention span is normally gone by page 3 and by page 11, I give up if I have been unsuccessful.

ThreadUp and other thrifting sites aren't for the faint of heart. It takes time, effort, focus, and, as I would find after a while, practice. But on the flip side, it also nurtures the ability to know what you are looking for. In order to search effectively and not end up with a digital cart full of items I don't really want, I have to be intentional in my searches and very selective about what I want — good skills to have in every area of life, especially when it comes to sustainability.

So just as I don't often go to my local thrift store for fun, I won't just dip into ThreadUp for some light searching. I will, however, when I'm in search of something in particular, in my size, probably in a specific color, and in the price range that I am looking for.

Luckily, thrifting is continuing to grow in popularity, especially the online kind. ThreadUp reported that 62 million women purchased second-hand products in 2019, as opposed to 56 million the year before. This is good to know, since 1 million people purchasing their next clothing item secondhand, instead of new, saves 6 million kg of carbon pollution.

ThreadUp resells and recycles up to 90% of the clothing it receives, preventing it from ending up in a landfill! This is where donating meets consignment.

While I had a fairly easy time fitting thrifting back into my life, I had never tried renting clothes. The whole idea made me almost as uncomfortable as thrifting. In fact, the idea of wearing something that *dozens* of people had worn, was even worse, but I decided I couldn't let that stand in the way of giving it a try.

I don't have the reason or the lifestyle to be a rent-my-whole-wardrobe kind of person, so I knew that when I tried it, it would be for something specific. I had a few business photoshoots planned, so I decided that this would be the perfect opportunity to experiment with renting and also get some shots wearing something fun that I would probably never own. My first rental was a success. I enjoyed having something new and exciting to wear for the photoshoot. The bonus was that it was delivered right to my doorstep and I didn't have to find permanent room for it in my closet. Returning the item was seamless, although making the trip to the UPS store was a bit of a pain. I am confident I will use the rental option again in the future when circumstances and opportunity align, especially since I know that renting as opposed to purchasing is in alignment with my sustainability values.

PRODUCT BOXES

There are more and more companies offering us the option to continually update our wardrobes, with new items of clothing delivered to your home regularly. When you stop to consider that you may or may not like the contents to begin with, this seems to create a cycle of waste.

Services like these allow you to purchase several items every month. You try them on in the comfort of your home. This is different from renting because instead of receiving the clothes and then using them for a time, you are simply given the option of purchasing and keeping things. This is a very easy way to keep a constant inflow to your closet, with very little to ensure that anything goes back out again — and that goes against the whole point of having a sustainable wardrobe! It removes the likelihood of investing in companies that have sustainable methods and pay their workers a living wage — or it requires you to do a lot more research on the pieces that have already ended up in your home.

I know that some people need a constant rotation in their closet for work and some people just love the subscription model. That's okay. But renting is another great way to keep the inflow without adding an excess of new items into the cycle.

Some of these subscription clothing boxes try to incorporate sustainable brands, but the vast majority don't seem to fall into that category. My bigger issue with services like this is that it feeds a cycle of consumption.

If you choose to use a subscription box program for clothing (or anything else for that matter) and it works for you — great. I have nothing against the brands or concept personally. But I implore you to be sure that you like your reasons and that your choices are sustainable — both financially and environmentally, in the long run.

RETURNS

When shopping online, it is helpful to have your measurements on hand. That way, despite the size variations between brands (and even lines or pieces within a single brand) you will be able to purchase items that are as close to your size as possible, minimizing the potential need for returns. If you're shopping on a secondhand site, like ThreadUp, you may want to visit the site of the actual brand and check sizes, particularly if you aren't sure if the item you are looking at ordering will fit properly.

The number of items being returned has gone up 95% over the last couple of years and these items may or may not be inspected, repackaged, and resold. Often companies find it easier to incinerate the items, and some brands refuse to donate these items for fear of cheapening their brand.

Sometimes, there is no choice but to return an ill-fitting piece, but if an item just needs a few tweaks, it may be better to seek the help of a seamstress or tailor.

KIDS CLOTHING

When I was a kid, I remember always trying to save my new outfits for a special occasion. I loved wearing a flashy new outfit on just the perfect day. I was the one wearing purple overalls edged with faux leopard print fur, the height of fashion.

I recall a period when my mother seemed to buy all our clothes from The Children's Place. I loved the cute outfits, even if they were less dramatic than purple overalls. What I remember most, though, is the chemical smell of the clothes. Nothing else I've ever smelled compares with that.

I didn't know it at the time, but The Children's Place was one of the companies that had clothing manufactured in the Rana Plaza factory, which became famous for its poor construction and ultimate collapse in 2011 and was responsible for killing and injuring thousands of people.[23]

The Children's Place still only ranks in the 29th percentile based on corporate social responsibility (CSR) and environment, social, governance (ESG) metrics.[24] Between the unmistakable chemical smell, the treatment of their workers — whether purposeful or inadvertent, and the low rating, The Children's Place is not a brand that I plan to ever use for my own children.

It is worth doing research when it comes to children's clothing. I've always had sensitive skin, and I can remember a day that I wore a brand-new sweater on a trip to a theme park only to remove it mid-day because painful and itchy red welts had erupted over my arms and neck. I definitely don't want to see the next generation exposed to the same harmful chemicals.

Thankfully, the principles for finding, buying, and sustainably maintaining kids' clothes are very much the same as those we have already covered.

When at all possible, secondhand or hand-me-down clothes can go a long way. Kids outgrow their clothes quickly, and instead of constantly buying new outfits, it is financially and environmentally sustainable to find clothes that are already in the cycle. Plus, there is already a vast supply of gently used clothing out there for kids.

As your child grows, and after you have saved the pieces with special memories or sentimental value, the best thing that you can do is pass on the outgrown items! Whether you donate them to a cause you want to support, or gift them to one of your friends, giving the items a second life is extremely valuable. My mother had many friends who passed clothes down to me over the years.

It is ideal to make sure that these items can be passed along by doing our best to take care of them. Babies and toddlers can be tough on clothes, but with proper cleaning, mending, and care, these items can provide another child (and maybe even more than one) with clothes fit for childhood's adventures.

And children can also suffer from having too many clothes. After a baby shower or two, many new moms find themselves with more outfits than their child could ever possibly wear! I'm pretty sure that my niece never wore the same outfit twice during the first two years of her life! At least it certainly looked that way. Before purchasing new items, we should be aware of how much we have, in what sizes, and what we are looking to buy. I totally understand the allure of little baby shoes but ending up with too many in the 6-9 month range and not enough after isn't going to be very sustainable for you or the planet.

WORKOUT CLOTHES

I spent years working out at the gym with my cell phone tucked into the waistband of my pants or in my hand. Neither of these was ideal. The phone crashed to the floor or slipped down my pant leg more times than I care to count, and sometimes it did both on the same day. But there was no way I was going to give up my cell phone. I needed a podcast or audiobook to be the background for my workout, sometimes inspiring me, sometimes calming me, and sometimes just distracting me from pushing my body a bit too hard.

Fortunately, two items helped to change this reality. The first discovery was AirPods, which enabled me to leave my phone in my coat instead of carrying it around with me at the gym.

When I moved a year later, and the gym was no longer convenient, I started running the trails near my apartment. Leaving my phone at home was not a viable option. My second discovery was workout leggings, pockets included. As with everything else women wear, pockets are revolutionary. Now I can't stand to wear workout pants without pockets. But since I only had one, I knew it was time to invest in a few more pairs.

The pair that I had was from Lululemon, and I did really like them. After some research, I determined that the company's sustainability practices were okay; not great, but certainly better than some of the alternatives. They seem to be moving in the right direction, although it is hard to see how many company statements are actually backed up by impactful action.

Luckily, I came across another brand I fell in love with pretty much instantly — Girlfriend Collective. I love the look, their inclusiveness, and the fact that they are based in nearby Seattle. But, of course, the best part is the company's sustainability practices.

I decided to purchase a pair of workout leggings (with pockets, of course) and try my luck with a workout bra, something that I have never been quite able to make work for me before.

Each pair of leggings made by Girlfriend Collective contains 25 recycled post-consumer water bottles which have been saved from a landfill. Girlfriend Collective also helps to prevent 18.61 pounds of CO_2 emissions and save 3.11 gallons of water through the production of each pair of leggings. Their bras are made from 11 recycled water bottles, which prevent 8.19 pounds of CO_2 emissions, and saves 1.37 gallons of water. The company's sustainable practices extend beyond the products. Their factories guarantee fair wages, safe and healthy conditions, and utilize zero forced or child labor — all things that will, hopefully, become the norm.

In my research, I came across discussion and debate regarding the potential harm to our skin from wearing products made from water bottles. Some water bottles contain BPA and other harmful chemicals, so the concern is that just as these chemicals can leach into the water inside the bottles, they could similarly leech into our bloodstream through our skin. There seems to be little to no evidence that this is possible and Girlfriend Collective differentiates between polycarbonates (plastic containing BPA) and polyethylene terephthalate (used in water bottles and other food containers, which is what they use to make clothing). They point out that if "it's safe for your sandwich, it's safe for your legs." The fabric made from the water bottles has been tested and is safe to wear next to your skin, and even the dyes that they use are eco-friendly — which is another area some companies fail on the sustainability front.[25]

When my leggings arrived, I fell in love pretty much immediately. They were well made, durable, and cute. Each time I put them on I was excited for my workout (or just to hang out around my house). And I was even more pleased by the constant physical reminder of my sustainability project.

For sustainability, we should wear the workout clothes we have, but if we need more, it's best to make sure that the company we support shares our value of sustainability. That doesn't just mean that the clothes are made from recycled materials, or their advertisements show someone out enjoying nature — this can all be a form of greenwashing, protecting companies from making necessary changes and holding us back from living our values. The companies that live their values across the board and that share openly about that are the ones that we want to support. Even if they don't do it perfectly yet, a concerted effort to strive for sustainability, both in word and in action, can serve as a guiding light to let us know who we want to partner with.

And wherever I may end up in my new Girlfriend Collective leggings, I know that I will always have my phone and my sustainable values close at hand.

TIGHTS

I competed in speech and debate in high school, so I went through more than my fair share of tights. A competition would last for three days so I would always pack 5 pairs of tights. I didn't want to walk into a debate round with a run in my stockings, an immediate knock to my credibility and professionalism.

I didn't always go through 5 pairs during a tournament, but the fact that I regularly packed that many shows that sometimes I did. Since I knew how many I needed, when the time came to stock up, I would run into Walmart and buy the 10 for $8 pack or whatever other set was the cheapest on that given day. Buying the cheapest option, of course, didn't produce the quality or longevity that I needed, thus continuing this infinite cycle.

I felt justified, though, because on the occasion when my mom would buy more expensive tights, or I would find a pair at the bottom of a basket in my closet, it would still rip or run. So, in my little high school brain, I felt the cheapest tights were the best value.

This was years before I started my sustainability project, and long before I started to consider that value was not just about my wallet but was also about the impact on the environment and the people around the world who were making products.

Although tights may seem insignificant and you may wonder whether they really have an impact on the environment at all, they do.

The largest environmental cost comes from the energy required to make the yarn used in tights since in order to make nylon, a great deal of heat is used to form strands from the fibers. So although we can invest in higher quality tights, take care of them, and even take steps to recycle them at the end of their life, the biggest environmental impact comes from our needing them in the first place.

I can't say that I will stop wearing tights or stockings of any kind, and I don't expect you to either. My go-to outfit when I'm not wearing athleisure wear is a dress with tights. But even as I age, I can't say that my luck with hosiery has vastly improved. I have stopped buying the cheapest ones, but the ones with higher price tags seem to have a limited lifespan, too.

I have a black pair that I have been wearing for over a year. When I recently noticed a small hole, rather than tossing them out, I took the time to sew it up. Unless they're sheer tights, I will sew up a hole or a run to make them last a bit longer. It doesn't always work, and it certainly doesn't make their lifespan infinite, but it does extend it a bit. I have some gray tights that I've had for close to five years. They are probably about 50% stitching now, but I do still wear them on occasion.

Every pair of nylon tights I tossed in the trash and that ended up in a landfill during my debate career will take between 30 and 40 years to fully decompose. This means that the tights I threw away in high school will likely still be sitting in a landfill when I get married, have kids, and they are competing in debate themselves. While it's not quite as bad as a foil balloon that never decomposes, or some lycra workout pants that could take up to 200 years to decompose, it's still a long time, and longer than many other kinds of clothing. A denim jacket can fully break down in a year and cotton socks in less than 5 months. Tights don't reflect the best side of the clothing industry.

In addition to being aware of where our tights end up, it's good to think about how they are washed. When nylon tights are washed, they often release tons of microplastics into the water. To prevent the microplastics from leaching into our water, we can wash these items in bags that will prevent the microplastics from escaping or use a tool to help capture them. If you don't have either of these means of catching microplastics and don't plan to invest in them any time soon, you can at least help to reduce microplastics by washing only full loads of clothing. When there is extra room for the water to swirl around the clothes, more microplastics are loosened and end up in the water.

There are also other tips for preserving tights to increase their longevity. These include putting damp tights in the freezer to make them last longer, washing tights in a garment bag, buying a larger size to reduce the amount of strain on the fibers, filing your nails before putting them on, and refraining from sitting on benches.

While some tips are more practical than others, we always have the option of buying tights that are more sustainably made or that just might last forever. During my research, I found a couple of brands that I hoped would hold the answer to sustainable hosiery. Although none of them are available at the local Walmart (or likely not your local anywhere), to support these brands and help advance our goals, ordering them online could be a worthwhile decision.[26]

The first brand I found was Sheertex, a company that designs pantyhose to last. And not just for a long weekend. The tights are made out of the same material found in bulletproof vests. So while your legs won't be bulletproof, the tights might outlive you.

One of the first things I noticed though as I poked around the Sheertex website was that there was no significant mention of environmental impact and sustainability. Compared to other companies where these are a top priority, Sheertex was definitely lacking. It seemed that although environmental benefit might be a side benefit of the tights, it isn't a primary goal or standard which guides their practices. When I first came across the company, I did find some references to sustainability, but the actions that the company reported to be taking were covered by blanket language, as opposed to detailing specific actions. Later, when I returned to the website again, I couldn't find that page, so perhaps I only imagined it.

Unfortunately, since the tights material is something that Sheertex has specifically designed, it isn't made from recycled materials in any form. And so far, there is no recycling program for the tights, so once they do wear out, into the landfill they will have to go. They are also more pricey than many other brands, ranging up to about $100 a pair. Seeing that price made the high school debater inside of me just about faint and wish for the days of the 5 for $5 sales. Luckily, post-high school me doesn't use price as the sole deciding factor — although it may be a determining one.

Another brand that came up consistently in my research was Swedish Stockings. As opposed to Sheertex, one of the three tabs on their website is dedicated to "sustainability," clearly indicating that it is one of their primary values. These products are made from pre- and post-consumer nylon waste, which is much less harmful than regular nylon production. And in their manufacture, the company strives to reduce emissions, water usage, and waste.

After the tights have been produced and used, the company offers a recycling program. If you mail in three or more pairs of tights from any brand, you can trust that they will be properly recycled. And if you provide your email address, you will receive a 10% discount code. The company isn't able to recycle old tights into new tights yet, since the technology that makes that possible isn't widely available. So, for now, the old tights are ground down and turned into tanks that separate grease from water to be used at gas stations, restaurants, and other establishments. The company points out that this isn't a really beautiful second life, but it is a very sustainable one, and keeps tights out of landfills.

Swedish Stockings is based in Europe, so they don't have a place for those of us on this side of the Atlantic to mail them to. Therefore, I'm not sure how financially or environmentally sustainable an option this is for Americans. The only upside to buying tights that have to be shipped halfway across the world is that they are light and compact, meaning transporting them requires less energy than something heavier and larger.

The Swedish Stockings brand also has a whole page dedicated to how to properly care for the stockings. I learned that tights only stretch properly from the bottom up. This means that to put tights on in the most sustainable way, you have to scrunch up the tights before sticking your foot in and then pull them up to your knee, repeat with the other foot, and then finally pull them up the rest of the way. You shouldn't adjust the tights after they're on to try and make them lay more evenly and you should try to distribute the fabric as evenly as possible as you pull them up the first time. If you miss the mark, the website says, you should take them off and start over, because they can only stretch from the bottom up.

The variety and prices at Swedish Stockings seem to be better than what Sheertex currently offers. Swedish Stockings offers socks, knee-high socks, leggings, and shorts, in addition to a selection of tights. The products seem to be within a $20-$50 range unless you are purchasing a set.

Swedish Stockings helps to differentiate their products by Denier count. The Denier of an item lets you know how sheer the tights are because it identifies the thickness of the fiber. A pair of tights that is 100 Denier will be pretty much completely opaque, whereas a pair that is 40 Denier will be sheerer.

Swedish Stockings also offers different blends with differing amounts of recycled material. Reviews I found online indicate that the ones made of 100% recycled material don't last quite as long as some of the other blends. The ones with the higher Denier count may also last longer. Ultimately, your selection is going to be dependent on the look you are going for. But if you're ordering from a brand founded on sustainability, you aren't likely to go wrong.[27]

Once again, I was pleased to see some sustainable options out there to serve as a counterpoint to the mainstream choices. But it is always disappointing to see how few companies are attempting to take environmentally supportive action. There are certainly some other companies starting to capitalize on this gap in the market and I am excited to see them expand. There can definitely be some more growth in this area of the market to keep our legs (and this planet) covered.

SOCKS

One thing that I can't seem to get to last is socks. Mine always seem to have at least one hole on the bottom. I've actually received comments about my socks being more hole than actual sock. This is one of the areas that I had been meaning to take care of, so I was determined to try to get it done in a sustainable and lasting way.

Remember, the first rule of sustainability is to use less and to use what you have. In my case, I had pretty much exhausted the latter option. I had used all I had and while the ones that remained could hardly be classified as socks any longer, I couldn't exactly give up wearing them completely.

The thick boot socks and the fuzzy slippers I love to wear around the house, I have had fewer issues with. Perhaps because I don't wear them as often, they seem to last a decent amount of time. My workout ankle socks, on the other hand, have an unbelievably short lifespan. I could get a new pair one day and by the next day, they would already be sporting holes! I don't know how or why, but they would.

I set out on my search for a sustainable sock. Luckily, there are lots of options out there and I'm sure that more will continue to appear. Harvest & Mill uses organic heirloom cotton in their socks which allows them to be dye-free. They are also completely made in the US with the cotton grown, spun, and knit right here! Teddy Locks makes socks with fibers made from certified recycled post-consumer plastic bottles. And since all of this is done in North Carolina, the socks travel less than 250 miles during production and are packaged using recycled and recyclable plastic-free shipping materials. Girlfriend Collective has also recently started making socks with 95% recycled plastic water bottles which can be recycled through ReGirlfriend as well. Conscious Step makes socks using Fairtrade and GOTS-certified organic cotton in ethical factories. Each design is also associated with a cause, so when you purchase a pair of socks, an associated donation is made to that cause. Pact is another brand using organic cotton in their Fair Trade-certified socks! And finally, MenoMieux produces eco-friendly socks and hosiery, some of which are made from recycled yarn from Swedish Stockings!

With so many great options, my feet are happy, and the old sock remnants can finally find their way into my textile recycling bag. They have served me well and walked many miles in my shoes. But now I'm ready to go the next ones in sustainable socks.

SHOES

Around 24 billion pairs of shoes are manufactured each year. Since there are only about eight billion of us, that's 3 pairs per year for each of us. I haven't purchased shoes for a couple of years, so someone out there has been buying my allotment.

As with everything else, making shoes requires resources. From oil to leather to cotton, as well as what is necessary to ship these materials to the manufacturer and then distribute them around the world, the entire process contributes to greenhouse gas emissions every step of the way.

A few companies are taking steps towards sustainability. For example, Adidas has launched FutureCraft Loop, an effort to design a completely recyclable running shoe, and they have partnered with Parley for the Oceans, a nonprofit that utilizes recycled plastic to create sneakers and clothes.

They have also recently worked with Allbirds, a company with the mission to create an eco-friendly, more sustainable sneaker (and also sustainable socks while they are at it!). Although both companies, and other manufacturers, are striving to use more sustainable materials in production — such as using recycled plastic or sustainably sourced sugar foam over virgin plastic, together they want to produce a shoe with the lowest carbon footprint possible.

The current carbon footprint of Allbirds is about 7.6 kg per sneaker, about half the emissions of a common alternative, and the company also invests in carbon offsets to reduce the overall environmental cost and neutralize their impact. We will talk more about carbon offsets in Chapter 4. Allbirds makes their shoelaces from recycled plastic bottles, the wool they use is produced using a process that uses 60% less energy than other alternatives, and the tree fibers they use in production use 95% less water than cotton. They are also a certified B Corp which verifies that their labor practices and products are sustainable and ethically produced, and they partner with Soles4Souls to give lightly used Allbirds new life and simultaneously help communities in need.

Together, Allbirds and Adidas have determined they can reduce the carbon footprint of a sneaker to about two kilograms, about the same as driving five miles in an average car or charging your phone 255 times, which is about as low as they believe may be possible.[28]

This collaboration certainly isn't the only sustainable way to buy shoes. Many companies are innovating in new ways. Ponto Footwear makes shoes from recycled and bio-based materials, like recycled leather, algae foam, and wood pulp while also donating to ocean cleanup. Rothys is famous for creating all of its shoes (and now other products, too) out of 100% recycled plastic water bottles and other post-consumer recycled materials. As demand and desire for sustainable solutions continue to rise, so will the incentive for more companies to innovate — or to partner with companies like Rothys and Allbirds.

Getting as much information as possible to make the best choice possible for whatever kind of shoes you are in the market for — whether flats, heels, or sneakers, will allow you to shop sustainably. So, too, is buying fewer than the 3 pairs of shoes allotted for you each year.

I've wanted to get a pair of Allbirds for a long time, but I'm still wearing out the sneakers I already own in preparation for getting some adorable Allbirds later.

CLOTHING BRANDS

I've mentioned several ways to avoid buying new clothes in this chapter, and I do recommend that whenever possible. I have also mentioned several brands that are trying to make a difference. I wanted to share a few more brands that have come to my attention as striving for sustainability. I haven't purchased from all of them, because there is very little I need in terms of clothing, and how sustainable would it be to purchase things I don't need, even from brands that are doing amazing things in the world? It wouldn't be. But although I haven't placed an order to date, many of these are on my list for the future as holes in my closet (and potentially my clothes) open up, or to purchase gifts for friends I know will appreciate them as much as I would.

Tentree, in accordance with their name, plants 10 trees for every item purchased and the company projects they will have planted over a billion trees by 2030. Customers receive a code so they can track the growth of their trees over time. They use ethically sourced and sustainable materials like cork, coconut, and recycled polyester in their products and also utilize ethical factories.

Everlane strives for both sustainability and transparency. They allow customers to see the factories where their products are produced and even break down the cost of the components of each item. They also maintain good relationships with their factories to ensure that employees are treated well and the products are produced well. Some of their newer product lines have also included items made from reused materials and recycled plastic bottles.

Since 2015, Reformation has been carbon neutral and they also score each item they sell with an environmental footprint to help consumers make an informed decision through a greater understanding of the environmental impact of each piece of clothing. The company creates items with sustainable materials and also upcycles when possible. They work to ensure those along the supply chain receive fair wages. Reformation also strives to protect deforested areas to offset the environmental cost of manufacturing. And once you are done with your pieces, you can sell used clothing to Reformation and earn a credit towards new ones.

Pact reuses old materials to remake many of the items they offer. They sell certified organic, fair-trade, non-GMO clothing, and work to ensure that each step of their supply chain is as sustainable as possible, even down to the way they produce cotton using much less water than traditional methods.

Levi's has released a new line of denim, Water<Less, which uses up to 96% less water than alternative products — which, as we know, use a lot of water. They are another company striving for sustainability in every step of their process. They are looking to use 100% sustainably sourced cotton in their jeans and recycle old jeans for use in home insulation.

Although H&M is considered a fast-fashion retailer, as we saw earlier, they are looking to move towards sustainability and have begun taking actions in alignment with that. Their Conscious collection is made with materials such as organic cotton and recycled polyester, and through eco-friendly fabrics and more sustainable production methods, they are working to reduce their environmental footprint. By 2030 H&M has announced they want to be using only sustainably sourced materials in all of their product lines. Only time will tell if that proves to be true.

The clothing company Amour Vert has zero-waste policies and strives to reuse items wherever possible, and when that can't be done, they recycle. They produce items in small batches so they don't end up with lots of unsold items. The items they do create are produced with sustainable fabric and non-toxic dye. For every item purchased, Amour Vert plants a tree. The company also follows a zero-waste policy and finds creative solutions to recycle and reuse items.

People Tree is considered one of the first sustainable fashion brands. It focuses on organic farming and sustainable practices at every level — from healthy working conditions to fair wages, and organic cotton to chemical-free dyes.

Eileen Fisher strives for sustainability through the materials used in their products and through ensuring the ethical treatment of the workers along the production line. They use innovative solutions to reduce fabric waste and also avoid air shipping which reduces carbon emissions. Used items are bought back to recycle, reuse, or to use to create art if it can't be resold.[29]

EVEN THE SUSTAINABLE, STRUGGLE

Remember, don't purchase an item just because it claims to be sustainable (remember to check) or because it is a brand you love. Make sure you love and will wear the item itself. There is no point in purchasing an item for ethical or sustainability reasons only to neglect to wear and care for it as it deserves.

Similarly, don't invest in a certain kind of clothing, just because it seems to be more sustainable. If you like to wear suits but can't find a brand that makes them out of recycled water bottles yet, you don't need to switch to athletic clothing simply because they might be considered more "sustainable." Take time to research until you find a brand that supports your ethical and environmental values. Then purchase that suit. Even better, rent a suit or buy one secondhand. Best yet, revamp the one you have in your closet with the help of a long weekend or a local seamstress. Invest in what you want to wear, care for, and maintain.

The conscious fashion journalist, Alden Wicker, encourages people to skip the "pity purchase." Don't buy items just because they are sustainable — especially if they aren't something you will wear or use and will just end up in the back of your closet. That would be a sustainable purchase and an unsustainable choice. You'll likely beat yourself up over it, which isn't good for you or any of us.

There is no such thing as a perfectly sustainable or ethical clothing choice. There are too many factors at play for that to be the case. But rather than getting distracted by making the "perfect" choice, or getting depressed that there isn't one, give yourself the grace to make the decision that you determine is best for you and the planet. With the information I have shared here, I hope you will be able to better maximize your responsibility to both.

As I stated earlier, none of the companies I've shared in this chapter are perfect, but most, if not all, are taking steps in the right direction. It is disappointing when companies don't live up to their stated mission or values, and it is disappointing when we do the same. As we strive for greater sustainability in our own lives, one of the ways we can do so is by expecting that from the companies we respect and support and by holding them to that level of accountability.

Although research has shown that about 88% of consumers want brands to help them be more environmentally friendly and some brands are starting to take steps in that direction, it is also up to us as consumers to put our money where our values are. The current trajectory of the fashion industry has it contributing 26% of the world's carbon footprint by 2050. That's a lot more carbon and a lot more clothes. If your closet doesn't currently reflect your values, that's okay, but now you know how to make sure any additions, do.

While all brands should look for ways to reduce their usage of water, land, chemicals, and fossil fuels, and instead utilize methods to reduce, reuse, reinvent, and recycle, the option to make sustainable choices doesn't end with them. We play a role, too.

Some of the brands most would consider sustainable, and that I listed above, have received backlash for a lack of transparency or a lack of substantive support for transparency. Everlane, for example, has recently been accused of not using sustainable materials in the production of many of their products, lacking real transparency in their supply chain at the supplier level and beyond, sharing insufficient environmental data, discouraging employees from forming a union, and firing some employees who had voiced support for one — although the company has denied that was the reason the employees were fired. Whether these allegations are true at some level or not, I have no real way to know, and whether you choose to take this information into account with your purchasing decisions is up to you. Everlane is doing a lot of innovative things. They were one of the first to disclose the production cost, factory information, and minimize or eliminate the traditional retail markup on their items. They are doing good work, but they can do better. So can I. And likely, so can you.[30]

If you are already taking some of these steps, I applaud you. Thank you for your sustainable choices. I hope that you will be inspired and encouraged to make even more such choices after reading this book.

None of the information I've shared here is intended to make you feel bad in your clothes — quite the opposite, in fact. I want you to feel fantastic in the pieces you have intentionally chosen, and even better when you know that the items in your closet are hanging straight in line with your values.

CHAPTER 4
APRIL: ON THE GO

Early in January, after the start of my sustainability project, I took a trip. My friend, Kaitlyn, and I took Amtrak's Coast Starlight Express train from Seattle to Los Angeles. The trip was something we had talked about doing for a long time and finally got it on the calendar in January. We had a great time playing card games, reading, watching the scenery passing by, and going all out in the dining car. When you book a sleeper car (which we did), all the meals are included in your ticket price! I would definitely recommend going that route — sleeping in a makeshift bed on a moving train is much better than sleeping upright in a chair on a moving train surrounded by people that you don't know. And the flourless chocolate tart was to die for.

It was an amazing experience. Over the course of the 35-hour trip, we went from the dreary rain of Seattle (it was exactly the kind of day that people think of when they think about Seattle), to the fresh snow of Southern Oregon, to a beautiful, warm sunset along the California coast.

But just a couple of hours into the trip, we realized that we were on the wrong side of the train.

Although we had great views, we were traveling south on the left side of the train — and since our primary goal was to experience the coast, which was on the right side of the train, we were a bit stuck. We probably could have asked to be moved, and we should have definitely requested a sleeper cabin on the right side when we made our reservations, but neither one of us had even thought about it. As it turned out, we didn't mind too much, and the views were great. Also, luckily, the cabin across from ours was unoccupied for most of the trip, so we could look through the open door and the inside window, even sneaking over to take pictures occasionally.

Because we were seated on the "wrong" side of the train, however, we also saw a lot of things that we hadn't expected. The phrase "the wrong side of the tracks" exists for a reason, and we saw countless examples of exactly what that phrase is referring to.

While we were surrounded by unlimited food choices and cozy in our private room and (if not entirely comfortable) beds, we passed hundreds of homeless encampments. Sometimes we'd see a large community living together, and sometimes it was just a solitary tent. My heart broke for these people.

And my heart broke for the planet. There was trash everywhere. So, so much trash. I am not trying to lay the blame for this on the homeless population. We know that these concerns are connected, and both of them deserve our help and attention.

The trash beside the train tracks wasn't the same as the trash I've seen from the freeway or along a country lane. It was thicker, denser, and it was everywhere. Sometimes it was piled up so high, I couldn't see the ground. Sometimes it was just scattered about, like puddles after a storm. Sometimes it was little things — takeout containers, soda cans, beer bottles, grocery bags, and diapers. Sometimes it was big things — chairs, mattresses, bikes, and even car parts.

While the trash was definitely hard to ignore, I had yet to understand the harm to the environment being inflicted by my trip.

REDUCING YOUR CARBON FOOTPRINT

One of the biggest ways that traveling impacts the environment is through carbon emissions.

All of us have contributed to carbon emissions, referred to as our carbon footprint, or the amount of greenhouse gasses emitted by something, such as someone's travel or the manufacturing of a product, over a given period of time. This period is generally a year, but you could calculate it for any length of time you want. Our "footprint" grows based on what we eat, our leisure activities, and of course, where, when, and how often we travel.

Recent research revealed that tourism has an 8% impact on global emissions, even though the predicted number was just 3%. Something that contributes 8% to overall emissions is significant but something we still managed to greatly underestimate. Fortunately, there are several ways that we can work to reduce this carbon footprint and canceling your next vacation doesn't have to be one of them.

Giving up travel completely is probably the fastest and most effective way to reduce tourism emissions, but I think we'd all agree that it is not likely to happen — ever. The second best way is simply to reduce our travel. As we've learned in the other areas of sustainability, if you can't give up something altogether, then doing less of it is the next best option. Fewer, but longer, trips can be a good way to reduce overall emissions, provided, of course, that we stay in the same place (or places) when we get there.

Air travel is the biggest contributor to carbon emissions, but the choices that we make after we deplane matter, too. Still, let's start with the airplane in the room.

The airline industry in the US consumed over 17 billion gallons of fuel in 2018 alone. This is, as you can imagine, a massive contributor to carbon emissions.

The first way that we can cut back on the environmental harm of jet-setting is to fly with airlines that are conscious of their emissions and are working to counteract them. Norwegian Airlines is one of the most fuel-efficient transatlantic airlines. And in December 2018, the airline Hi Fly took the first plastic-free flight. Several others have committed to using less plastic or no plastics on their planes. We can reduce our plastic use on planes by bringing a water bottle, snacks, and other items we might need while in the skies.

As more companies join the ranks of green travel, there will be more ways to see the earth without damaging it — hopefully ensuring that it can be preserved to be explored and enjoyed by generations to come.

Carbon offsetting is one of the primary ways that people can help to equalize their carbon "debt." This is like when we eat too much at Thanksgiving, Christmas, or on Taco Tuesday, when we recognize the extra calories consumed and get to work to burn them off. Instead of calories, carbon offsetting happens when we recognize the greenhouse emissions produced by our flight and take action to utilize renewable energy products to help repay our "debt."

If I fly from Seattle to New York, a trip of about 2,800 miles, my trip will incur approximately 1.07 tons of CO_2 emissions. The airline could offset these emissions by participating in programs that plant trees, install clean energy options in developing countries, or establish "green" energy plants, etc.

If the airline doesn't have a carbon offsetting program, we can book flights through programs such as Flygreen, in order to help fill that role. Flygreen receives a fee from the airline which is used to offset the CO_2 emissions from your flight — either partially or completely.

Another option we can choose is to keep track of our air travel and develop a personal carbon offsetting system which we can "pay" at the end of the year. I'll talk more about this later in this chapter.

Of course, carbon offsetting is an imperfect option, and certainly not a solution to carbon emissions, but since we will continue to travel and expend large amounts of CO_2 for the foreseeable future, taking positive action to counteract the problem is far better than ignoring it.

Another way we can reduce emissions is to take a direct flight, which is also timesaving. By taking one flight instead of several, we are cutting down on the overall mileage, and reducing the number of times we have to take off and land, which contribute significantly to the amount of carbon emissions. This may not be an economically sustainable choice for everyone, or every trip, but it is something we can consider and take advantage of whenever possible.

I have always flown economy class. It's not my favorite, but I plan to stay there because flying in first or business class results in 3 times more emissions per person — probably just because you get 3 times as much space.

Once we have landed, choosing public transportation, such as buses or trains, will further reduce our carbon footprint. Biking and walking are generally best but aren't always an option. When they are, though, it's a good way to burn extra calories, so we can enjoy more of the local, seasonal foods we favor!

If each of us tries to incorporate a few of these different ideas into a part of our trip, we will each be making an impact.

Planes, trains, and automobiles aren't the only modes of transportation with a high environmental cost. I've been on a single cruise, but it was enough for me to decide that cruising is a pretty great way to travel. Unfortunately, the environmental footprint of the trip doesn't look as good as the blended margaritas served onboard.

Reports estimate that cruise ships pollute more than 1 million cars combined and that per person, the carbon footprint of a cruise is greater than air travel. Although, technically, a cruise *is* the vacation, many people have to also fly to begin the cruise, which adds insult to injury. I live near Seattle so the cruise dock is a quick drive away, but not everyone is that fortunate!

The negative effects don't end there, because once on board, the air quality on the ship is reported to be as bad as some of the world's most polluted cities. So much for fresh ocean breezes.

Although I think that working to offset our carbon footprint is a powerful way to understand and take responsibility for our impact on the environment, the term doesn't have a great history. The term "carbon footprint" was popularized by BP, the 6th largest polluter in the world, when it launched its "personal carbon footprint calculator" in 2004. This was a way to shift the responsibility for emissions (and a lot of other environmental issues) from companies like BP, to consumers. And while we, as individuals, are not the largest polluters in the world, we do have a role to play.

CARBON FOOTPRINT CALCULATORS

While initially intended, at least partially, as a means to transfer environmental responsibility to individual consumers, carbon footprint calculators serve a purpose and do exactly what they say. While exploring options for sustainable travel, I came across dozens of websites and blogs that referenced various carbon footprint calculators. We contribute to carbon emissions in all areas of our lives, but travel is definitely one of the major ones, which I think is why these calculators are frequently mentioned.

If you're curious about what the carbon footprint of your recent travel has been, or what it is in total considering your lifestyle, housing, dining, shopping, and transportation choices, you can plug this information into a carbon footprint calculator. There are several great options available at Trip Zero, World Wide Fund, and World Land Trust, or by checking out footprintcalculator.org or carbonfootprint.com. The more exact input you have, the more precise the output will be, but don't let that hold you back from plugging in whatever you know and taking a peek at your estimated emissions.

Some of the calculators allow you to make an offset directly through them (but make sure it is through a qualified company if you use that option!), or you can plant trees with the USDA Forest Service Plant-a-Tree program or utilize a service like terrapass.com.

A common form of offsetting is paying to have native trees planted. Even this, however, has some downsides. If the same types of trees are always planted, this can ultimately harm the biodiversity of the surrounding area, even though it also has the result of more trees absorbing more carbon dioxide. Just keep this in mind as you decide how and through whom to offset your emissions. There are programs helping to increase prairie grasses which store carbon in the soil, and others helping companies transition from using harmful chemicals to safer alternatives, while others are capping older landfills with cement to contain the methane gasses. While forestry is an important tool to offset emissions, these alternatives are also important. The carbon these programs are helping to offset is substantive, measurable, and verifiable.[31]

Be sure to check though that the company you are purchasing your offsets from is living up to its promises and standards. You can do this by looking to see if the company is certified by services like Green-e, evaluated by another third-party, logged into an official registry, or discloses these standards on its website.

As in all areas, transparency and accountability are foundational, and where they are lacking, it is best to steer clear (and then work to enact change).

When I entered my personal information into the various calculators, I was saddened by the results. They weren't terrible, but there were definitely areas where I could be doing better, and I set out to do just that.

I also decided to check back in December and do the calculation again to see if I had made progress. Then, based on the new results, I would do a carbon offset.

If you want real-time access to your footprint, you can use an app like Joro which is designed to help you understand and manage your footprint. You will answer some initial questions and connect a credit or debit card to allow the program to automatically estimate the emissions from your purchases. Although the program won't know what each line item you purchased was, it will use the answers you gave in the assessment to make assumptions and recommendations. In addition to these tips, the app can also suggest classes and articles about how to have the most impact while reducing your footprint. The first users of the app reduced their carbon footprints by about 10% and the founder, Sanchali Pal, pointed out "if everyone in the world did that, it would be like removing half the world's cars," which is not an insignificant impact.[32]

It is irrefutable that the emissions created by individual humans are unable to compete with the emissions generated by large corporations, but if I want those institutions to be held accountable, I know I must start by holding myself accountable. And as I was consistently reminded by researchers and analysts throughout my research, every action helps.

We can work to change the standards for companies, but we can also take the steps to reduce our emissions in our own lives. Both are important, and for a few dollars, I can afford to do my part.

ROAD TRIPPING

One of my favorite modes of travel is the "road trip." They're made even better with the appropriate snacks, a solid soundtrack, and good company.

Depending on the length of the trip and the number of travelers, driving may also be a superior sustainable option for travel.

Of course, one of the biggest things to consider when taking a road trip (of really any distance) is the vehicle we will be using. While we may not get to choose the specific airplane that takes us to a destination (or its size, capacity, or efficiency), we can make this choice when it comes to the vehicles we drive.

This is one of the areas where size does matter. On a longer road trip of 2,500 miles, i.e. from Los Angeles to New York City, a typical SUV will generate almost 3,500 pounds of CO_2, a standard car, on the other hand, will generate about 2,700 pounds of CO_2, and an efficient car will generate about 1,950 pounds of CO_2. In a situation like this, it may actually be more environmentally conscious (and time conscious, let's be honest) to take a flight, which will generate under 1,000 pounds of CO_2 per person. So, unless we're planning to stop and enjoy the sights along the way, we don't always have to avoid air travel to make the sustainable choice.

If, instead of New York City, our destination from Los Angeles was San Francisco, a trip of about 350 miles, we see a pretty similar pattern. A typical SUV will generate almost 500 pounds of CO_2, the average car will generate close to 400 pounds of CO_2, and the efficient car will generate close to 300 pounds of CO_2. A flight between these two cities averages out to approximately 225 pounds of CO_2 per person.

In either scenario, driving a hybrid or electric car is a more efficient option, and while they can't eliminate CO_2 emissions entirely, they do help to lower the numbers. The key is to have an idea about the impact of our choices.

Whether you are buying, leasing, or renting a car, the more you plan to drive, the bigger the environmental impact — or the smaller, if you make a sustainable choice. I won't mention any specific brands or models here, innovations are constantly being made in this area. But whether you're buying your next car, or renting one for a weekend trip, taking time to do a bit of research is definitely worth it.

We've already learned not to buy products we don't need, just because it is a new, sustainable option, especially if we already have a similar product at home. Generally, the same goes for cars. Replacing a car with a shiny new model, even one with new "green" features and great MPGs, comes with significant inherent environmental costs. Tons of materials are required to produce a new car, no matter how environmentally friendly it may be.

Argonne National Laboratory has determined that the impact of consuming the resources used to produce a new hybrid car will be canceled-to out through the long-term use of the car. But by continuing to use what we already own and buying used when it is time for an upgrade, we will help to reduce our impact.[33]

Carpooling is another way to help, regardless of the type of car we drive. The average car driving 20 miles across town generates almost 22 pounds of CO_2 but making the same trip with three friends will reduce our emissions per person to less than 6 pounds of CO_2. If you live in a rural area, carpooling may not be possible, but there may be times that it's an option to be explored — whether in your car with friends or by sharing an Uber ride with a stranger.

So, if there is a more efficient option available than a road trip, that's probably the sustainable way to go. But if hopping in the car is the best choice, I'll be the first to grab the snacks.

Another way that road trips can help us maintain our sustainable standards is through the things we bring. A cooler or bag dedicated to snacks (sans excess packaging) is likely to be a more sustainable and healthier option overall.

Igloo recently released a fully biodegradable cooler. It is made with recycled tree pulp and is designed to be the alternative to similar Styrofoam options. Since we know that Styrofoam may take centuries to break down, this seems like a very sustainable solution. Of course, we want to use the cooler (or three) we already have in the garage, but when we need to pick up a new one, this might be it.

I like to travel with every cup holder in the car filled. This is another perk of the road trip and allows me to avoid having to buy more bottles and cups along the way. If your cup has a capacity that is clearly marked, some places will allow customers to pay for a specialty drink at a restaurant or coffee shop along the road without the need for a disposable cup!

If you want to reduce your waste as much as possible during a road trip (and space isn't an issue), you might consider carrying an extra container to store compostable items. If you will be staying in one place for several days, you may find a local farm or grocery store that accepts items to be composted (Google can probably help with that!).

I took several months-long cross-country road trips with my family while I was growing up and I hope to take an even longer one in the future. I dream of a year or two spent on the road, working and traveling, learning and experiencing. Who knows if it will ever actually come about, but I think it would be a great trip. And although I would contribute to higher carbon emissions in some ways (more travel), I would also be lessening it in other ways (living on the road means fewer emissions from home). Plus, I would be able to incorporate ideas like slow travel and ecotourism to help cut emissions further. If you feel as I do and want to live an on-the-go lifestyle in a sustainable way, I hope this book will both encourage you to believe that both goals are possible, if you pursue them through the lens of consciousness.

SHOP AND EAT LOCALLY

Traveling provides an amazing opportunity to support local communities. Frequenting small, locally owned businesses supports the local economy, especially in places where tourism is an important source of income. I will admit that the area where I struggle most with this is with food. When I'm traveling alone and don't know an area well, I am often tempted to patronize a chain restaurant I am familiar with. But I've never left a Red Robin in Anytown, USA convinced that I just had the best dinner of my life. However, I have walked out of a small Mexican eatery knowing that I just had the best queso I've ever eaten, and a diner with the best burger, and a quaint brunch spot that had the best pancakes. By going local in a new place you can have an amazing dining experience and support sustainability at the same time.

Even better, be on the lookout for organic restaurants, those that work with local farmers, or grow their own ingredients. If you've traveled a long way, you probably don't want to eat food that has traveled just as far. Eat local. Eat seasonal. And eat less meat (don't worry, we'll get there).

STAY LOCAL

Just as it pays (or sometimes costs) to shop and eat local, staying local is something else to consider that often comes at a high environmental price. Hotels are currently responsible for 60 million tons of emissions each year.

When searching for a hotel that is working to reduce emissions, check for certifications like the Sustainable Tourism Eco-Certificate, EarthCheck, and Green Globe. Many other certifications cover a range of environmental issues, from composting, to building materials, to solar panels. It is worth asking about and doing a bit of research for the certifications local to the area where you are staying. If you want to vet a hotel even further and you are in the US, you can also check its Energy Star Rating.

TRANSPORTATION AT THE DESTINATION

Traveling a long way for vacation or business (not all travel is just for pleasure) carries a high environmental cost. However, we can make a big difference based on the amount and type of transportation we use when we reach our final destination. We should try to walk, bike, or use public transportation, if possible. I know this isn't always realistic, I'm from Seattle, after all, but even a small reduction can make a difference. And I've learned that one of the best ways to explore a new place is by sightseeing on my own two feet (zero emissions required).

Walking, biking, carpooling, and riding buses, ferries, trains, or other forms of public transportation tend to be more environmentally friendly. Walking and biking are also better for your health, a win-win.

Obviously, the best and simplest means of transportation is our own two feet. But, if we're being honest (or at least if I'm being honest), that is very rarely how I get around. Sure, I walk from the car into the store. I also run every morning for exercise. But rarely do I go anywhere without energy usage and the expulsion of a polluting substance.

If you live in, or are visiting, a large city, you are in the perfect spot to make sustainable choices. If you don't, that's okay, and I'm with you. At times, I've needed to drive somewhere so I could exercise and work out. Where I live now, I can run all around the neighborhood, but I must drive to get groceries and meet up with friends. Life is all about give and take, but there are always ways that we can find to improve our sustainability no matter where we live.

I have to drive almost every day and there are few alternatives available to me (no carpools, Uber drivers, or buses). Biking isn't an option, either. Even if I were able to locate a driving alternative, many options, while better, don't necessarily have the environmental benefits I'd assumed. Research done by the University of California in 2017 found that between 49% and 61% of ridesharing trips (i.e., Uber or Lyft) either wouldn't have been made at all or would have been made by either walking, biking, or public transit, if the rideshare wasn't an option. So, although it may have been cheaper, more convenient, or more efficient for the rider, these trips actually ended up resulting in increased congestion, traffic, and emissions.

Another study done by the University of Colorado determined that in Denver the use of a ridesharing service increased the average miles driven by 84%. This is largely because this option for public transportation is cheaper and drivers are more likely to increase their traveled miles.[34]

Generally, when we utilize a ridesharing service, we save overall emissions when compared to driving our own cars separately and alone, but this isn't always the case. So, I recommend that you use your best judgment when deciding whether, and which ridesharing service, to call.

ECOTOURISM

Ecotourism is designed to facilitate travel with a focus on bettering the environment — both the planet itself and the lives of the people who live on it. Often, the money you spend on ecotourism benefits the causes supported by the places you are paying, i.e. animal sanctuaries. About 95% of the revenues from ecotourism is returned to the local economy, as opposed to only about 20% of the alternative.

Of course, it is unlikely that all the trips you want to take or will take fall into the category of ecotourism, but these are always an option, especially if you are looking for a way to get back to nature and support causes you care about at the same time.

ENVIRONMENTAL EXCURSIONS

As with shopping, staying, and eating local, supporting local companies that offer tours or other activities is another sustainable choice. Just as shopping local at home helps to keep money in our communities, when we travel, we have the opportunity to support other local communities. If you want to go above and beyond, do some preliminary research to ensure that you are supporting companies with sustainable (i.e. doesn't offer tours in areas or close to animals that should be left undisturbed) and ethical (i.e. local people are employed and paid fairly) practices.

BE AWARE OF LOCAL CUSTOMS

Although this may seem somewhat unrelated to sustainability, the people we meet and the experiences we have during our travels are infinitely important and are part of the overall reason we are pursuing sustainability in the first place. It all comes back to our desire to respect, honor, the care for people and places we visit around the planet.

SLOW TRAVEL

When I first heard the term "slow travel," I immediately associated it with the kind of traveling you have to do when you're with your grandparents or have a car full of kids. But actually, anyone can utilize the principles of slow travel in pretty much any situation.

There is no single right way to do slow travel, but for most of us, it means staying in one place longer and making the most out of it as sustainably as possible, as opposed to traveling to lots of different places. [35] It is like minimalism for your passport.

It can also involve utilizing more of the local transportation options (and simultaneously less of them), consuming fewer resources, or choosing to travel to lesser-known places, instead of the bigger landmarks. It can be all of these things or none of them. But utilizing the principles of slow travel in some way will bring environmental benefits.

When I consider my history, I see several examples of slow travel. When I was growing up, my family would often drive to a timeshare in the middle of Washington State to enjoy a week relaxing at the lake. We didn't fly, which reduced our environmental impact, and the drive itself was just a few hours. Another plus was that once we arrived, we walked everywhere, including the grocery store, the farmers market, church, pool, and even the shaved ice stand. Everything we needed was right there. Plus, since it was a time-share rather than a hotel, we used the same linens and towels for the entire week. While having to make my bed on vacation wasn't my favorite thing, looking back I don't regret it at all and I'm glad those sheets weren't washed every night. We also did most of our own cooking and used things that we brought from home — a positive sustainable score, too.

I have very fond memories of those weeks in the sun (and sometimes the snow) at the lake. While it wasn't a time to experience a new place or culture, it was still a vacation done in a slow travel kind of way.

Trips I've taken to England and Africa had different purposes and were experienced very differently. You probably don't want slow travel for every vacation, but if you're willing to take the ride, I think that you'll find slow travel can be just the ticket.

STAY SUSTAINABLE

A seemingly small but significant thing we can do when we travel is continuing to maintain our sustainable habits, no matter where in the world we are. I'll share more in later chapters about the specific habits I've adopted and the products I've incorporated into my routine that have helped me to lessen my environmental impact even as I travel. By maintaining my momentum while on the go, I stay sustainable.

One small way is to bring a reusable water bottle to refill. An increasing number of airports and other public places have dedicated spots to refill water bottles. Some airports even have a meter that reports the number of plastic bottles that have been eliminated through the use of the water bottle filling station. I love this reminder of our collective positive impact.

Refilling water bottles isn't always an option, however. When I traveled to Africa a decade ago, we carried bottled water with us everywhere, because our immune and digestive systems may not have been ready to handle the local tap water. The availability of sustainable clean drinking water around the world is its own issue, but the important takeaway is that wherever you are going for travel, do your research and then make a conscious choice based on what you've learned.

One of my pet peeves about traveling and hotels is the miniature soap and shampoo bottles offered to travelers. If a hotel has 100 rooms, for example, this would mean that 100 mini bottles of shampoo, conditioner, and lotion could be used and discarded every day, up to 300 little plastic bottles just thrown away and likely to spend decades in a landfill. And that's just one hotel. My small hometown in the Pacific Northwest has 3 hotels, but I don't even want to guess how many hotels operate in nearby Seattle. That's a lot of miniatures bottles.

I suggest that we always bring these products with us and make sure that we dispose of them properly. This will eliminate the waste and will also increase the likelihood that these items will be recycled, whenever possible. It may mean that we have to take our empty shampoo bottles back home with us to be reused again or recycled, but this is always worth the effort.

Another easy way to reduce your footprint while traveling is to maintain some of the same smart habits that you do at home. Do you really need all the lights on? Do you really need to sleep with the television on? Do you need to take a 40-minute shower? You can reduce your energy and environmental impact while still enjoying your trip.

Once you have checked in to your locally owned hotel (or even if you're staying at a huge international chain) your choices inside the room can also make a big difference. Many hotels have started to request that we reuse our sheets and towels multiple times. When we do, it has a huge environmental impact. We don't wash the sheets and towels at home after every use (at least, I hope you don't by this point in the book), so it is worth questioning whether the ones we use at a hotel need to be. According to the EPA, about 15% of commercial water use is by hotels. And the Smithsonian has reported that reusing towels can reduce energy costs by 17%. That number will improve even more if we stretch the time between washes and if we can enlist more people to join us.

I'm not asking you to sleep on dirty sheets or use smelly towels, but I am asking you to consider if the choices you're making are sustainable.

Another small change I recommend is to become conscious about the temperature in your hotel room so as to not exploit either the AC or the heat. Just because you won't personally be responsible for the electricity bill doesn't mean you need to go overboard. Some hotels strive to be energy efficient or have renewable energy systems, so if there is one at the location you're heading, that could also be a sustainable choice.

With all of the smartphones in use today, it is surprising that many people still feel a need to print out travel itineraries, boarding passes, and driving directions. The sustainable option is to utilize the technology at our disposal to reduce the need to print out travel information.

In addition to a smartphone, another way to maintain momentum is to compile and carry a sustainable travel kit. The following items can help reduce our carbon footprint: insulated and refillable water bottles and hot cups (better yet, use one that can serve as both a water bottle and a hot cup!), cloth napkins, handkerchiefs, reusable cutlery sets, containers to carry food, snacks, or leftovers, and a reusable shopping bag. We can also travel with our own snacks (ideally, sans packaging). It also helps to have a means to clean the travel kit components, particularly if an outing is projected to last more than an afternoon.

Keep in mind that the items you already own are always better than the "sustainable" ones you'd have to purchase. The bamboo cutlery set in the little pouch is nice, but so are the utensils you have at home. The same goes for straws, cups, bags, and everything else.

If you are packing for a flight, opt for bamboo over metal, bring refillable TSA-approved bottles for soap, shampoo, and conditioner (and a reusable clear bag to carry them in), and a refillable water bottle. But don't forget to empty the water bottle before you get to security and remember to fill it again when you get to the other side. You'll thank me later.

EATING OUT (OR IN)

Although I eat out regularly (I visit my favorite Mexican place at least once a week), I thought I should talk about dining in versus take-out since we generally eat out more frequently while traveling. This is an area where our sustainability values may be a bit more challenging to act on. Remind yourself *why* you are striving for sustainability. Decide in advance what you are going to do before you place your order.

Although restaurant dining doesn't usually incur the high environmental cost of takeout, it's worthwhile, when possible, to research whether the restaurant uses disposables. For example, if they are offering plastic straws, you may want to be ready with your metal one or be ready to go without.

Some restaurants may offer real and disposable utensil options. If possible, always look for reusable utensils rather than disposables. If you ask in advance for a real fork or cup, restaurants are usually more than happy to oblige. We can also bring our own tools or utensils with us.

I have even heard about people bringing compostable items home with them after eating out so they can be properly disposed of. I have yet to do that, but I am conscientious about the number of paper napkins I use.

If there's a possibility you might take home leftovers, it is a good idea to bring along a container for them. The end result is no disposables in the garbage, less cost to the restaurant, your fridge looks sleek instead of being stuffed with Styrofoam, and you'll be ready to reheat the leftovers later.

Dining in at a restaurant (as opposed to takeout) is one way to automatically reduce waste (and the overall number of dishes), but if I'm being honest, there is little that I enjoy more than eating amazing restaurant food in my pajamas, on the couch, watching reruns of The Big Bang Theory.

The biggest way to minimize waste in take-out is to bring your own containers for the food. It's best to ask if that is something you can do when you call to place your order. If you choose to do so, it's best to order, at least the first time, when the restaurant is not overly crowded or busy and you have time to state your case. An easier alternative is to order your food in the restaurant and then box it up in your own containers when it is served.

Local restaurants tend to be a bit more understanding and may even appreciate that you are saving them money by not using their containers! They also may be interested to learn more about your sustainability efforts and the ways you are striving to make your community and the world a greener place. And remember to be polite and tip well, if possible. If a restaurant refuses to accommodate you, it is best to go along and use that information when deciding where to get takeout the next time.

Some restaurants will serve their to-go items in compostable containers or in paper bags or wrappers that can be composted. Yes, that Taco Bell burrito wrapper, Burger King hamburger wrapper, and Subway sandwich wrapper can be composted. In some cases, you may want to check whether heavy-duty items (like "compostable" forks or clamshells) can be composted in a backyard composter or if they will only break down an industrial composting facility. We will talk more about composting in Chapter 7, but for now, if you are willing to take disposables because you know they are compostable, just make sure to take the extra step to compost them. Tossing them into the trash can defeats the point.

Recently, I was happy to see one of my favorite fast-casual chains sharing about the steps they have taken to become more environmentally friendly. While some of this is on the store level, down to the lightbulbs they use, they also are striving to make the products they use green. They use paper bags for packing orders, recyclable cutlery, strawless lids for their cups, and compostable bowls. But I noticed that the company didn't share about *how* they ensure the cutlery is recycled, bowls composted, or bags disposed of properly. Since many people take these things to go, the company can't control what happens to them when they leave the restaurant. And if those that are discarded at the restaurant end up in one big trash bag, they aren't being handled properly either.

PLASTIC STRAWS

Plastic straws tend to get used the most often when people are on the go and the environmental impact of plastic straws is something that we have heard a lot about in recent years. Research shows that approximately 500 million plastic straws are used by Americans every day and each one may take anywhere from 100 to 200 years to break down. Actually, they just turn into smaller and smaller pieces of plastic, leaching into the soil, ending up in our water, and being eaten or ingested by marine life. They increase the toxicity of the ocean, disrupt ecosystems around the world, and producing them requires large amounts of nonrenewable resources and fossil fuels.

Straws are a relatively small issue when it comes to sustainability and only 0.03% of ocean plastic pollution is attributable to them — as opposed to 46% from discarded fishing nets. However, by volume, 0.03% makes sense, and this is something that I can control in my own life.

So, while the number of straws in the ocean may be relatively small in the grand scheme of things, we can still act on behalf of our planet and to live a more sustainable life. Straws are still important. They are one more example of how we often prioritize convenience over sustainability but the elimination of them is an easy fix.

The best option is to take a reusable straw with you whenever possible. It may seem awkward at first to remove it from the glass, and take it home, but the inconvenience doesn't make it inconsequential.

I have metal straws in my house that I have had for years and I use them all the time in smoothies and other cold drinks. They work great when I'm on the go, too. Reusable straws can be made of glass, silicone, stainless steel, or bamboo. Some are designed to be portable, others are not. Some come in a carrying case, others do not. There are countless options, and as long as they are reusable and responsibly made, you really can't go wrong.

There are disposable alternatives to plastic straws as well. But the paper ones still require a significant number of resources to produce — in some cases more than their plastic counterparts, even if they break down easier — and often they do, in the bottom of your drink.

Granted, you can always just go completely strawless, so if that's more your speed, that's a sustainable option. But if you're in the drive-through lane or a cup at the restaurant still carries a smudge of lipstick from the last guest, you might want to have a reusable straw at hand.

WATER BOTTLES

It was a long time before I realized that water bottle companies only produce half of the product. They aren't making water; they're actually just in the business of making bottles.

Whether you carry a water bottle around with you all the time, or just when you know you'll need one, the sustainable choice is always to utilize a reusable one.

If the statistics about microplastics and BPA in plastic water bottles aren't enough to turn you off, the sustainability argument hopefully will. The production of plastic water bottles requires about 17 million barrels of oil every year — enough to fuel 1 million cars for that length of time. In addition, producing just 1 pound of plastic requires 22 gallons of water. So making 1 liter of bottled water actually requires 3 liters of water.

Bottled water is over 1,000 times more expensive than tap water to the consumer, and over 40% of it is drawn from the tap anyway. You can save both money and the environment by giving up single use plastic bottles.

I admit that it's easy to forget to bring a water bottle, so I keep a couple in the car at all times. I can easily grab one from there and take it with me into a meeting or on a run. When one is empty, I take it into the house to refill it and then put it back in the car right away or by the door so I don't forget. If I do, I always have a backup (or two) at the ready.

The most sustainable reusable water bottle option is the one that you already own — and chances are, you do. Buying another one, even if it is trendy or attractive, won't necessarily help to instill this habit, and instead will add one more thing into the cycle. I'm still using the ones I've had for years, and since they are stainless steel, they'll probably last forever. If you need one or want an extra to make sure you always have one available, there are lots of good options.

There are places in the world where plastic water bottles provide the only clean drinking water option, and in times of crisis they are of vital importance, but a hot afternoon at Disney World doesn't make the cut. If each of us will reduce our use of these single-use water bottles as much as possible, we will help to reduce the 50 billion plastic water bottles currently bought every year in the United States.

HOT CUPS

I live near Seattle, the home of Starbucks, so I am used to seeing a coffee shop on almost every corner. I don't have a completely caffeine-fueled life-style, but I do find myself stopping at a local coffee shop with great regularity. Usually it's to meet a friend for coffee, to work in between meetings, or just because I want to fill a craving.

I like routine and familiarity. Starbucks feels both homey and local to me, even though I've been in stores everywhere from Dallas to Orlando to Boise. So, while I certainly want to continue to visit, I also want to ensure that I cut down on waste and reach my sustainability goals.

The most sustainable option (environmentally and financially) is to stop frequenting these places as much or give them up entirely. While I was willing to cut back on my visits, I didn't want to give them up altogether. Instead, I started opting to get my coffee at the independent local establishments near me. Although I always knew what I would get when I went to Starbucks, from what my drink would taste like, to the music, to the atmosphere, I began to enjoy meeting friends at more unique places where I would often be surprised. A coffee shop atop a ridge brought me chai in a "for here" mug as I journaled and watched the sunrise over the foggy bay below. The coffee shop built into the corner between two buildings makes a great mocha, even if you do have to stand in the wind while your drink is being made. Another one down the street is frequented by customers that have the cutest dogs!

I've had fun trying out different local spots. Some I visit with friends and others I prefer to go to alone. Most importantly, these businesses have been supportive of my sustainability efforts. Most of them happily use a to-go cup that I carry with me or will make my drink in a "for here" mug if I don't have anywhere to go. Some even offer spaghetti noodles as stirring sticks, instead of wood — a very sustainable solution if not also an odd one.

In this way, I get to make sustainable choices, but I also get to support local businesses, a sustainable choice wherever you live.

While Starbucks will provide you a "for here" cup upon request, during my many years of visits, I've seen this only a handful of times. In fact, only about 1.5% of the drinks served at Starbucks are served in reusable cups or mugs. Although Starbucks caters to a large contingent of to-go customers (just 20% of the drinks served are consumed in the store), there is still room for improvement. Starbucks sells reusable cups and mugs but reusing them at the store has yet to become the norm, while it's more frequently done in local establishments.

If every customer used a reusable cup for both in-house and to-go orders (I know, that would be a huge leap, but it would be pretty impressive) we would save thousands of trees, millions of liters of water, and over a billion kilograms of CO_2 emissions each year. Bringing and using your own cup is another way to cut back on your carbon footprint!

Anywhere between 16 and 58 billion paper cups are used and thrown away in the United States every year. That is a staggering number — and only partially (although maybe largely) attributable to Starbucks. A large number of these cups are used with hot liquids and thus, aren't made solely out of paper, but rather, out of a combination of plastic, paper, water, and other waste. 20 million trees are cut down every year and 12 billion gallons of water are used to produce them.

Just as bad, these cups can take over 20 years to decompose. When I think of how many cups I have tossed and never thought of again (until now) and the fact they will still be around in 20 years, my heart breaks a little.

McDonald's reportedly sells over 137 million drinks that will be served in disposable paper cups every year. Costa Coffee, one of my favorite places to get coffee in England, sells over 140 million. There is no research or number pointing to how many cups Starbucks contributes every year, and while that doesn't surprise me, it does leave me worried. Especially because estimates range up to 4 billion cups a year.

Thankfully, using reusable hot cups is becoming more accepted, and some companies, even Starbucks, are trying to innovate the most effective ways to normalize this practice. Hopefully, in the near future, this will become the norm, but until it is, we can be trendy and different by bringing or asking for a non-disposable cup. If you don't have the option to do so, it is best to go straw-less, lid-less, and stopper-less — regardless of whether you like your coffee iced or hot.

And if you are at a place that will accept your cup, I especially like the insulated ones that can keep drinks hot or cold. But whether you have a cup for each purpose, or one that does both, you are making another important and necessary environmental effort by helping to reduce our consumption of disposable cups.

CONSIDERING THE COST

When you're on the go, it can be harder to act in line with your values because you are out of your normal routine. But you can still find ways to live your sustainable values without slowing down at all.

I decided to review the previous year to consider what kind of ecological footprint my trips may have had. Although I don't normally travel often, I was shocked to realize how many trips I took in the year before I started my project. Early on, I attended a conference in Texas, and while I was there, I took a short trip over to Waco, the home of the Magnolia empire. A few months later, I headed to southern California for an aunt's wedding. Both trips were enjoyable, but they required a lot of driving in addition to air travel.

My third trip of the year was a family affair when we spent a long weekend in Idaho. Again, it was necessary to take a few long drives in addition to the flights.

Finally, in the early Fall, I traveled to the Northeast for another conference, which required the most driving in addition to being the longest flight.

All of these trips were to accomplish a necessary purpose; none were just about rest and relaxation. And while I enjoyed all of these trips and have great memories, I was surprised by the accumulation of miles, both flown and driven.

When I traveled to England a few years ago, I was only vaguely aware of the environmental impact of the trip. But I realize now that even my much shorter trips, while generating much less overall waste, can certainly add up. This assessment has left me feeling grateful for the travel opportunities and now, with my greater knowledge and perspective on the environmental costs of traveling, I now know what I could or would have done differently and what I should do in the future.

Several years before I began my sustainability project, I came across a review of the book *Zero Waste Home: The Ultimate Guide to Simplifying Your Life by Reducing Your Waste* that surprised and saddened me. In the book, the author shares about her experience decreasing her family's amount of yearly waste until all of it could fit into a Mason jar. As you can imagine, she had to employ some pretty drastic tactics to accomplish her objective. The review I read expressed appreciation for the book's ideas and insights, but also scolded the author for the annual international trip she made to visit family, due to the environmental cost of the flight. In the author's defense, when I actually read the book a few years later, I noted that she did, in fact, acknowledge the environmental harm of those trips and shared ways to reduce the harm to the environment from traveling.

It is probably not realistic to assume that even the most ardent environmentalist will be willing to give up traveling entirely. In fact, many environmentalists travel all over the world to share about the causes they care about. And I doubt most of them could fit their collected waste into a Mason jar at the end of a year. I know I certainly could not.

In summary, although I was shocked and disheartened by all that I learned about traveling in April, I don't think that the alternative is not to travel. There are so many things to learn and explore and it is on these adventures that we experience all that this amazing planet has to offer. Fortunately, there are ways that we can travel that are mindful of our need to collectively strive for increased sustainability.

We all must do our best to live out our personal values in the ways that make the most sense to us. I am not perfect and my life is not entirely sustainable. It probably never will be. But it remains important that we continue to do our part and make the best choices that we can.

So if one day you are sitting next to me on a plane, just know that I care about the planet and I will be paying my carbon offsets at the end of the year.

CHAPTER 5
MAY: SKINCARE

By this point in the year, I had become a regular visitor to the website for the Environmental Working Group, searching for cleaning products that were both sustainable and nontoxic.

I have to admit, however, that my association with the EWG goes back even further. Several years ago I was listening to a podcast where someone was discussing the EWG's Skin Deep database and the app that they developed to help you determine what health risks were hiding in your makeup bag (which sounds like a teaser for the nightly news).

When I got home that day, I downloaded the app and spent some time scanning various products in my medicine cabinet to see if I was filling myself with toxins. I don't know if the app wasn't working, or if none of the products I used at the time were in the database, but I never received any results, just a message that my "item was not found." I soon deleted the app and forgot all about it, continuing to slather my face with products that did more internal harm than external good.

Thankfully, my sustainability project intervened to ensure that, at least going forward, I will be using what's best for both the planet and my body. All of my research for this book was conducted through an internet browser, rather than through the app, so I still have no idea if the app works. But the information on the website database is liquid (foundation) gold.

It was important to me that the sustainable choices I made were also nontoxic and healthy, and I knew the Skin Deep database would help me figure out which products fall into that category. If I really wanted to be completely sustainable, I could avoid using facial products and makeup altogether, but that's not my ultimate goal. My goals are nourishing my skin (so I don't look like I'm 60 years old before I am) and preserving the planet.

So, the hunt for sustainable, non-toxic makeup and skincare products was on. Little did I know this would be harder to find than a goose that lays golden eggs — and all I was after was a little foundation.

I quickly realized I was going to be forced to make some difficult decisions.

THE TRADE-OFF

My dilemma was perfectly illustrated by a trip to Target.

A few days after my first mind-bending jump into the Skin Deep database on the EWG website, I found myself in the makeup aisle with foundation as the last remaining item on my shopping list.

It was Monday. It was late. I had just come from an hour-long barre class and I was exhausted from the strenuous workout and a long workday. I hadn't had dinner and my mood was bordering on hangry.

I scanned the aisle, almost, *almost* wishing I hadn't started this journey so I could skip over to the Maybelline section and pick up my shade — 120. It was so close. Right there.

But from what I had learned on the EWG website and my commitment to the sustainability project as a whole, I knew I couldn't give in, as tempting as it was.

Instead, I continued to scan the shelves. Pacifica brand had done a good job across the board from what I'd seen on the EWG website. I found a shade that I thought would work. I looked at the price. It was expensive — almost double what I had ever spent on foundation. But I was doing it for my health, I reasoned, not to mention for the planet. So I tossed it in my basket and headed to self-checkout.

Once I was home and had eaten, I decided to double-check my purchase. With a Big Bang Theory rerun playing in the background, I pulled up the EWG website, feeling apprehension as to what my search might reveal.

I typed in the brand and the product.

A yellow number 4 popped up.

What?! How could this one product that I picked from a fairly nontoxic line be in the moderate danger zone? I felt exasperated; a bit at the brand, but more so at myself. I hadn't bothered to visit the EWG website with my smartphone as I stood in the aisle to double-check that I was making a good purchase.

Worse, when I tried out the foundation the next morning, it was great; definitely better than what I'd used in the past. It was smooth, not overly pigmented, and lasted for most of the day. While I knew I would need to use up this product, I also knew I wouldn't be able to bring myself to purchase it again.

So, the next time I found myself in Target, standing in the makeup aisle, I put down my basket and pulled out my phone. I scanned the aisle, again and again, typing different brands into the EWG search bar. I found just two products that were "verified" by the EWG. W3ll People and Mineral Fusion.

I had previously researched W3ll People and knew it was a brand fighting for sustainability. However, the foundation in stock was a stick foundation (in a plastic tube), about the size of my ring finger, and double again what I had paid for the last foundation. I knew that nontoxic would cost more, but this felt extreme. I would probably use it up in a week!

I decided to go with Mineral Fusion, which was also EWG verified and came in a slightly larger glass bottle at a pretty comparable price point. This time, I went home knowing I had made a good choice — at least for my skin.

When I put it on the next morning, I wasn't really thrilled. It was too light (completely my fault) and gave questionable coverage. I decided that when it was gone, I would give Mineral Fusion another shot, in a slightly darker shade. If I still didn't like it, my search would begin again.

Some of my readers may think that my desire to seek out non-toxic products is overkill. After all, isn't the point of this book to encourage making sustainable choices? Why bother to trade-off? Why not just opt for sustainability?

Unfortunately, just because something is nontoxic, doesn't mean that it is sustainable, and vice versa. There are very few items available that are both.

I want to make choices that benefit the earth and my body because if I don't, my actions won't be sustainable in the long run. And the chemicals I'm trying to avoid in my skincare and makeup can't be good for the environment either.

After much deliberation, I reached an unfortunate trade-off. I determined that for products like shampoo (which we will discuss in Chapter 6), I was willing to sacrifice a little of my nontoxic criteria to make sure that what I was using wouldn't end up in a landfill. However, when it came to skincare products like foundation, I wanted to stick to nontoxic products, even if it meant more plastic.

CHEMICALS

The EU has banned or restricted 1,300 chemicals from being used in the production of cosmetics. Canada has banned 600 chemicals. The US Food and Drug Administration, which was founded in 1938, has only banned or restricted 11 chemicals. That's a shocking discrepancy and a major problem for those of us in the USA.

In his book *What's Gotten Into Us*, McKay Jenkins says "chemicals in Europe are considered guilty until proven innocent. Here in the United States, it is the other way around."

Congress hasn't voted on the regulation of cosmetics in over 80 years. The last legislation passed was the Food, Drug, and Cosmetics Act of 1938 which prohibited selling cosmetics containing a "poisonous or deleterious substance," or any "filthy, putrid, or decomposed substance." It is both fascinating and terrifying that in the US cosmetics remain, for the most part, an unregulated industry. Congress has passed safety standards for drugs, food, toys, and medical devices. Everything from electric blankets to cough suppressants and laser scanners to pesticides has been regulated. But not cosmetics.

What's worse is that many multinational brands produce cleaner and safer versions of their products to sell in Europe, as opposed to the counterparts sold in North America.

An average woman uses 12 products every day which may contain 168 different ingredients. Does anyone really know what those ingredients are and what they do? If so, chances are, it's not the consumer. Less than 10% of the over 10,000 chemicals used in the cosmetic industry have been tested for safety.[36]

And that is where the EWG comes in.

Since there is so little testing and review before cosmetics and other personal care products are released (basically none), the EWG performs testing on the back end. Although it would be nice if the US government required testing, or banned some of the most harmful chemicals, at least the EWG is alerting consumers.

Similar to the rankings for cleaning products, the EWG has a ranking system for cosmetics and body care products that starts in the "green zone." These are the products that are considered to be less dangerous and receive an "EWG Verified" (the best overall ranking) or are numbered 1 or 2. If a product is rated between 3 and 6, it falls into the "yellow" zone of products that are considered to be a moderate risk. Products rated from 7 to 10 fall into the "red" zone and are considered to be the highest risk.

If you buy products from any major brands, it is worth taking a few minutes to check out where they fall on this scale. From there, you can make a personal, informed decision.

The EWG website is available to help you or you can do research on your own, but I want to discuss some of the chemicals that find their way into many of our skincare products which are known to cause harm, from allergies to cancer.

Some groups list the "toxic ten," while others reference the "dirty dozen." Unfortunately, there are more than ten or twelve chemicals to avoid. Many are worse than dirty, and some are more than toxic. But here are the ones that surfaced again and again during my research to protect your skin (and yourself) against.

- Butylated hydroxyanisole (BHA) and butylated hydroxytoluene (BHT) are found in lipsticks, moisturizers, exfoliators, and fragrances. Some studies have reported that they can cause liver damage or alter your thyroid hormone level. Further, the National Toxicology Program classifies BHA as a chemical that is "reasonably anticipated to be a human carcinogen."

- Aminophenol, Diaminobenzene, and Phenylenediamine are also known as coal tar dyes and are used often in hair dye. They are a byproduct of coal processing and are a known human carcinogen. In Europe, much of their use in hair dye has been banned. But in the United States, hair stylists (and their clientele) are exposed to these chemicals in hair dye almost every day.

- Parabens serve as antibacterial agents and preservatives to prevent contamination of our cosmetics. The European Commission's Scientific Committee on Consumer Products has warned that some longer chain parabens may be endocrine disruptors, cause reproductive harm and other developmental disorders, interfere with hormone levels, and are considered to be carcinogenic.

- Synthetic fragrances (nearly 4,000 of them) are harder to identify because they are used in everything from shampoos to lotions and aren't always clearly labeled. Because "fragrance" can be used as a general term, some of the chemicals that fall under the term may not actually have anything to do with scent. In the United States, companies aren't required to list the chemicals in their fragrances since laws still exist to protect the secret ingredients in a company's product formula. And the EWG has found that across 17 name-brand fragrance products, an average of 14 chemicals were not listed on the label. Since the chemicals in fragrances can vary, they can be linked to allergies and rashes, and even to cancer and nervous system damage. Some fragrances act as a neurotoxin, which can cause irritability, hyperactivity, and depression. Opting for unscented or fragrance-free products would be the perfect solution, however, research shows that the chemicals used to elicit the lack of a scent are just as harmful (if not more so) than the ones added to incorporate a pleasant odor. Many of these chemicals that are commonly passed off as "fragrance-free" are described below.

- Sulfates are a chemical I was familiar with before the start of my research. I have relatively curly hair and I was told early on that I should avoid using shampoos containing sulfates. But this restriction should probably be extended to everyone. Sulfates are the ingredients in shampoos and other cleansers that do the cleaning, however, research has shown that these chemicals are absorbed rapidly and can cause skin irritation and acne and may disrupt the natural oil balance of your skin.

- Phthalates present another set of problems. These chemicals keep products flexible or soft and are often used in nail polish, deodorant, perfume, and hairspray, and are also used outside of beauty products to soften plastic. In fragrances, they work to combine the scents together. Research has shown that the chemicals in phthalates can cause endocrine disruption, respiratory problems, and headaches. I mean who hasn't gotten a headache after putting on hairspray, standing next to someone wearing a little too much perfume, or just walking past the local Bath & Body Works store? The phthalates may be the cause. Pregnant women are advised to avoid all products with phthalates since they can lead to birth defects and reproductive issues. This is a chemical garnering more and more attention, fortunately, and like parabens, alternative products are now labeled "phthalate-free."

- Oxybenzone is a chemical that is used in sunscreen. An important product, science has suggested that every one of us should wear sunscreen every day to avoid skin damage from sunburn. But studies have shown that oxybenzone may disrupt hormone production, which rivals sunburn for negative impact.

- Propylene glycol is used as a skin-conditioning agent but according to the EWG, it has been linked to dermatitis and hives, two things I want to avoid.

- Petrolatum is mineral oil jelly. I used it all the time when I was growing up. Commonly known as Vaseline, it was the major ingredient in the chapstick I used to use on my lips. It is intended to help lock moisture in the skin, or it can be used in your hair to boost shine. But it becomes a hazard if it hasn't been refined.

- DEA, or diethanolamine, is a major additive found in many of our products. It is the chemical that makes cosmetics creamy and soaps sudsy. Research shows that it can cause skin irritation. The European Union classifies DEA as a carcinogen with the potential to cause serious damage to health. Its use is completely banned in the UK. So, I think I'll pass on the suds.[37]

- Teflon is one of the brand names for PTFE, one of thousands of fluorinated chemicals known as PFASs or PFCs. When we hear Teflon, we picture nonstick frying pans. You may not realize that it's also in your makeup bag. Through testing, the EWG found Teflon in 66 different products sold by 15 major brands. Beyond Teflon, they also found 13 different PFAS chemicals in nearly 200 products from 28 brands. Teflon and other PFASs were found in makeup, sunscreen, shampoo, and shaving cream, many of which are household names. PFASs have been linked to cancer, thyroid disease, and a reduced effectiveness of childhood vaccines. The Skin Deep database lists the products that contain PFAS, or you can look at your product labels. PFASs are often identified with "fluoro" in the name.[38]

- Artificial coloring is made from coal tar and should be avoided in food, drink, and makeup. These chemicals are typically labeled as FD&C, D&C, or Red 6.

- Toluene, a chemical commonly found in paint thinner and which is also used in hair dyes and nail polishes, has been linked to interference in hormones and immune function.

- Lead has been found in a variety of lipsticks. Yuck.

- Formaldehyde isn't just used for science class (I remember hoping to be sick the day that frog dissection was scheduled in high school biology). A derivative of formaldehyde, formalin is a preservative used to keep beauty products fresh. Unfortunately, it has been linked to cancer.

Armed with this information, you now know many of the primary chemicals to you may want to avoid. Unfortunately, many products don't list the chemicals they contain.

But the worry doesn't end there. If we combine "clean" products with ones we already have in our makeup drawer, or if we just continue using the same products we always have, we are mixing chemicals. There is no real way to know how our cleanser, moisturizer, toner, and foundation (and maybe concealer, highlighter, blush, contour, and any other number of products) will combine and interact — especially if they are from different brands. While products are tested, they aren't tested in combination with other products from other brands. So, while a moisturizer might be fine on its own, there is no way to know how it will combine with everything else on the palette of your face.

Everyone's genetic makeup plays a role as well. We exercise and eat well and moisturize, but we also watch Netflix and eat doughnuts and sometimes leave a little mascara under our eyes at bedtime — but very few people would think the moisturizer or mascara residue could have the biggest negative effect on their health.

Chemicals are terrifying. I've suffered from eczema since I was a toddler when my doctor prescribed a skin medication that was toxic given my age and stage. Luckily, I've learned how to manage my eczema and can hide most of the rough itchy patches from the outside world. But, the effect that chemicals can have on our bodies, some for the rest of our lives, is profound.

Companies continue to use these chemicals because they are cheaper than more natural and healthy alternatives. And, if consumers and the government aren't forcing change, it is easier and financially rewarding to go with the status quo. Although I hope that governments will begin to enact changes, or companies will decide to act in the best interest of consumers, in the meantime, we can do our best to bring change — starting with our personal makeup bags.

The information I have shared here is not comprehensive. It is intended to increase awareness and to act as a starting point for further research. The chemicals listed above appeared consistently in the material I read. Unfortunately, there are hundreds and thousands more like them being used, to make our skin bronze, glow, and sparkle, while also potentially aggravating pre-existing medical conditions or planting seeds for new ones.

If you are interested in learning more about the chemicals used in cosmetics and other personal care products, I encourage you to utilize the Skin Deep database. While we want to care for our environment, we also want to ensure that we maintain our health so we can enjoy it, too.

THE COST OF CLEAN BEAUTY

The use of chemicals is not our only concern when it comes to skincare products. The way that these products are tested and approved is another area of major concern.

While there is no universally approved definition of the term "clean beauty," it definitely comes with a higher price tag.

Unfortunately, this is to be expected because the thing that makes some products "dirty" is the substitution of less costly (and healthful) ingredients. If a company is spending more to incorporate clean and/or sustainable ingredients in its products, additional money will be spent on administration, research, testing, reporting, and sourcing. If the final product and the packaging are sustainable as well, the investment increases further.

Ideally, the higher price won't remain high forever. As demand for clean beauty products grows, companies will be able to produce them in greater quantities which will improve efficiency and reduce costs per unit.

If you are ready to begin using clean products but find the cost prohibitive, start by purchasing small sample sizes. You'll be able to make sure that you like the products before you spend the additional funds. Plus, it is always a good idea to test products before buying a large quantity, because the use of natural, plant-based materials may introduce some potential allergens and irritants. But, note that this approach will generate more environmental waste in the short term.

It is okay to figure out what "clean beauty" means to you personally. You can decide what products you want to use, what "standards" you want to follow, and what price you want to pay. As long as we stay informed and try to make sustainable choices, we'll be on the right track.[39]

ANIMAL TESTING

If the section on chemicals scared you, this one will break your heart.

Animal testing is a horrific practice but it is still used by many major brands at the time of this writing. I was shocked during my research to see animals being injected with, or covered in, substances that may, eventually, lead to death.

One particular image stuck with me. A small white rabbit, cowering at the back of its cage. Its eyes are red and bloodshot. The face, covered by streaks of mascara. No animal should have to go through that irritation and pain for me, or anyone.

The makeup brands that use animals for product testing include Bobbi Brown, Sephora, Revlon, Maybelline, Benefit, MAC, Rimmel, Wet and Wild, and Nars. Unfortunately, this horror doesn't end at makeup, animal testing extends to other businesses including 3M, Acuvue, Air Wick, Almay, Always, Aquafresh, Arm & Hammer, Band-Aid, Bounce, Bounty, Braun, Burberry, Calvin Klein, ChapStick, Clarisonic, Clean & Clear, Clinique, Clorox, Crest, Dior, Downy, Dr. Scholl's, Drano, Estee Lauder, Febreeze, Gillette, Glad, Glade, Head & Shoulders, Ivory, Jimmy Choo, Johnson & Johnson, L'Occitane, L'Oreal, Lancome, Lubriderm, Lysol, Mary Kay, Michael Kors, Mr. Clean, Nair, Neutrogena, Nivea, Off, Olay, Old Spice, Oxiclean, Pampers, Pantene, Pledge, Post-it, Prada, Procter & Gamble, Raid, Ralph Lauren Fragrances, S. C. Johnson, Scrubbing Bubbles, Sensodyne, Shout, Spray 'N Wash, Swiffer, Tide, Tommy Hilfiger, Valentino, Venus, Vera Wang, Versace, Vicks, Victoria's Secret, Walgreens, Windex, and Woolite.[40]

There are so many companies exploiting animals, and, sadly, mine is not a comprehensive list. These are the brands that I recognized easily and assumed my readers would also be familiar with. It is heartbreaking to realize that so many of the products I have used, some of which are still in my home, were developed at the expense of innocent animals. At this discovery, I felt shocked, lied to, and raw. Animal testing taints companies large and small — from luxury brands to cheaper knockoffs, and long-established firms to startups.

The companies and brands on this list have either tested their products on animals themselves or paid a third party to carry out the tests. Some will deny that they use animal testing, while still using the same chemicals and substances that have been tested on animals in their products. Others have been unable to demonstrate that either the finished product or its ingredients were not tested on animals.

I hope that in the near future these companies will change their practices and be removed from this list.

The argument given to justify animal testing is that it protects humans. But the fact is that these products also undergo human testing once they have "passed" the animal testing phase. The statistics show that 92% of the drugs that passed animal testing fail during the human safety trial. Thus, the vast majority of animal testing (and the pain and suffering endured by said animals) is for nothing, and the end result is the death of an estimated 50,000 animals every year.

If the thought of mice and rats suffering doesn't move you, consider the Beagles that are routinely blinded in the testing of soap and shampoo.

We must end animal testing. We cannot save the planet while simultaneously destroying the animals that call it "home."

LABELS TO LOOK FOR

We need to identify the terms found on product labels, so you'll know what you are (or are not) buying. A product identified as "vegan" means it has been produced without any animal products or animal-derived ingredients. "Natural beauty product" means that the product contains no synthetic (man-made) chemicals. Ideally, "cruelty-free" products have not been tested on animals, however, companies try to skirt the issue by testing the ingredients on animals, but not the finished product. If a product is labeled "100% cruelty-free" you can be sure that no part of the research or manufacturing process utilized animal testing.

A product that is 100% cruelty-free and vegan is not tested on animals and contains no animal products. If a product is cruelty-free but not vegan it has not been tested on animals but may contain animal ingredients (such as beeswax). A product that is vegan but not cruelty-free doesn't contain animal ingredients but may have been tested on animals. The following logos may help to identify whether a product is vegan or cruelty-free.

The "cruelty-free and vegan" logo is used by People for the Ethical Treatment of Animals (PETA). PETA is sometimes criticized because they don't perform regular audits or verify ingredient suppliers. Two other logos to be aware of are the leaping bunny and Choose Cruelty Free (CCF):

The leaping bunny tells you that regular company audits are performed, that ingredient suppliers don't use animal testing, and that the company is re-accredited periodically. You will never see the leaping bunny on a brand that sells cosmetics in China, where animal testing is required. Interestingly, products made in China aren't necessarily animal-tested, just products that are sold there. Products identified with the leaping bunny are not required to be vegan, so some may contain animal ingredients. The second logo, for CCF, identifies brands and products which restrict the use of animal ingredients and which have ensured that none of their ingredient suppliers test on animals. They don't conduct regular audits but they require re-accreditation. (Consumer warning: Look closely when these logos are used on products because some brands may use logos with a similar look but that are not officially accredited and as such, may not have the status they are claiming.)

If you are committed to buying products from companies that don't use animal testing, knowledge is our greatest weapon. Thanks to the internet and our ability to access it through our phones anytime and anywhere, there is really no excuse for unconscious, indeliberate action.

The next time you need to purchase toothpaste, foundation, or laundry detergent, take the extra 30 seconds to make sure you are supporting a company that has pledged never to test on animals. The same goes for your next online order. Once you know that what you are buying is vegan and/or cruelty-free, you won't have to worry about it again. And on behalf of those 50,000 innocent creatures, I thank you.

MAKEUP BRANDS

Now that we have discussed many of the nuances behind the products we use on our faces, I'll share about a few brands that are taking steps to break the mold, without breaking the compact. What you are looking for in a makeup brand is perhaps different from what I might want, so this information is a jumping-off point for you to do your own research as it pertains to what belongs in your makeup bag and on your skin.

RMS Beauty was created when the founder, Rose Marie Swift, discovered through a blood test that her blood contained high levels of pesticides, heavy metals, and other chemicals. RMS Beauty uses organic material to formulate their products. (Note: The EWG has ranked some of the RMS Beauty products higher than others, so do a little research before you place an order.)

W3LL People is the brand that I recognized on the shelf at Target. They are verified by the EWG and have always worked to ensure that their products are clean, cruelty-free, and gluten-free. They also strive to incorporate plant-based substances wherever possible.

Kjaer Weis offers luxury makeup products, many of which are certified natural or certified organic. Many of their products are available with a refill option, which is great for those looking to reduce their waste and make sustainable choices. (Note: Unfortunately, not all of these products have been rated by the EWG, and those that are have had mixed results, so do some checking before you place an order.)

ILIA Beauty makes natural and organic products. Each of their products reportedly contains 85% bioactive ingredients which have been sourced from organic farms and made in an organic certified lab. They are Leaping Bunny certified, but as of this writing, they have not yet been reviewed by the EWG.

Zao Organic produces makeup that is vegan, gluten-free, chemical-free, and organic. It is another brand offering a reusable refill system to reduce waste. The reusable external packaging is made from bamboo which is durable and ultimately, compostable. They have received verification from Leaping Bunny, ECOCERT, and COSMEBIO. (Note: The products that have been reviewed by the EWG have had moderate mixed results, so research is your friend.)

Elate makes sustainable and zero-waste makeup products. The outer shell of the casing is bamboo and the makeup itself sits in recyclable metal canisters. They are also a Certified B Corporation, vegan, cruelty-free, and certified by Leaping Bunny and Beauty Without Bunnies by PETA. Their products are about 75% organic because they opt for fair trade products over organic alternatives when they are unable to ensure both. The company focuses on ethical marketing, sustainable practices, and is working towards becoming the first waste-free cosmetic company. With each order, they donate one tree through One Tree Planted, an environmental charity that helps to reforest after fires and floods and strives to protect habitats and their biodiversity around the world. (Note: Elate has not been reviewed by the EWG.)

I encourage you to search for products and brands that avoid harmful chemicals and are cruelty-free. The EWG is a great resource to come back to again and again — ideally before you place an order. If you also want zero-waste or a more sustainable makeup routine, I urge you to look for products packaged in bamboo, glass, or stainless steel. Avoid anything with a pump — since those are notoriously hard (if not impossible) to recycle. You may also want to look for brands offering a refill option, which provides an added bonus. The packaging and the metal refill components are often fully recyclable.

Mascara can be a hard product to find a sustainable substitute for, but there are some options. The mascara sold by Elate has a compostable bamboo shell and a recyclable inner tube. Kjaer Weis offers a refillable mascara, or you can purchase mascara in a glass jar like from Lush, or a metal tin like one sold by Bésame, and use a separate washable and reusable plastic wand. In these cases, the jars can be recycled or refilled, and the used wands can be sent to wildlife rescue organizations where they are used in the care and cleaning of birds and animals.

If you still cannot find products that meet your standards, or if you just want something different, you can, of course, always DIY your own makeup. I am all for natural alternatives, but this is not something I want or plan to do. I find that store-bought options tend to last longer, due partly to the added chemicals which extend the product life, but which also ensure that a bad day won't end with coffee grounds from homemade mascara in my eyes and running down my face.

As I was deciding what to buy, I agonized more than I had at any other point in my sustainability project to date. I wear minimal makeup as a general rule and typically buy one product at a time. However, I found myself spending hours on individual company websites and visiting the EWG website again and again, in search of viable products to try.

After extensive research, I finally settled on Elate. I placed an order for foundation and concealer. Sadly, although these products worked reasonably well, they weren't what I had hoped for. Although I could have forced myself to use them permanently, I decided I ultimately didn't want to. The overall cost to get these tiny palettes to me was unsustainable. I realized that in the process, I had become stuck on the idea that my makeup products needed to be zero waste and perfectly sustainable. Even after months of research and education, I had to remind myself that the only thing that is truly sustainable is the thing that is truly sustainable for me (or for you). Oftentimes this looks like building habits we can continue, supporting causes we care about, and spending money on products that we will continue to buy and want to use.

The end result was that I went back to some of my old favorites. They weren't all refillable and they didn't necessarily come wrapped in compostable paper, but I made certain that they were highly rated by the EWG and were, therefore, products that I felt comfortable using on my skin. All matched the level of sustainability that I intentionally decided on. I use mascara out of a regular plastic tube, but I buy foundation in recyclable glass and then take the extra time (sometimes a lot of it) to clean and recycle it.

Although perfect sustainability doesn't exist, sustainable sustainability does.

MAKEUP BRUSHES

The best makeup brushes are the ones you already own. Unless you are pretty young, you probably already have a great set, and if you're anything like me, you already own more brushes than you will ever use. I have a set that I purchased several years ago. I didn't have sustainability on my mind at that time, but I've used those brushes ever since. I recently became convicted, however, because I wasn't taking care of the brushes as well as I should.

As in every other area of life, the most sustainable thing I can do is to use my makeup brushes for as long as possible. I don't need to buy sustainable ones with bamboo handles. What I do need to do is take care of my brushes so they will last.

All I needed was soap, water, and a clean towel, and now they look beautiful and feel almost brand new. If you have special brush cleaners or tools, use them! If you decide that these are just more products you don't need, good for you. But if, you decide they are an important part of your routine, please be sure to clean and recycle the bottles when you're done.

There may come a time when you need new brushes or want to give some as a gift. When you are looking to purchase, avoid those labeled "natural," as this often means the bristles are made of animal hair. Brushes labeled "cruelty-free" can still utilize animal hair because technically the label only applies to product testing. Some companies claim that using hair from animals is technically harmless, but the majority of the hair in makeup brushes seems to be a byproduct of the meat or fur industries, which aren't really harmless.

I recommend brushes that are labeled "vegan." These brushes are made with synthetic fibers so you won't be rubbing animal fur on your face. While these aren't optimal, there are no sustainable or plant-based options available yet. They will last longer and deliver a better overall experience than animal hair and the bristles are less likely to dry out, are more resistant to bacteria, and are hypoallergenic.[41]

So although the brushes may be synthetic (for now), some brands, like 100% Pure make their bristles from recycled PBT plastic bottles. This won't be compostable, but at least the material is already on its second life! And many brands offering sustainable makeup brushes do make the handles out of wood or bamboo — two materials that can be composted. You just have to remove the bristles first.

Sustainable brands that I discovered are EcoTools, Everyday Minerals, Antonym Cosmetics, The Body Shop, 100% Pure, Bdellium Tools, NVEY ECO, and others. Additionally, some makeup brands, i.e. Elate, carry vegan brushes. Since I did not need makeup brushes during my research for the sustainability project, and I likely won't for the foreseeable future, I don't have any personal experience with these brushes. But I wanted to give you a good starting place just in case you are looking for some.

Brushes can also be bought second-hand, although that is further than I am willing to go in the interest of sustainability. If you are like me and decide to buy new brushes, I recommend that you buy only what you need and will use regularly, rather than a whole set. Out of the 12 piece brush set I purchased years ago, I only consistently use one brush. ONE.

The bottom line is always: make the most of what you have, care for it, and when you do need something new, consider used first. If you do purchase new, commit to taking care of it and then dispose of it in the most responsible way possible.

FACE MASKS

I enjoy an occasional Friday night spent with a close friend watching a chick-flick while devouring a few great snacks and trying out a new face mask. Face masks may be easy to brush aside or ignore because they're such small contributors to the overall waste in the world. I get it. We just want to relax, kick back, and indulge in a few moments of concentrated skincare. Unfortunately, those masks that are so easy to add to our shopping cart, will ultimately end up in a landfill and many contain chemicals that will make their way into the ground.

Luckily, there are sustainable options. First, there is the DIY face mask you can make at home with ingredients you already have on hand. Or you can look for sustainable face mask options from companies like C'est Moi, which has facemasks that are EWG verified with packaging that can be recycled through Terracycle, or Alder New York, which offers vegan and EWG verified face masks packaged in 30% post-consumer recycled plastic jars or a single-use pouches. And, as always, if you already have a favorite brand, please make sure to check the ingredients before you next spread it on your skin.

FACE WIPES VS. WASHCLOTHS

When the time comes to remove our makeup at the end of the day, we have an opportunity to make another sustainable choice. Have you seen photos of cleansing wipes floating with the fish in the oceans or washed up on a beach? I confess that for a long-time I was a consumer of disposable makeup wipes. But when I started this project, I knew that how I cleanse my face was another thing I was going to need to change.

Face wipes, whether you use them for removing makeup or just cleaning your face, are designed to be single-use and are made with polyester, polypropylene, rayon fibers, cotton, or wood pulp, most of which aren't biodegradable. They aren't just bad for the environment, however. Most of them are soaked in harsh chemicals which can disrupt the pH balance of your skin, strip natural oils, and remove the acid mantle which provides a protective layer to the skin to keep out dirt and impurities and seal in the moisture and natural oils.

Reusable wipes and washcloths are a great alternative, and the good news is that most of us already own some. In truth, I didn't actually have any washcloths when I started this project. Since I'd spent a lot of time on the Marley's Monsters website in February, however, I knew they had what I needed: reusable rounds.

Adjusting to reusable rounds took some time — not only because the feeling on my face was totally different but because they didn't, at first, appear to have the same cleaning power as the chemical-laden facial wipes I was used to using. Having to wash them frequently with the rest of my laundry was another adjustment. I purchased the dark-colored rounds so that they will hopefully last longer and show less makeup staining. Once I grew used to these changes, they integrated well into my daily routine. To be honest, this wasn't my favorite swap, but I remind myself that it is one that is making a difference to my face and to the earth.

LIPS

One of the small ways I feared that I had a negative impact on the earth was through my ChapStick consumption. Until the last few years, I always considered myself as a red-lipstick-and-high-heels kind of girl. But those who know me well know that I am really very much the opposite. When I finally accepted that I actually lived a ChapStick-and-flats lifestyle, I became cognizant of just how much ChapStick I regularly consumed.

At approximately the same time, I realized that ChapStick is one of the companies that tests on animals. I haven't used the ChapStick brand for quite a while but I continue to refer to the alternative products by that name.

Lip balm, the correct and generic term, remains a major part of my daily routine. I use it when I am in the car, at my desk, and before I go to sleep. I keep one in my purse and my backpack, and within reach when I'm both on the couch and in my bed. I also have a tin on hand filled with a dozen stand-bys. Many of these have been given to me as gifts or as marketing freebies. On the one hand, I am grateful for lip balm because I can't stand the feeling of dry lips. On the other hand, I know that these small cylinders of plastic (200 million of them each year) don't simply disappear or regenerate when the balm is used up but rather, end up in the trash.

Unlike some other makeup and skincare products, this was not one that I could live without (it's who I am, remember?). So although I wasn't willing to eliminate lip balm from my routine, I knew that if I found an amazing brand and I subsequently didn't need to use it as much or as often, I would definitely be on board with that. Unfortunately, the plastic to product ratio is often quite high. To avoid unnecessary plastic waste, we can purchase zero waste, cruelty-free options with compostable tubes like those from Ethique, Blue Heron Botanicals, and Package Free. Although these products aren't reviewed by the EWG, the ingredients are almost all recognizable (no complex, unknown chemicals here). They all also offer vegan options. Axiology also makes zero-waste makeup crayons for your lips and beyond.

Supporting sustainable companies almost always comes with added benefits. Blue Heron Botanicals saves a baby turtle with every purchase, and since I owe this book and my sustainability project to a turtle, this is a no-brainer!

As with many of the other personal care products we've discussed, you always have the option to make lip balm at home. You can even add a tint if you want more color. All you need to begin is beeswax and you're good to go. There are other options, too, if you prefer to make a vegan lip balm. I'm happy to stick with what is good for the environment and my lips — and saving turtles is an added bonus!

TOOTHBRUSHES

There isn't too much to say in this area. The plastic toothbrushes that we pick up from any drugstore or dentist are not the most sustainable options. Unfortunately, neither are the electric ones, no matter how expensive.

A study conducted at Trinity College Dublin in collaboration with the Eastman Dental Institute at University College London analyzed the impact and carbon footprint of electric toothbrushes, standard plastic toothbrushes, plastic toothbrushes with a replaceable head, and bamboo toothbrushes. It is probably no surprise that electric toothbrushes were found to have the greatest negative environmental impact. And as you might expect, plastic toothbrushes with a replaceable head and bamboo toothbrushes have the most positive, or the least negative, impact.[42]

If you want to make a sustainable choice, opt for a bamboo toothbrush. Bamboo grows quickly and spreads easily, and it also has antibacterial properties, which is an ideal quality in a toothbrush.

Unfortunately, there aren't many completely compostable or biodegradable toothbrushes on the market, but some are being developed. Most contain some amount of plastic, even if they claim to be 100% biodegradable. Brush with Bamboo, however, has created bamboo toothbrush with 100% biobased bristles made completely from plants and with no petroleum. With a bamboo toothbrush, the handle can be composted but you will need to pull or cut the bristles off first (if they are plastic). If you don't compost, or have a composting program in your area, you might know someone who does. Some people also use the handles for craft or garden projects, although I don't fall into either category.

Another option is to get a toothbrush with bristles made from pig hair. Personally, I think this sounds disgusting and unsustainable on a large scale, not to mention very un-vegan. Pig hairs are hollow, too, which could allow bacteria to multiply and which is the last thing you'd want.

There have been arguments that utilizing bamboo in the production of products reduces the amount of land that can be used to cultivate forests to offset carbon emissions or increase biodiversity. While this may appear to have merit on the surface, there is no real way to know that if the land wasn't used to grow bamboo it would actually be utilized for these purposes. Bamboo grows quickly (about 1,000 times faster than hardwood trees), uses minimal water, absorbs more carbon, produces up to 35% more oxygen, is low maintenance, doesn't need to be replanted (it self-generates from its roots — which is annoying when it is in your backyard but great when you are growing it for production) and doesn't need pesticides.

Since the production of plastic toothbrushes doesn't require land and significant resources like bamboo toothbrushes do, it appears initially that they have a small environmental impact. Ideally, plastic toothbrushes would be recycled, or at least have the heads recycled when it is time to replace them (dentists recommend replacement every three months). Unfortunately, this isn't something that is conventionally available or commonplace. And we are well aware of the overall impact of plastic anything on the environment. So, we are left with the decision of what we want to do next.

Some people have ditched toothbrushes altogether and use miswak or neem sticks instead, which come with minimal to no packaging. I can see how this is a sustainable option, but not one that I am inclined to experiment with.

I do want to acknowledge that some people need to use electric toothbrushes for a number of reasons. If that is you, or if you just love your electric toothbrush, that's okay. You can still be a person who values sustainability, is living a sustainable life, while using an electric toothbrush. It's our collective responsibility to try to find areas where we can make those modest adjustments that will allow us to have a smaller environmental footprint overall — with our toothbrushes or in other ways.

TOOTHPASTE

One of the first sustainable swaps I discovered as I began researching better ways to care for my face and body was toothpaste tablets. Approximately 1 billion toothpaste tubes are thrown away every year in the United States alone. That's about 31 tubes every second; a staggering number. Tablets may be a sustainable alternative. They are often sold in reusable glass jars and the refills typically come in compostable or recyclable containers.

Bite is at the forefront of this market. They offer glass jars to store your supply of toothpaste tablets and the refills are sent in compostable pouches. The packaging consists of recycled newspaper and the mailing boxes are fully recyclable. There are other companies and even Etsy stores that sell toothpaste tablets online, but Bite currently has most of the market share and does the most advertising.

While I am definitely on board with the sustainable packaging and quite like the aesthetic that the glass jars provide, I will admit I was skeptical at first. The thought of brushing my teeth with something like a Pepto Bismol tablet felt like a difficult transition. I lectured myself that this was, after all, my project and I wasn't going to give up simply because I didn't want to experiment with toothpaste. So, I went online to place my first order from the Bite website. As I clicked around, I grew increasingly unconvinced of the overall sustainability of the product in a surprising way.

Bite operates primarily on a subscription model. Although I know that this works very well for many people and for many different kinds of products, I tend to be wary of subscriptions, as they are not financially sustainable for most people in the long run.

Bite's generic mint tablets sold in the large size jar are $30 for a 4 month supply of 248 tablets. This comes to approximately 62 tablets a month, which is enough to brush twice a day for 31 days a month, for the four months of the supply. However, that means that over a year the total price comes to $90 — per person.

Without the subscription, the cost of the jar would come to $48 according to the website, but I couldn't find a way to purchase that option. I assume that this price is based on the small jar which sells for $12 each for a one-month supply. The small size was the only option I found that didn't include a subscription. If you decide to forego the subscription and purchase the small jar, you would have to purchase a new jar every month, since there doesn't appear to be a refill option available for the smaller quantities. This would add up to approximately $144 a year — per person.

These figures seemed high to me as a person who has historically spent about $12 a year on a few tubes of toothpaste. While it's not that I couldn't afford to purchase from Bite, I'm not sure that I want to dedicate that much of my monthly or annual budget to a single personal care product. And looking to the future, I wasn't sure I would want to multiply that by 4 or 5 once I had a family. While toothpaste tubes can be shared and squeezed and stretched, tablets probably cannot.

In the end, I decided to switch gears and focus primarily on conventional toothpaste tubes, albeit ones that can be recycled. Thanks to the increasing awareness of companies and consumers on the impact of their actions, several brands have released toothpaste tubes that can be recycled.

I know that recyclable and reusable are not the same thing. However, for this product, I decided that I would be happy with a recyclable option.

I decided to try Davids toothpaste which is vegan and verified by the EWG. Unlike conventional tubes, Davids comes with a small crank, enabling you to get every last drop out of the tube. A fun feature, and really practical, especially if you're like me and have never been able to consistently squeeze the tube from the bottom. Davids tubes are made out of metal, so they can be cut open, cleaned, and recycled. Even the cap and the crank are recyclable.

Another toothpaste option is Tom's of Maine. Although Tom's toothpaste has mixed reviews with the EWG, there are a few recycling options when it comes to their tubes, which can be recycled through Terracycle. The company is also working to convert all of its tubes to number 2 plastics, which can be recycled curbside (no cutting or cleaning required, apparently).

Thanks to the actions taken by these companies, and increased consumer awareness, hopefully, all toothpaste brands will be moving to sustainable or recyclable tubes in the near future.

It bears repeating, of course, that the recyclability of these materials depends on how and where they are processed. Doing a little research will help you determine what option in your area is most likely to have the desired result.

There are other potentially clean and green options for personal care products like deodorant and toothpaste. The first option is always to make them at home.

I decided not to pursue this route for a couple of reasons. Protecting my teeth and maintaining a clean mouth and healthy gums is a top priority for me. I probably could make my own toothpaste at home, but I don't have the confidence that whatever I made would be as good as what I buy for oral hygiene. Plus, I've never had a cavity, and I would like to keep that streak going as long as possible.

So, while I have health and safety reasons for not wanting to make toothpaste, those reasons don't necessarily extend to other products, such as deodorant. But I lead a busy life, and don't want to spend my Saturday afternoons trying to DIY whatever I currently need in my bathroom drawer or makeup bag. But, if you have time or think it would be really fun to try brewing up your own products, then I encourage you to do just that! There are countless internet blogs and YouTube videos that will tell you everything you need and give you step-by-step instructions.

If after all this, you plan to stick with your favorite toothpaste, try to avoid the ones containing microbeads. These often end up in oceans and waterways, absorbing bacteria along the way, and are eaten by fish which harms both the fish and, ultimately, the rest of the food chain.

If you plan to stick with the non-recyclable tube option, please check the ingredients with the EWG to see if your brand is one that has partnered with Terracycle to take back empty tubes.

FLOSS

I hate to admit this, particularly since both my dentist and hygienist could potentially read it at some point, but I never floss. I have healthy teeth and gums, and I've always hated flossing. I considered skipping this section altogether, even though I will have to start flossing at some point in the future. When I do start though, it certainly won't be with the floss that my dentist hands out.

The floss that most of us use not only comes in a plastic case but is also made from plastic. It's coated in chemicals to allow it to slide over and between our teeth with ease. These same chemicals can be found in things like Teflon, and have been linked to cancer, reproductive problems, dementia, and other serious health issues.

A sustainable alternative is to opt for floss made out of silk. Another option is nylon, which is vegan but isn't biodegradable. You may also want to look for floss that comes in a refillable jar or canister. Quip and a few other companies have released or are developing a refillable floss pick. Of course, another option is to use a Waterpik or other electric flossing device.

I have several years' worth of floss from my dentist, but I will probably invest in a reusable floss pick at some point.

What to do with all of the unused floss? I'm thinking about passing it along to someone who flosses regularly, along with the suggestion of a floss pick for the future as well.

Sustainability has transformed my habits in the best way possible and has also helped me help the planet. And if your habits involve the use of traditional floss, fortunately, there are a few sustainable options available.

BRUSHING YOUR TEETH

When I was little, I used to watch *Barney & Friends* with the purple dinosaur on television. I remember Barney teaching his audience a song about brushing their teeth that reminded us "to never let the water run." As a result of Barney's sage advice, I've never struggled with the temptation to leave the water running when I brush my teeth. I don't recommend that you learn the song, but it makes an excellent point, especially if you, like me, are striving to live a more sustainable life.

The EPA reports that leaving the water running while we brush wastes up to four gallons each time. If you brush twice a day, multiply that number by two, and by the number of people in your household to see how many gallons of water are being wasted each day. It's estimated that approximately 1 in 3 people leave the water on while they brush.

Every choice we make impacts the world, including the water running down the drain. The thousands of other choices we make each day matter, too. The primary question to answer is whether we are making consistent choices while being conscious of the potential impact. It is my hope that you and I will make our choices with intentionality, conscious of the impact they will have on us personally but also on the planet and the creatures that inhabit it.

CHAPTER 6
JUNE: BODY

I'm not going to lie to you — this chapter touches on some very personal subjects, but, in the interest of full disclosure, I have presented my complete journey, in all its sweaty glory.

Sweat, however, is not the bodily fluid we are going to start with.

THE BLOODY TRUTH

Disclaimer: In this section, I discuss the feminine cycle including periods, pads, tampons and menstrual cups, and everything in between. If this subject does not apply to you personally, you may want to skip ahead to the next section. I guarantee it will be just as unpleasant, but bloodless. At least, I hope so.

Now for those of you who are still with me, let's get to it.

The average woman will use between 11,000 and 17,000 tampons or menstrual pads in her lifetime. Most pads and tampons on the market today are produced with cotton and cellulose. As we have learned, cotton production isn't easy on the environment, but rather is heavy on both water consumption and pesticide usage. Similarly, cellulose, a wood product, requires trees and chemicals; lots of them. Since a large portion (between 15 and 30% according to the World Wide Fund) of the wood traded around the world is traded illegally, it is likely that some portion of the cellulose comes from this wood.

When the wood is harvested and sold, it is transported to a treatment and processing facility before being transported to its final destination. Ultimately, this wood product makes its way to our homes. If the product arrives in plastic wrap of some sort, the plastic has also undergone a similar process, requiring additional resources and producing additional emissions.

After consumer use, the product will make a final journey to the landfill.

At the outset of my sustainability project, I suspected that this would be one area where I would need to make a switch.

Menstrual cups are the most popular alternative to tampons and pads, but you can find other alternatives. Ultimately, all of these products function in the same way, with the same result. There are several companies that produce sustainable products, such as the period cups from Nixit, Saalt, or DivaCup, which use 100% medical-grade silicone without chemicals, plastic, or dyes.

If you prefer to stick with cotton tampons, you can opt for an applicator-free option like the ones sold by Veeda. If you prefer an applicator, Dame offers a self-sanitizing, reusable tampon applicator. This eliminates the excess plastic waste which otherwise ends up in the landfill.

If you prefer pads to tampons, you might want to consider period panties. Saalt, also a producer of menstrual cups, offers Saalt Wear, which are sustainable and leakproof underwear made from 55% recycled water bottles. The company also donates 2% of sales towards period care, menstrual health, and the education of underserved communities. Thinx and Knix also produce period panties. Aisle produces a reusable pad and panty liner which snap together with wings and can be tossed in the wash after use.

The products you decide to use, like everything else, will depend on your comfort and lifestyle. Keep in mind, however, that the sustainable product you will actually use will always be the better option than the one that you think you should use but never do.

These items are also the most financially sustainable. A cup that may last for years can cost as little as $20, whereas a box of disposable tampons, which costs $7.00, may last just a few months. Over the course of your lifetime, you could spend over $3,000.00 on the purely disposable alternatives.

While the sustainable options may seem more expensive upfront, and it appears easier on your wallet (in the moment) to just grab a box of tampons, in the not too distant future these products will have more than paid for themselves — and there won't be any additional environmental costs to pay down the line. It goes without saying, of course, that if you already have some of the less sustainable options mentioned above on hand, you should probably start there and use what you have.

However, in addition to the environmental cost, we also have to consider the cost to our bodies of choosing the disposable options.

First of all, both tampons and pads contain plastic. A pad has as much plastic as 4 plastic bags! So while you may be successfully reducing your plastic use in the kitchen, this is another area to consider. Both of these disposable products have also been bleached, and I think it's safe to assume bleach is not a substance any of us should willingly want in or on our bodies.

A recent study in the US found 24 endocrine-disrupting chemicals in 7 categories of feminine hygiene products, including pads, panty liners, and tampons and the study concluded that "the estimated exposure doses of phthalates, parabens, and bisphenols through the dermal absorption pathway from the use of pads, panty liners, and tampons were significant."[43]

I don't know about you, but substances that have come into close contact with pesticides, and/or contain those kinds of chemicals, aren't things I want to have in close contact with me. Technically, feminine hygiene products are regulated by the FDA, but as we learned in Chapter 5, this doesn't necessarily mean they are all safe or healthy to use.

SHAVING

As I promised, this section should be less blood-related than the last one. At least, if you're careful.

Over 2 billion razors and refill blades are thrown away in the U.S. every year. Until now, I was part of that statistic.

One of the easiest, if not the cheapest, swaps I knew I needed to make was to get rid of my disposable razors. I'll be honest — although I'd tried the fancy razors with the replaceable heads, my frugal side never really got on board. I preferred the completely disposable razors that come in packs of 12 for $2, definitely not sustainable for the planet, but good for my wallet. Plus, I reasoned those inexpensive razors lasted just as long as the more expensive ones so I wasn't really creating more waste in the long run. But, when this month's challenge rolled around, I knew that this was another area where I could be doing better.

Those looking for increased sustainability turn to three primary tools for unwanted hair removal — the electric razor, straight-edge razor, and safety razor.

Electric razors, while fast and efficient, require a lot of resources to create and operate — like electricity.

Stainless steel safety razors, like those sold by Leaf Shave or Kappi, are a frequently used alternative. They can be repaired and fully recycled if they need to be. The straight single blade doesn't need any pressure, you can just slide it along your skin in short strokes and at a (slight) 30-degree angle.

When a blade has served its purpose, it can be recycled, but should not be tossed in with the recyclables. Since most recycling plants still have some faction of human employees sorting the material, we want to make sure to keep them safe. You can use or make a blade bank for collecting your used blades and to ensure safe and efficient recycling once it is full.

Straight-edge razors sound vaguely terrifying in that they don't need their blades replaced, just sharpened. If you're looking for a zero-waste option and have a steady hand, this may be the way to go.

If you prefer to avoid razors altogether, you could opt for sugaring, waxing, or laser hair removal, or give up on shaving entirely. I won't judge! Let's just take sustainable action and keep the people who make recycling possible, safe.

SHAVING CREAM

You can't have peanut butter without jelly, and you can't have razors without shaving cream — or can you? This is actually a product that I do without, opting to use conditioner instead. This works great for me and makes my conditioner a 2-in-1 kind of product!

Since I know that's not for everyone, you might opt to make your own shaving cream, use a bar of soap, or get an alternative product like the shave soap bar from Package Free (unrated by the EWG but with recognizable ingredients).

SWABBING OUT

Another issue that is not very pleasant to think about and discuss is earwax.

People primarily use cotton swabs to remove earwax. If you don't engage in this exercise, you can skip this section. But if you enjoy having clean ear canals, there are some sustainable options.

Although a cotton swab is a relatively small piece of plastic, as we've learned, plastic in almost every form is detrimental to the planet, especially when it is incorporated into the daily routines of millions of people.

As I started my research, an image came to my mind that I'd seen in passing ages ago and nearly forgotten. It was a picture of a seahorse floating along grasping a cotton swab more than three times its size by its tail. Seahorses often use their tails to carry seaweed or other things that belong in the ocean. Cotton swabs don't fall into that category. In my research, I came across this photo, or similar photos, over and over again. It broke my heart because I know that this is not how things are supposed to be.

Of the 8 million metric tons of plastic that are dumped in the oceans each year, anywhere between 1% and 6% can be attributed to cotton swabs. With so many people using them every day, I shouldn't be surprised.

Of course, there is also the environmental cost of producing disposable cotton swabs in the first place. The process requires fossil fuels, and preparing the fossil fuels for production requires extracting, transporting, and refining them for production. Although the footprint created by a single swab may not be large, collectively, they add up — just as they do in the oceans.

Producing disposable swabs also contributes to emissions and the resultant poor air quality, as well as water and ground pollution. While this is true of many manufactured products, cotton swabs are no exception. And as we already know, the production of cotton requires a lot of land and other natural resources as well. This can negatively affect air quality and biodiversity, with the result that cotton is one of the most environmentally damaging crops on the planet.

1.5 million cotton swabs are produced every day, but thankfully, we don't have to continue to contribute to that number. We can switch to a reusable option, such as the ones made by LastSwab — although there are also other silicone, stainless steel, and bamboo options on the market.

There are two kinds of swabs produced by LastSwab, one for cleaning out your ears and another for use in applying or removing makeup. I purchased the former and will admit that getting used to it required some time. Since the swab wasn't covered with cotton, it was a bit harder than I was used to. Ultimately, though, this difference just led to me being more careful in using it. Similarly, it is also less absorbent than cotton swabs, but so far that hasn't been a major issue.

My LastSwab is easy to clean and that extra step adds only a few more seconds to a ritual that used to end with something getting tossed in the trash can.

Like most things, cleaning the swab immediately after use is the best option. Thankfully, it can be cleaned with soap and warm water, both of which are usually close at hand.

You may be wondering about what to do when you are traveling, but my LastSwab has been a great option on trips, too. This one reusable swab takes up less room than the disposable ones I used to pack and allows me to maintain my sustainable habits on the go.

There are some alternatives to a reusable swab. Companies such as The Humble Co. and Well Earth Goods offer bamboo swabs, which can be composted. That means they are less likely to end up in the tail of a seahorse, but you have to be willing to take the extra step. And while the bamboo alternative is certainly better than plastic, it is still a disposable item.

The idea of a reusable swab may seem repulsive at first, but when compared to the use of hundreds, and perhaps thousands, of the disposable versions that we use once and throw away, this is a great option to reduce your waste with one simple change.

Of course, you can also give up swabs altogether and as with so many other things, that is probably the most sustainable option. And probably the one all doctors and health experts would support. But I wasn't ready or willing to do that at this point, and in case you aren't either, some of the alternatives may serve you (and your ears) well.

COTTON BALLS

Another popular product that I have never really been in the habit of using is cotton balls. Unfortunately and unsurprisingly, the same sustainability issues with cotton that we discussed previously apply to this product, too.

If you like to use cotton balls to remove makeup or anything else, you could consider switching to a washcloth instead. Alternatively, some of the products applied with cotton balls can be applied using a spray bottle or can be squeezed into your hands and then applied. I know many people who have made this switch who have been shocked at how much further the product seems to go when most of it isn't being absorbed by a cotton ball!

NAIL POLISH

Few things make me feel more pulled together than painted nails. I can pull my hair up into a bun, add a bit of mascara and cardboard-coated lip balm, but it is knowing that my nails are polished that proves I am on top of my game — and everything else. The bad news is, I've also seen what even a few weeks of wearing polish can do to my nails.

Nail lacquer is designed to survive showers, hand washing, dishes, gardening, and everything else we do on a regular basis. Many people will see their nails crack before the polish does — whether that's because of the polish or not is a different issue, however.

Although nail polish containers aren't particularly sustainable, the bottle is generally made of glass, which can and should be recyclable, as long as it has been properly and thoroughly cleaned.

What's inside the bottle is another issue. The fact that most polish can only be removed with a strong chemical remover should be a red flag. Many nail products contain chemicals suspected (or known) to lead to negative health effects, including asthma, cancer, reproductive harm, and other issues. Employees in nail salons are particularly susceptible since they spend so much time working with these products.

When purchasing polish, look for brands that are "5-free" — these contain no formaldehyde, toluene, dibutyl phthalate, formaldehyde resin, or camphor. The first three of these chemicals are known to cause cancer or reproductive toxicity, at least, per the State of California. Some brands may advertise as being "3-free," meaning they don't contain those three chemicals. But I really don't want to put anything containing the latter two chemicals on my skin or nails either.

Hopefully, nail polish brands will continue to remove these harmful chemicals from our favorite colors, shades, and lines without ruining their efficacy. But until that day comes, it is up to us to be aware of what we buy and put on our nails to maximize personal health and sustainability.

PERFUME

Another product that may have just as many harmful chemicals as nail polish, and that we may need to be even more concerned about, is perfume.

I don't wear a lot of fragrances, and when I do, it has always been the inexpensive brands, which are sadly full of endocrine disruptors and other harmful chemicals. As I researched, I soon realized that I would need to look at different types of fragrances going forward. I decided to begin by using up all of the remaining products I had before making a new purchase while being careful to spray it only onto my clothing and not directly onto my skin.

If fragrance interests you, or you love a certain scent combination, you can always make your own perfume. If not, try to ensure that you purchase your signature scents from a company that doesn't add parabens, phthalates, synthetic fragrances, or any of the other named chemicals.

If you can find a healthful and sustainable fragrance that you like in a refillable bottle, that's even better! If not, opt for glass containers whenever possible — it's likely to be beautiful to look at while it lasts, and when it's finished you can reuse the bottle for something else or clean and recycle it.

Even though I'm not really into perfume, there are many enticing scents and brands that are ranked highly (or even verified) by the EWG, making them personally sustainable and safe for your skin.

DEODORANT

If you decide not to seek out a sustainable scent, or even if you do, you probably also need to seek out a sustainable deodorant. It's a good idea to do some due diligence and check what the EWG has to say about the one you're using.

I first experimented with natural, nontoxic deodorant when I picked one up at Target at the start of my sustainability project. It wasn't really in line with my month-by-month plan, but I had yet to put an end to my impulsive and consumerist habits.

I regretted the purchase quickly, and only partially because I hated it. The deodorant itself was almost liquid. So even though it came in a stick, I had to smear it on with my fingers. It was pretty disgusting. And worse, the longer I wore it, the worse I felt like I smelled. And when it came to daily exercise, I found that it didn't hold up to the sweat factor.

But it was even more than those things. Whenever I found myself sweating, even just the tiniest bit, I felt like I smelled horrible. Like a boy's high school locker room after a face-off in the finals with a rival school. I wanted to live more "naturally," but clearly, that impulsive purchase wasn't the best option for me. As I have had to remind myself many times over the course of my project, even though it claims to be sustainable, without doing a little research you can never be completely sure.

Fortunately, by the time June rolled around I had made time to focus on making healthy, sustainable choices for my body. And I found a few better options for me, after searching for dozens of hours through the EWG Skin Deep database, of course.

By Humankind makes a great deodorant with a refillable tube and it's ranked a 1 by the EWG. This is a rare combination and makes it one of the best options for both the planet and our bodies that I could find. It has no harmful chemicals and, on their website, By Humankind jokes about it being natural enough to eat. Since the product also has no aluminum or parabens, it can't technically be called an antiperspirant, since those ingredients are required by the FDA for such a label to be given. But since these ingredients aren't generally considered healthy, it may be worth it to go without the label. It must be noted, however, it may take a few weeks for your body to cleanse itself of toxins when switching to a more natural formula.

Nuud is another deodorant option (or what they call an "anti-odorant") that claims to last from 3 to 7 days. It doesn't contain aluminum, parabens, petrochemicals, salts, cheap perfume, or vague chemicals. The tube is bioplastic (made from sugarcane) and is packaged in a biodegradable cardboard box. The lid, however, is made from regular plastic. It is cruelty-free, 100% vegan, and I've heard, doesn't leave marks on your clothing. Unfortunately, it has yet to be reviewed by the EWG, but the information provided by Nuud directly makes me hopeful.

Some smaller online shops offer a block or spherical deodorant that is supposed to last for years. If you go this route, make sure the packaging it comes in is as green as possible. Even though these products are likely not reviewed by the EWG, they are more likely to be made with ingredients you recognize. And if you choose to opt for even more sustainability by making deodorant for yourself, go for it. There are lots of people online who can show you how and tell you why.

LOTION

While we're on the DIY subject, creams and lotions are another product that many people attempt to make for themselves. Once again, I'll take a pass, but I can see why it is something that people could find to be fun.

Luckily for me (and you, too, if you're like me), there are sustainable lotion choices that don't involve a pot and an afternoon in the kitchen.

Body butter and lotion bars tend to be more sustainable options compared to lotions sold in plastic bottles. Often, they either come in a zero-waste, reusable, or at least recyclable container. They also tend to last longer because they don't have any water added.

Earthley makes lotion bars that are vegan, cruelty-free, and Leaping Bunny certified. They come packaged in a metal tin and are rated a 1 by the EWG. Chagrin Valley makes non-GMO lotion bars with locally sourced, minimally processed ingredients. They also use 99% plastic-free and recyclable packaging and most of the lotions are rated highly by the EWG.

WASHING UP

We've covered a lot of chemical-laden products and some pretty nasty topics in this chapter, so let's end by talking about sustainable products that will clean all of that away, at least metaphorically. Whether or not you identify with "team showers" or "team baths" (although I don't think I've ever actually met anyone who identified exclusively with "team baths"), I hope that some of the tips in this section will help you become more aware of the dirty environmental impact of getting our bodies clean.

Until I moved out and had to pay for the electricity to heat my own shower water, I never paid much attention to the time I spent standing under the spray. But even that was nothing compared to the attention it got when I started working on the research for this book.

To begin, I read whatever I could about the environmental impact of showers. I purposed to become more aware of the time I spent in the shower by using the stopwatch feature on my phone. Since I'm super into time management, I thought I had a pretty good idea of how much time I spent in the shower, and I always gave myself a time deadline for when I needed to be done and ready to move on to the next thing.

The results of my personal research were very interesting and enlightening. I quickly saw a pattern. Those showers where I took time to shave hovered around the 15 minute mark, while the ones where I didn't shave still lasted about 10 minutes. While these numbers weren't horrible, I knew that they were only this low because I was acutely aware of the stopwatch in the background. I didn't stop to relish the warm water as I ordinarily would. Trust me, I've taken plenty of 30-minute showers in my day — and I'm not proud to admit it. Even though I wasn't overly disappointed with my initial results, I knew that I needed to make some improvements going forward.

In the US, showering accounts for almost 17% of residential indoor water use annually. While I found several tips to reduce the amount of time I spend in the shower to cut down on energy and water usage, I was surprised that there was no real suggested time frame for optimal shower length. This was one more thing on my sustainability journey that didn't appear to offer an easy answer or solution.

The first, and most obviously sustainable suggestion, is for us to simply work at taking shorter showers or to shower less often. Singing into the shampoo bottle or practicing your Oscar acceptance speech may need to be cut back if you want to improve your environmental footprint. While there is certainly a threshold of time required to get your hair and body clean, there are a few things that can be done to reduce time and water usage.

I shower two or three times per week, which is considerably better than the five to seven times per week I showered in college. This works very well and also minimizes the time I have to dedicate to my hairdryer (which is another win for the planet). This schedule keeps me clean and keeps my water usage to a minimum. While I don't time myself with every shower, I do utilize the stopwatch on occasion to keep myself accountable. As we all know, we manage what we monitor.

There are a couple of other options (beyond shaving seconds off of our shaving time) for reducing the environmental impact of our showers. The first option is to install a low-flow or smart showerhead. 250 billion gallons of water could be saved every year if every household in the US switched to a low-flow showerhead. The water saved could supply more than 2.5 million U.S. homes with enough water to last an entire year. Think about that for a minute. While this number may not be 100% attainable, it is certainly a positive goal to aim for.

If you are building a new house or are looking for a new showerhead, please consider purchasing a low flow or smart option. If you do decide to upgrade to a smart showerhead, your old showerhead can be recycled as a donation to a program like Habitat for Humanity. Although this means that it may be installed in another house to use the same amount of water as before, it also means the showerhead won't be languishing in a landfill!

However, if you have a showerhead that you like and aren't ready to purchase a new one, there are several other options to consider that can reduce your water and energy consumption. And you want the benefits of lower-flow without having to replace a showerhead, you can install an aerator to the existing showerhead, which will reduce the flow from the faucet and result in a savings of between 2 and 16 gallons of water each day.

Since I live in an apartment, I didn't have the option of installing a new showerhead. However, I was pleased when I took a close look at the one I have and realized that I didn't need to! It is a Delta showerhead and uses 1.75 gallons per minute (GPM). Anything less than 2 GPM is considered to be a low-flow showerhead, and the average showerhead uses about 2.5 GPM. I will admit that when I first moved into my apartment, I found the shower spray to be a little softer than I was used to, but I quickly adjusted to it and currently enjoy the knowledge that I am reaping the positive benefits of a low-flow showerhead. If you aren't sure if you have one, it is worth taking 30 seconds to check.

Once I knew how many gallons of water I was using per minute in the shower, a quick calculation showed that I was still using over 17 gallons of water with each shower. This is better than the average of 25 gallons used during a typical 10-minute shower, but I wanted to explore more options to continue to reduce my usage.

I experimented with a process known as "Navy showers." Although I have lived all of my life near a Navy town in the Pacific Northwest, I didn't know that "Navy showers" was the term for a practice that my dad told us about when my siblings and I were growing up. In a "Navy shower," you start out under running water, but you turn it off once you are sufficiently wet. Then you soap up thoroughly before turning the water back on just long enough to rinse off. This technique saves water and avoids wasting soap which can be washed away before you are ready if the water is running.

This method initially sounded detestable to me. I feel cold much of the time and being under the warm water in the shower is one of the few times I feel completely warm! Additionally, I hate leaving the shower wet and cold, so the idea of standing in the shower wet and cold, and then risking a sudden spray of cold water when turning the water back on to rinse off, definitely didn't appeal to me.

I knew that the "Navy shower" wasn't something that I could get behind every time, so I decided that I would use this method only on the days when I shaved. That way, I would turn the water off while I shave, since the water normally is more of a hindrance than a help anyway.

I must admit, I hated this change to my shower routine. But when I implemented the practice, it meant I was able to ensure that I was using only 10 minutes' worth of water during all of my showers. Although that is still a lot of water, it is a good starting place as I work to continue improving in this area and slowly reduce the water and energy that I use to get myself clean.

During my research, I came across some additional ideas that I didn't experiment with, but which may work for you! One idea is to create a music playlist that is only as long as the time you want to spend in the shower. Alternatively, you could set a timer for the shower length you want and program a favorite song to play when it is time to get out (or a song that you hate if that would motivate you to get out of the shower a little faster)!

Another idea is to reduce the water temperature just enough that it makes you less likely to linger in the shower longer than you need to.

Some people also suggest using products that serve multiple uses — like 2-in-1 shampoo and conditioner. This could potentially save time and money in the long run, but while this may work for some, I knew that it wouldn't work for me and my hair.

Another suggestion I found encouraged sticking a bucket under the faucet before you hop into the shower while you wait for the water to heat up. The water can be saved to water houseplants, mop floors, or perform any number of tasks rather than be wasted.

The final suggestion I found was to ensure that you use any downtime in the shower to do something else, i.e. while the hair conditioner is setting, you can use the time to wash your body. This suggestion seemed to me somewhat obvious, but if it is a revelation for you, then you should be able to knock a minute or two off of your shower time.

Showers aren't the only source of water usage in the bathroom, however. If you prefer baths, the universal environmental advice is to switch to showers. The average tub takes about 36 gallons of water to fill, but if you're not filling it to the top, you're probably only using 20-30 gallons. Provided that you aren't showering for more than 10 minutes using a regular showerhead, or 15 to 20 minutes with a low flow showerhead, you will be saving water and energy by taking a shower instead of a bath. Of course, if you take a longer shower, the environmental positives begin to decrease.

I enjoy a relaxing bath from time to time as much as anyone. But it's important for each of us to be aware of how much water we are using, and the frequency of our baths. If each of us will cut back a little, or use less water to fill the tub, we can make a big difference.

One related suggestion I came across urged that we reduce our shower times leading up to a planned bath. In that way, we can feel that we have "saved up" enough water to justify it. To my mind, this seems to require way too much mental energy and may involve a degree of stress, which is usually the very thing that people take a bath to eliminate.

Other recommendations suggest saving bath water and using it to do laundry or water your plants. That is something else that I don't think I would ever take the time to do, but if you want to, then do it! And please send me pictures, I would love to see your method for getting all that water outside.

SHAMPOO + CONDITIONER

Unfortunately, many of the issues we discussed in the last chapter, like harmful chemicals and deadly animal testing, apply to shampoos and conditioners, too. I won't repeat all of that here, but you should know that the same problems apply in this area, too. If you've ever gotten shampoo in your eyes, I hope the memory of the pain will remind you about the harms of animal testing and give a voice to those animals that can't voice an opinion of their own. If you need a refresher on chemicals or the brands that test on animals, return to Chapter 5 for the list of the ones to avoid.

Fortunately, the EWG offers help in this area, too. The Skin Deep database doesn't just cover cosmetics, it also covers everything from sunscreen to shampoo, and nail polish to perfume. It is worth checking the database to see where your current products rank, whether or not you intend to switch to different, more sustainable options.

In the US alone, over 552 million plastic shampoo bottles are thrown away every year. That means that one of the easiest swaps you can make when it comes to shampoo and conditioner is to switch to the product in bar form. Bars require less packaging, and the packaging is likely to be easy to clean and recycle.

I learned during my research that not all shampoo bars are rated very highly by the EWG, but there are a few. By Humankind has a highly reviewed shampoo bar that is ranked a 2 by the EWG. The shampoo bars by HiBAR contain no sulfates, silicones, or parabens but have mixed results according to the Skin Deep database. Ethique is another common brand making these products with mixed results. Before you purchase either, be sure to check out the particular product you are considering with the EWG. There are many brands like Briit Botanicals that are not yet reviewed by the EWG but that are cruelty-free, use sustainable packaging, and contain no artificial fragrances or colors.

Another option is to switch to a refill-based shampoo and conditioner routine like those from Plaine Products. You can also opt for hair and body products like those from Seed Phytonutrients with recyclable and biodegradable paper bottles, or recyclable glass bottles and aluminum tubes. The company has also partnered with TerraCycle to create a free recycling program for the pumps from their products.

BODY WASH

I'll be honest, I've never been a huge fan of body wash in bar form. They always leave my skin feeling dry — much more so than a purely liquid version. But going into this month, I was more than willing to give up my plastic bottles for a bar soap if that turned out to be the more sustainable option. Unsurprisingly, it was.

Many of the major brands have a line of bar soaps. Before purchasing, I recommend that you check the one in your shopping cart with the EWG, and ensure that the product is cruelty-free, and meets any other designations you are looking for.

The packaging for bar soap tends to be on the sustainable side. But when purchasing bars of soap, look for those with as little packaging as possible and where the packaging can be recycled or composted.

If you must purchase a product in a bottle, look for the same designations, and be sure to clean and recycle the bottle once it has reached the end of its use.

To apply body wash, you can use your hands, a washcloth, or opt for something like the natural loofahs from Boie which are antimicrobial and recyclable.

Unfortunately, many bar soaps (and other body products) contain palm oil. Palm oil is the least costly oil but comes with an extremely high cost to the environment. Sadly, the demand for palm oil is high, too. In some countries, rainforests are burnt to the ground to create more land for palm plantations. This not only disrupts the lives of the locals and animals, but also harms the ecosystem. Both organic and non-organic palm oils are controversial at this point. Not only that, but since rainforests play such a major role in storing, absorbing, and processing carbon emissions, the result is further increasing overall emissions into the atmosphere. So, be sure to check any soaps for palm oil before purchasing.

USE WHAT YOU HAVE

I will admit, I have a lot of personal care products, including lotions, shampoos, and body washes, accumulated from I honestly have no idea where. Additionally, I have 8 bars of soap in the cabinet along with various products aimed at keeping my eczema under control.

Before making sustainable choices, I knew I needed to start by using what I already had, since these products were technically already part of the cycle. So while all of that is important to living a sustainable life going forward, I also wanted to be able to start to explore more sustainable options. So for June, instead of just maximizing the suds from the bottles already in my cupboard and shower, I wanted to be able to try out new items to experiment with what my sustainable practices will be going forward. Plus, this wouldn't be much of a chapter if I just said, "I used what I had," although that may be just the message some of us need.

I did make a concerted effort (both before and after June) to use all the products taking up space in my bathroom. And once I did, I also made sure to properly dispose of the containers to the best of my ability. While that may or may not have been something I would've done before, I made sure to take the time to thoroughly clean and recycle what could be, compost what could be, and throw away the things I knew didn't have any other potential final destination.

As I wrote this book, I realized more and more that I could come off as a super gross person — washing my clothes only a couple of times a month, showering just a couple of times a week, and whatever it was that happened with that first deodorant I tried. But then I took some time to consider where the ideas about what it takes to be a "clean and tidy" person originated. Society, prompted by advertisers, pushes the message that we need to shower every day, wash our clothes after every wear, and still only wear each distinct outfit once. And these messages are the cause of many of the environmental issues I am writing this book to combat. They are harmful, costly, and wasteful.

I understand if you think that some of my habits are weird, or annoying, or even gross, but I challenge you to question the foundation of these beliefs and consider the impact of this messaging on you and the environment.

Throughout these months as I was focused on finding sustainable solutions for face and body products, I discovered many brands and products that didn't work well for me but might serve others. Regardless of the particular products that you and I choose to use to care for our bodies, it is our shared motivation and intention toward sustainability that binds us together.

CHAPTER 7
JULY: FOOD

We've all chased "healthy" food trends at one time or another. Coconut oil was the first big one that I remember. For a time, people were falling over each other to buy coconut oil because it was found to have health benefits for cooking, skin care, dental cleaning, etc. People were incorporating it into absolutely everything. They were even eating it out of the jar! The research was in and coconut oil was all the rage. Eventually, new research suggested that coconut oil wasn't the miracle food we'd all hoped for.

I still use coconut oil. I often use it to make popcorn. While microwave popcorn is easier, and movie theater popcorn is dripping in melted butter, both of these alternatives are much less healthy than coconut oil. So while coconut oil may not be the perfect health food, or even the best popcorn oil, it still has some health and taste benefits that I appreciate.

Health crazes are often the result of the impossible standards for beauty and fitness that our society imposes. To many of us, "looking good" holds a very high value. And this "ideal" doesn't simply apply to our physical appearance. Our homes must be pristine, our schedules coordinated, and our clothing never-seen-before.

I hadn't realized how caught up I had become in this looks-obsessed culture until I saw a picture of an orange on Instagram. The orange was shriveled, misshapen, and covered in bumps. It was unlike anything that I had ever seen in a grocery store, and that was exactly the point. You'd think I would have realized back in May that beauty, especially sustainable, ethical beauty, is much more than skin deep, but apparently, the message had yet to fully sink in.

I will share more about Imperfect Foods, the company behind the image of the ugly orange, later. But that orange was a surprising and intriguing start to the month of July, as I was fully focused on food. And the problems, I would soon realize, were much deeper than surface level.

MEAT

Before I began my sustainability project, I knew that one of the best and, in one sense, easiest ways to drastically lower the environmental impact of what you eat is to not eat meat. The research and statistics on this are pretty undeniable.

Raising animals for food generates more greenhouse gases than all modes of transportation combined.

It also contributes to rainforest destruction. Over 136 million acres of the Brazilian Amazon region have been destroyed and up to 91% of that destruction is due to animal agriculture. Approximately 10,000 acres of the rainforest are cut down every day to make room for this; that's an acre every 9 seconds.[44]

Raising animals for food also uses an enormous amount of water; accounting for about 55% of the total water consumption in the United States. It is the leading cause of freshwater pollution as well as the current levels of die-off in the Great Barrier Reef. Ironically, it contributes to world hunger since these animals consume 50% of all grain produced globally. It also utilizes 45% of the world's livable land.

It requires the death of other animals (ones we don't actually eat) through habitat destruction and the resultant reduction in wildlife. The USDA is responsible for the deaths of 2.7 million wild animals which have been killed to make room for livestock to be raised for food.

While these statistics are somewhat shocking on their own, it may be helpful to break down the environmental impact of our lifestyle choices. A vegan lifestyle, for example, has a smaller environmental footprint than others, but how much of a difference? And what about vegetarians?

During my research, the people who eat meat (of which, I am one) are referred to frequently as "meat-eaters." I've never felt more like a dinosaur than when I came across that phrase. And although that is likely a large part of the point, I have decided to use the term "omnivore" here instead, because unless you are a T-Rex, you likely don't subsist on meat alone.

Everything that is produced for us to eat has some kind of a carbon footprint, and it is not too surprising to find that anything that requires that other things must also be produced in the process will have an even larger footprint.

Animals, like cows, tend to be toward the top of the scale, largely because of their size and how much they eat. For example, beef generates about 13.8 kilograms of carbon for every 1,000 calories of meat produced. Tuna generates 5.3 kilograms of carbon for every 1,000 calories. Pork generates 4.5 kilograms of carbon for every 1,000 calories. Chicken generates 3.4 kilograms of carbon for every 1,000 calories.

The carbon footprint of dairy products is also pretty high. Cheese generates 4.5 kilograms of carbon for every 1,000 calories of product produced. Cow's milk produces 3.2 and eggs, 3.1. Of course, all foods produced have a carbon footprint, but they are typically much lower than meat, and a bit lower than dairy products. For example, rice generates 2.1 kilograms of carbon for every 1,000 calories of product produced, potatoes generate 1.5 kilograms, and tomatoes and beans generate 1.4 kilograms.

To put these numbers in a frame that we can relate to, the food eaten by a vegan would have generated on average about 2.9 kilograms of CO_2 per day. The food eaten by a vegetarian would have generated about 3.8 kilograms of CO_2 per day. And the food eaten by an omnivore would have generated about 6.5 kilograms of CO_2 per day.

Put in another way, if a four-person family of omnivores was to give up both meat and cheese for just one week, the reduction in CO_2 emissions would be greater than if that same family stopped driving for 35 weeks. The production of just one kilogram of beef generates as much CO_2 as a car that is driven 155 miles. Similarly, if the entire human population became vegan by the year 2050 (something that I don't think anyone would agree is realistic), overall food-related carbon emissions would drop by 70%.

Sadly, the environmental impact of food production doesn't stop with CO_2 emissions. We also have to consider the land used to produce our food. Did you know that it takes three times more land to produce food for a vegetarian than for a vegan? The number increases to 18 times for those of us who are omnivores. As we saw previously, meat production has contributed to the leveling of 80% of the Amazon rainforest. Overall, the animals we raise for food occupy approximately 80% of the earth's agricultural land but only contribute about 20% of the total calories that we consume.[45]

Another point to consider is that not all of the livestock we consume is being raised on open farmland, with grass underfoot and the clear sky above. Actually, about 50% of this livestock comes from factory farms in the United States.

Regardless of where our livestock is raised, another environmental consideration is the huge amount of waste they create. In fact, the waste produced by all of the animals we breed is a whopping 130 times greater than all of the human waste generated by the United States population.[46]

All of this animal poop is created because these animals consume a large amount of the crops grown in the United States. About 60% of the corn and 47% of the soybeans we grow will go to feeding the livestock that will later feed us. While this might not be a major problem here in the USA, we need to be aware of the fact that globally 82% of the hungry children around the world live in countries where most of the food produced in that country is largely fed to livestock that will ultimately be sold to Western countries for consumption there.

Another way to look at this is to consider that 16 kilograms of grain can be used to feed a single cow or 20 people. Although it wouldn't be what we would call a well-rounded meal, at least 20 hungry people would have eaten. On the other hand, if this grain is fed to a cow, far fewer people will ultimately be fed (1 kilogram of the beef from that cow will only feed 2 people). And in much of the world, a lot more than 18 people are going hungry.

To recap, in the United States alone, 41 million tons of food are fed to 7 billion units of livestock each year, which in turn produces just 7 million tons of food. Right now there are 701 million people in the world that are hungry. If the grain we use to feed livestock was used to feed the hungry around the world, the United States alone could feed up to 800 million people annually. This would be more than enough.

With a reduction in the number of livestock raised for food, we would be able to raise more than just grain for the hungry. Each 1-acre tract of land that would have produced 137 pounds of beef could be used to produce up to 40,000 pounds of tomatoes or 53,000 pounds of potatoes — a vast difference.

This is a perfect example of how so many of our issues are interconnected. Hunger could essentially be eliminated if it weren't for our overproduction and consumption of meat products. Unfortunately, a similar picture can be seen in our food waste — but we'll get to that.

Raising livestock for consumption also requires an enormous amount of water each year — about 15 trillion gallons. Growing the grain that our livestock consumes, watering the livestock, and preparing the slaughtered livestock for our consumption requires lots of water. The production of just 1 pound of beef requires nearly 18,000 gallons of water. One hamburger requires 660 gallons of water. Similarly, it takes 576 gallons of water to produce 1 pound of pork, and 468 gallons of water to produce 1 pound of chicken. The elimination of just 1 pound of meat from our weekly diet would save more water than if we chose not to shower for six months. These statistics make those few minutes I shaved off my shower time seem pretty insignificant.

To be fair, as we have discussed in previous chapters, it takes a lot of water to produce just about anything. For example, it takes 7.9 gallons of water to make 1 cup of tea, 449 gallons to make 1 pound of rice, 108 gallons to make 1 pound of corn, 216 gallons to make 1 pound of soybeans, and 119 gallons of water to make 1 pound of potatoes.[47]

But just because the production of everything requires water doesn't mean that everything requires the same (or even remotely similar) amounts of water. It takes about 300 gallons of water to produce the food a vegan will eat in a single day whereas a vegetarian diet will require about 1,200 gallons of water to be expended. An omnivore's typical diet will require about 4,000 gallons of water per day. In effect, it will take less water to produce the food that a vegan will eat in a year than it will take to produce what an omnivore will eat in a month.

Water consumption can't be the only concern, but it is a big part of the total picture, and when our goal is sustainability, it is an important factor to consider.

Another consideration may be our stewardship of the animal kingdom. About 59 billion animals are slaughtered for our consumption every year. If we remove the approximately 8% of the population who are vegetarians or vegans out of the equation, the omnivores among us account for the deaths of 8.5 animals per year.

Each of us needs to own our individual and personal responsibility for this. We need to be willing to understand how our food is raised and processed.

Although I never thought of myself as an animal person since I'm afraid of big dogs (and some small ones, too), the more I researched, the more I realized that I am. Especially when you consider that the catalyst for this whole journey was a story about a sea turtle, and later when I was broken over animal testing for makeup and skincare products. So I share these uncomfortable statistics to give you a full perspective of what is going on and to motivate you to decide what kind of changes you want to make.

And it isn't just that eating meat, on the whole, is unsustainable, it is also the way we go about producing it that needs to be looked at.

Pigs bred for food live about 6 months before slaughter, compared to a normal lifespan of about 12 years. Male dairy calves live 1-24 weeks, while those raised for beef live approximately 18 months, instead of the 20 or so years that they might have lived.

Chickens bred for eggs live about 5 months instead of 15 years. The male chicks (born without egg-laying potential) are ground up alive or are suffocated. Approximately 500,000 of them receive this fate every single day. Chickens bred for meat last 6 weeks, instead of 8 years. And this list goes on and on. Lambs, turkeys, and everything else you see in the meat case were killed long before they would reach the end of their natural life, purportedly to help support ours.

The quality of these animals' short lives is also notable. Cows are not designed to consume corn (rather grass and other roughage), but because corn is cheap to produce, requires less land, is abundant, and is often subsidized, we feed them corn, which causes acidosis, a buildup of acid in the bloodstream. This condition often leads cows to suffer from bloating, diarrhea, ulcers, liver disease, and a weakened immune system leaving them more susceptible to disease.

When they are slaughtered, it is estimated that between 15% and 30% of the cows will have abscessed livers. Sometimes the number ranges up to 70%. In order to combat this, cows are given antibiotics. Interestingly, a majority of the antibiotics sold in the United States, about 80%, are used in animal feed to help continue this cycle. [48] But ultimately, if we are what we eat, we know where those antibiotics will end up.

Sheep, chickens, pigs, and every other kind of animal we consume are bred, treated, and exploited for us. The life of a dairy cow isn't much better than a beef cow, but I'll get to that later.

I have heard it argued that animals exist for our consumption, so if we aren't raising animals for that purpose, then what is the point of raising them. In fact, many of the animals that we consume serve other purposes.

It is also interesting to consider that around the world, the animals people eat vary greatly. The fact that dogs are eaten in parts of Asia shocks us in the United States, just as much as our consumption of beef leaves other cultures horrified. This begs the question, if there are animals that we value highly enough to not eat them (and in the case of cats, actually let them control our lives), why shouldn't this apply to all animals?

No matter your culture or belief system, I think that it is almost universally acknowledged that animals existed before humanity did. Although we were the ones who named, classified, and cared for them, we have also been the hand of pain, death, and extinction.

You may be asking yourself, what would happen if we stopped raising animals for food. To be honest, I'm not entirely sure. Without the push to raise animals for food, the number of animals being forced to procreate would drop and perhaps level out to a more sustainable number. But just as trees don't exist merely to become toilet paper, animals don't exist solely to feed us.

It is interesting to watch people ditch plastic straws and switch makeup brands to save animals from the effects of pollution, product testing, over-consumption, and unsustainability, but then turn around and consume them without a second thought.

I don't say this to generate guilt or shame, although you may be feeling an emotional response as I did. Much of this is so very heartbreaking and it can seem hard to know how to make a difference. Fortunately, an increasing number of people are making a change.

The Economist recently reported that about a quarter of young people between the ages of 25-34 in the US say that they are vegetarian or vegan.

And a National Geographic poll found that Americans between the ages of 18 and 34 are more likely to be exploring vegetarian options. About 43% of young adults are looking to consume less or no meat. And although the number isn't quite as high, 26% percent of American adults over age 65 are looking to reduce the amount of meat they consume. About 33% of those surveyed said they are making more meatless meals because of higher prices and fewer options at the store. Although this number isn't 100%, and likely never will be, every percentage point results in fewer animals being killed for consumption.[49]

In the event that you ever run into me and see me eating bacon, a BBQ chicken pizza, or ground beef tacos, I have made the decision to begin by reducing my overall meat consumption to a maximum of once per day.

If you are a vegetarian or vegan, I am proud of you and grateful for what you are doing for the planet.

I will share several other ideas for increased sustainability around our food consumption, but first, I want to begin by telling you why I have decid-ed — for now — not to become a complete vegetarian. This is illustrated by points from two of my favorite authors.

Author Brené Brown has said that she has been married so long that now when a fight begins, she can fast forward in her head and say with almost complete certainty how that disagreement will end. Even though I have so much life ahead of me and so many choices ahead, I feel like I have a similar ability: an ability to play the tape of my life through to the end.

With all of the knowledge that I have acquired in researching this book, I feel quite certain that there will be a time in my future when I will no longer be able to justify eating meat and I will become a vegetarian, possibly even a vegan.

But I feel unready to make this drastic change in my life now. I'm not even 25 years old, so much of my life is still ahead of me.

Author Gretchen Rubin says that one of the ways to change your habits is through lightning bolt moments, and it was one of those moments that led her to give up carbs and sugar, a decision she has stuck with for years.

While my feelings about food consumption didn't come to me like lightning bolts, striking an instant change in my life, I experienced them as a smaller electricity jolt — maybe the equivalent of sticking a fork into an electrical socket. It was the recognition of the impact of my choices and the overall sense that I will not be able to continue as I had been indefinitely.

In truth, I feel this way about a lot of things. For a long time, I have made the conscious decision not to "put my phone away an hour before bed" as many experts suggest. I have decided that I know I will start that practice, probably in the not too distant future, but for now, I want the ability to work, journal, research, and scroll until I go to bed. But, when I play that tape to the end, I know that this choice will not last forever.

Lightning bolt moments happen for all of us. I had one when I read the story of the sea turtle in *How To Give Up Plastic*. I knew from that moment on that I had to do things differently. The same applies to writing this book. As quickly as the idea came to me, I knew I had to write it.

If you've had a lightning bolt moment concerning plastic, chemicals, or meat-eating, I encourage you to explore that further. Lean into the experience and let it change you — both for the person you will become and the good you will be doing for the planet.

I am always amazed by certain people: vegetarians, families with only one car, and the people who can fill a mason jar with all of the waste they generated in a year are included. I am inspired by them, even if I am not yet ready to make all of the same decisions. I support and even applaud them in those choices, and I feel hopeful that they would support me in mine.

No matter where on the continuum you fall, forward progress is better than none at all. And, at least from my perspective, it's okay not to skip ahead to the end of the tape all at once.

From my spot on the continuum, however, I will make all of my future choices through a stronger, more enlightened lens. For example, I often opt for a salad instead of a burger, choose the vegetarian option when possible, and eat smaller servings of meat. I think that part of my inability to jump in with both feet at this junction stems from my "moderator" nature (another idea popularized by Gretchen Rubin). The idea of giving something up completely and forever is a really difficult choice for me to make. Especially since I am also an Upholder (another Gretchen Rubin term) and once I make the decision, I know there will be no going back. And the obligations and rules for myself that I create around that will likely only grow stricter. Something similar to this has happened with my consumption of milk.

MILK

I grew up drinking cow's milk. Then, years ago I was offered goat's milk by a friend and I couldn't wrap my head around the fact that this "milk" came from an animal living in my friend's backyard. Drinking it felt wrong somehow. So I didn't. But I continued my consumption of cow's milk, as long as it didn't come from my neighbor's cow, that is.

I didn't know anything about dairy milk production back in the day, but I do now, and it isn't pretty. Since cows technically and originally produced milk to provide for their calves, to kickstart the production of milk, these cows are artificially inseminated. Once they have given birth, the process starts over again. The fate of the calf isn't pleasant, either.

All calves are taken from their mothers within 72 hours of birth. Male calves are sold to become veal. They are often kept in dark crates for over 5 months to keep their meat tender. They frequently suffer from diseases such as anemia, pneumonia, diarrhea, and some have their muscles atrophy so they can barely walk. Then they are transported on average more than

1,200 miles, about the distance from Boston to Disney World, but once they arrive, they are most certainly not in the happiest place on earth.

Female calves are often sentenced to the same fate as their mothers. They are dehorned and drugged to produce as much milk as possible. This is done through genetic manipulation, intensified herd management, and selective breeding. In 1970, the average cow produced about 9,700 pounds of milk or 4,400 liters. According to 2017 statistics, cows are expected to produce 19,000 pounds of milk or 8,618 liters per year. [50] That means the quantity has doubled in just a few decades.

Up to half of the milk-producing cows will suffer from inflamed breast tissue. Another half, on average, will become lame from the living conditions or from being constantly pregnant. When a cow has reached the end of its expected milk-producing window, it will be slaughtered and the meat used for cat or dog food, or to produce hamburger meat or soup.

Despite the increase in meat alternatives in restaurants, grocery stores, and fast-food chains, the sale of meat has not declined. In 2015, the per capita beef consumption in the United States was 54 pounds. That number actually increased to 58.1 pounds per capita in 2019.[51]

Of every five pounds of beef sold, one pound is likely from a Holstein or Jersey cow, which was decommissioned after serving as a dairy cow. Since the meat isn't generally high-enough quality for steak, it will be ground and sold.

Research suggests that in 2019 former dairy cows were used to produce 7.7 percent of the beef put on the market. Although overall milk sales have been declining in recent years, the production and consumption of other dairy products is rising, with the result that a large number of cattle will continue to give their lives for our consumption.[52]

The cost of dairy products, unfortunately, doesn't end with the cost of the cows themselves. Dairy production also requires lots of land, electricity, water, and grain (and more water and pesticides to grow the grain), not to mention the greenhouse gasses emitted by the animals themselves. If cattle were a country, it would be the third-largest contributor to greenhouse gas emissions in the world. A recent report by the Institute for Agriculture and Trade Policy (ATP) found that 13 of the largest dairy companies in the world create the same combined greenhouse gas emissions as the State of Florida, the nation's 3rd most populous state. Although gas from cows may seem a little bit humorous, these statistics are just more evidence of the impact that a single industry can have on the planet as a whole.[53]

And greenhouse gases aren't the only thing cows are giving off. A farm with just 2,500 dairy cows will generate the same amount of waste as a city with a population of 411,000 people.

Now that we know the truth about dairy production, let's look at some of the alternatives to animal milk, some of which are a bit more sustainable and a lot more humane.

In my research, I came across an article on almond milk and its supposed lack of totally environmental friendliness. Growing almonds is often water-demanding (some reports say it may take more than a gallon of water to grow one almond), can cause groundwater depletion, and risks endangering the bees. Pesticide Action Network has reported that the bees face a 30% death rate due to the pesticides used to grow almonds. They recommend other kinds of milk, such as soy and oat, that are better from an environmental production standpoint. Oat is known to be relatively easy to produce and since it is grown to feed livestock, there is generally excess that can be used. But I don't really like soy or oat milk. And I know that soy milk isn't the best option for women to drink for hormonal reasons. I could try and make myself like soy or oat milk and ignore the research regarding the impact such a decision could have on my body, but that's not a choice that will probably be sustainable for me in the long run. And I would still be choosing a milk (soy or oat) that has a higher carbon footprint than its almond alternative. Almond milk isn't the most sustainable alternative, but it is still definitely more environmentally friendly than dairy milk.

Producing milk of any type requires water, and oftentimes, a lot of it. It takes nearly 12 times more water to produce dairy milk than almond milk; my milk of choice. It takes about 8 gallons of water to produce a pound of almond milk as opposed to 90 gallons for dairy milk. That's a significant change just for taking a few steps and grabbing a carton out of a different section of the dairy fridge.

Producing a single glass of cow's milk will require about 1.8 square miles of land and 125 liters of water. It will also generate .6 kilograms of CO2.

A single glass of rice milk, on the other hand, will require about .06 square miles of land and 54 liters of water. It will generate .3 kilograms of CO_2. A single glass of almond milk will require about .1 square miles of land and 74 liters of water. It will generate .14 kilograms of CO_2. A glass of oat milk will require about .14 square miles of land and 9.6 liters of water. It will generate .18 kilograms of CO_2. Finally, a glass of soy milk will require .12 square miles of land and 5 liters of water. It will generate .2 kilograms of CO_2. For those who get lost in the numbers, the net result is that drinking any non-dairy milk is better for the environment than drinking cow's milk, although the production of each kind varies slightly in the resources required and the emissions released.

I opted for almond milk for several reasons, not the least of which is that I prefer the taste and therefore it represents the most sustainable option for me. Remember, our goal isn't always to make the "perfect choice," it's about making the "best choice," one that is sustainable for us in the long term.

Overall, I am very happy with the decision I've made and the impact it will have. Although I slip up occasionally and end up with dairy milk in my coffee, whether because it slipped my mind or someone else buys me a drink, I try to remind myself to focus on growth over perfection.

That is my motto for how I approach milk, and pretty much all the rest of sustainability, too.

Unfortunately, the dairy problem doesn't end with milk. It extends to yogurt, cream cheese, cottage cheese, and, yes, cheese, in addition to sour cream, ice creams, and, well, cream. It should come as no surprise that the dairy used to make these products is produced in the very same way, from cow's milk, and the environmental impact is extrapolated out from there.

This is another area where I strive to be imperfect. The idea that I will never eat ice cream again is a stumbling block to 100% commitment. But the idea of eating ice cream occasionally, or even rarely, while exploring dairy-free options, such as sorbets and popsicles, seems manageable. Again, there are no perfect or right answers. Wherever you're at on your journey of sustainability, or if you are just starting out on the road to sustainability, I support you and want to cheer you on. If you are ready and able to jump into the non-dairy or vegan camp, or if you just want to make a few changes to your lifestyle, that's awesome. And if you aren't going to change anything at all, you are at least making the decision consciously and with all the information you need to decide.

Of course, this section wouldn't be complete if I didn't acknowledge those individuals who make their own dairy/non-dairy products, whether by keeping cows or goats, or utilizing plant-based options. While doing this does help to alleviate some of the ethical and environmental stresses, it does not remove all of them. If you choose to support your sustainability this way, I applaud you. But if you, like me, know that the best you can do is move a few feet over to the non-dairy shelf of the refrigerator aisle, I think you deserve a round of applause, too.

THE JUG LIFE

If you decide to keep cow's milk in your diet for any reason, you can opt for sustainability while purchasing milk, and also reduce waste in the process by purchasing milk in glass jugs. You will pay a little more as a deposit for the jug, but the glass jug can be returned for reuse and you generally receive your deposit back as a credit toward your next purchase.

This option supports sustainability in several ways. First of all, using glass over plastic is a clear win. Plus, the fact that the jug will be sanitized and reused without having to go through any sort of recycling process saves energy and reduces emissions. Not only that, but if you are purchasing milk from a company that sells milk in glass jugs, chances are they are a smaller local farm with more sustainable practices. This may not be true 100% of the time, but it's a safe assumption.

While smaller health food and organic produce-based stores are likely to carry milk in glass, some of the larger retailers might, too.

The only downside of the glass jugs is the need to return them to the store. This is another example of how making the sustainable choice may take a bit more effort but is completely worth it.

Another option is to look for a local delivery service. Check to make sure that the company that will drop off the milk in a glass jug (and maybe other local, organic produce as well) right to your front porch — and pick up last week's empty jugs.

Dairy, like everything else, has an environmental footprint, and not a small one at that. But if you want to stick with dairy, even small choices, like purchasing it in glass or from local farms, can help to reduce the impact. Being sustainable doesn't have to be hard, and sometimes it even dresses up the refrigerator (a glass jug will always look better than plastic).

GROCERY DELIVERY

Thanks to the innovations of the modern world and the enduring hassle of going to the store, grocery delivery has emerged (and for more than just milk in glass jugs!). Although in many areas you can get grocery stores to deliver, there are other, more sustainable alternatives to consider before you place your order.

Imperfect Foods delivers food that many grocers would otherwise reject as too small, too large, asymmetrical, or otherwise imperfect. These items would often be thrown away, but now are finding their way into our homes and onto our plates.

Another option in some areas is Zero Grocery, a plastic-free delivery service that uses reusable containers that you simply return when they are empty. I hope to see more companies and services like this. Be sure to investigate the options that may be available near you.

There is some controversy over the sustainability of grocery delivery and other similar industries, and we will examine that more closely in Chapter 8.

FARMER'S MARKET

I understand the pull of grocery delivery but working from home makes me look for more opportunities to get out, not less, so I was excited to get out of the house and pay a visit to the local farmer's market.

Towards the end of the month, I grabbed some reusable bags and headed to the farmer's market. Although I was a bit skeptical at first and somewhat wary of the potentially higher prices, I ended up being pleasantly surprised.

It turned out to be a great opportunity to choose natural foods, support the local economy, and benefit the environment.

One of my goals for shopping locally was to shorten the supply chain for my food. Buying from a farmer's market means the food was grown on a local farm, transported to the market, and then taken home to be eaten. When I buy food from a grocery store, the supply chain is much longer. It starts at the original farm or manufacturing plant where it has been grown or produced, then it is transported to a packaging and distribution center, moved to the store, and finally to my home. A food delivery service, like the ones mentioned above, does add a few more steps (the distribution, packaging, and delivery are all separate processes) to get it from production to my plate.

I could technically shorten the supply chain even more by buying from a local CSA or even growing it myself. These options aren't readily available to me at this time, so I settled on the farmer's market as the best option for now, but CSAs and home gardening can be great sustainable options. I hope to be able to experiment with both of these options at some point.

The people I met at the Farmer's Market were all extremely kind and helpful, and it was nice to be out in the early morning air.

As I brought home my haul, I loved the idea that all of these items were fresh and from the local area! It was also rewarding to know that I was supporting farmers and their families, the unsung heroes of our communities and the world as a whole. Another perk of having fresh food in the house is, of course, eating it! I guess it seems somewhat obvious but having healthy options accessible greatly increases the chance that I will eat them.

The produce sold at farmers' markets is likely to have been harvested within the last several days. It didn't have to travel countless miles like most of the produce sold in the US, which has traveled over 1,500 miles to find its way into your cart. It's not only the distance this food has to travel, but also the fact that it is harvested long before it reaches ripeness. Bananas, for example, are often picked up to a month before they will arrive in stores and are artificially ripened. Now you might not find bananas at the farmer's market (at least not near Seattle), but the fruit you do find will likely be fresher. And while we're on the subject of bananas, whether you're buying them at your local farmer's market, Trader Joe's, or somewhere else altogether, opt for the lonely ones. Bananas have a fairly large carbon footprint to begin with, so we don't want the singles just tossed in the trash, but that is often what happens to the single bananas left behind at the end of the day. Choose the lonely banana, and maybe grab one for your friend, too. You won't regret it.

Purchasing from a farmer's market allows us to eat seasonally. When berries are no longer in season, we can switch to whatever comes next. You probably won't find everything you want or need at your local farmer's market, but just being in contact with local farms, and the seasonal nature of food, will make you think about how blueberries ended up in the supermarket in January.

You may learn more than you wanted to know. Many of the largest berry manufacturers exploit their workers and use child labor. These people often receive poor wages, unsanitary working conditions, and sexual harassment. Shopping locally, whenever possible, not only helps to support your community but keeps money away from organizations that don't care for their communities.

UGLY FOOD

I think I have always understood on some level that less than 100% of the produce grown ends up on the grocery store shelves. It's rare to see a bruised banana or a crooked cucumber. Looking back, I remember a time my family went apple picking for a day. When we were done, the farmer helped us sort all of the apples that we picked. Some of them were spotty looking, others had bruises from a recent hailstorm, and others were just misshapen and ugly, but the farmer reminded us that despite the outward blemishes, all of these apples were okay to take home and eat. Which we did. As we sorted, however, a good portion of the apples we'd picked, probably 20% to 30%, were riddled with worms or had fallen on the ground. The farmer couldn't sell those, so they would never be eaten, except by the horses on the farm.

Before this sustainability project, I had never really thought much about that. Now I realize that just because I never see spotty, bruised, wormy, or oddly shaped apples in the grocery store doesn't mean they don't exist. So what happens to those apples, and all of the other fruit and vegetables that aren't close to perfect?

Unsurprisingly, they don't make it to the market, or if they do, they may be discarded. If they get a little bruised during their time on the display floor, they will often face the same fate.

Services like Imperfect Foods provide a way to get our hands on the food items that may not be as aesthetically pleasing as you are used to seeing at the grocery store, but that are just as tasty, albeit a little more unique in appearance. The real win is that sending these items to our stomachs is a much more sustainable option than sending them to a landfill.

And of course, visiting the local farmer's market or CSA will also give you access to both beautiful and ugly foods — with the benefit of them being locally grown!

PLASTIC FOOD

This section isn't really about plastic food, although I did love my toy kitchen growing up and some of the meals I made there looked delicious.

I'm referring instead to the reality that frequently when we purchase a head of broccoli or a cucumber at the market, we often find it wrapped in plastic. That may not seem like a very big deal (it's only a little plastic), and it keeps the food clean. But most of the fresh food we purchase that is wrapped in plastic was grown in dirt and should be thoroughly cleaned before it is consumed — plastic or no plastic. And unfortunately, that thin layer of plastic isn't recyclable most of the time.

Thankfully, fresh produce items can generally be found, at least in some places, without this extra, unsustainable, and unnecessary addition.

It's also concerning that there are so many food items packaged with plastic even when the product isn't fresh. Think about those pasta boxes that come with a little window so we can see the noodles, even though a picture of it is also shown on the box. Barilla has recently removed the plastic window from some of their boxes, and while I haven't seen them at my local store yet, I will certainly pick those over the alternatives with a plastic window.

Even small changes like this are still important. It is through these small acts that we support sustainability.

BYOC (BRING YOUR OWN CONTAINERS)

You know you've officially entered adulthood (and not in an exciting way) when you are thrilled that a bulk-based, organic-centered grocery store is coming to your town.

My town has always had one store with bulk options, but they always felt limited, and I wasn't in the habit of shopping there. But when I heard this new store was opening in my area, I felt like a kid in a candy store, but one lined with rice, broccoli, and dried beans.

If you are planning to purchase items in bulk, make sure to bring your own containers, if possible, to avoid using more plastic with your purchase. The idea is to cut back on excess packaging — and to save time decanting the groceries when we get home.

If possible, you can get fresh meats and cheeses in your own packaging (or at least compostable paper) from a local butcher or in the deli section at the grocery store. The same may go for the local bakery or the bakery section. Always inquire.

Local restaurants are another source of local foods. You could get tortillas from the local taqueria or pizza dough from the pizzeria on the corner. And chances are, you can probably use your own container! This is also another way to support local businesses. My all-time favorite salsa is from a nearby Mexican restaurant, and although I don't buy it in my own jar, it comes in a recyclable container.

Not all of the products we need will be sold in bulk or sold in a way that we can use our own containers. When that is the case, choosing recyclable packaging is the next best option, and then making sure to actually clean and recycle it properly. Some things (like medications) come in packages that can't be recycled or reused in any way, and that's okay, too.

Sustainability is an art, and the best artists are not starving, but are well-fed, healthy, and happy.

THE DUMP DILEMMA

One night, while watching a scary movie and trying to distract myself, I started scrolling through my county's website to find out more about the trash and recycling processes that are in place.

Sadly, I came across something scarier than the movie I was watching. It was a simple sentence that said all of the trash from our county was taken to a landfill in Oregon. Since I live near Seattle, Oregon is a solid 3-hour drive away — and that's if traffic is good.

I realized then that the people in my community, including me, are generating tons of trash that is destined to sit in a landfill, and all of that trash has to be hauled hundreds of miles, in big trucks, creating additional carbon emissions, to be deposited, decompose, and create additional carbon emissions.

Talk about something that makes absolutely no sense.

I shouldn't have been surprised by this revelation after learning in January just how far my recycling travels. But at least those items were being transported to hopefully be remade into new things. The trash that I (and everyone else in my county) was generating was going to travel hundreds of miles to sit and decompose over a period of hundreds of years. This had no silver lining. It was bad for the environment I was fighting to protect.

COMPOSTING

Once I knew how far away the landfill was, I knew I had to start making some changes. The first was one that I resisted for a long time. I tried to think of ways around it, excuses not to do it, or reasons why I didn't need to include it in this book. But I finally couldn't get around it anymore. Even though it was hard to think of myself in this way, I knew I needed to start composting.

When I first began researching the county's trash relocation policy, I also looked into their composting service. I am very grateful and proud that they offer one! Unfortunately, it does not extend to where I live, at least not at this time. So I was on my own.

Since food waste contributes 330,000,000 pounds to the garbage generated in North America every year, I knew it was something I had to do. Composting benefits the environment by recycling organic resources and by keeping those resources out of landfills, where they are unable to break down properly. It also saves water by acting as a fertilizer, retaining moisture, and reducing water runoff.

At first, I hesitated to start composting because I wondered if I generated enough waste to make it worthwhile. I quickly learned that I do. Although previously, I generated about one bag of trash each week, once I started composting, I was able to reduce that amount further. And most of what used to make my trash can smell badly was now in the compost bin instead of the trash!

I learned that in Washington State, where I live, about 42% of what the average household throws away could have been composted instead. And the impact of composting is undeniable. According to research from the Composting Council, if the food waste from everyone in the United States was composted, it would have an impact comparable to removing 7.8 million cars from the road, something that is unlikely to happen until we invent those hoverboards from Back to the Future 2.

The average household in the United States generates about 650 pounds of organic trash, most of which ends up in a landfill. In fact, landfills are about 60% organic matter. This is an issue since the organic matter is mixed with inorganic, which hinders its decomposition, preserving it instead, and resulting in a term you may remember from middle school biology — anaerobic decomposition. And as the organic matter sits, rots, and decays, it generates methane gas, a greenhouse gas 23 times more potent than CO_2.[54]

Once I had gotten over my shock about the traveling trash and I worked up the courage to see what the county had to say about composting, I returned to their website. Since I had already checked at an earlier date and was not eligible for the county's compost program, I just wanted to see what benefits this new habit would have on my local (and global) environment.

For the people who are in the county's composting program, instead of having their organic waste travel hundreds of miles, it is instead processed in the county next to ours! This greatly reduces its journey and the emissions at all levels, since the emissions not only come from the trucks necessary to transport the trash to Oregon, but also from the organic material in the trash (that could and should have been composted) which will produce methane gas because of the low oxygen conditions in the landfill.

Not only that, but since food waste is often heavier than other kinds of trash, it also takes more energy to transfer them to a landfill. This results in increased emissions, which is especially sad when you consider that the composting center is so much closer than the landfill to begin with.

With composting there is literally no downside! Especially if you live in an area with a city or county composting program, all you have to do is place food scraps into a different container and maybe wheel an extra can down to the street corner every few weeks. If you are doing the composting yourself, there is a bit more work involved, but you get to use the end product yourself or you can share with grateful neighbors!

Composting is much more than just throwing food scraps into a bin, it is actually a little tiny decomposing ecosystem, which is kept in "balance." You must have a mixture of "green" items that are high in nitrogen (the food scraps, grass cuttings, and so on) and "brown" components that are high in carbon (dry leaves, paper scraps, hay, etc.).

You can't compost all food scraps. Generally a compost bin shouldn't include meat, dairy, or cooked greasy foods. I was surprised to find that you also shouldn't include citrus, banana peels, or onion. These items have higher acidity and natural chemicals which can kill the worms and other microorganisms in the compost, and which slows down the decomposition process. Plus, citrus peels take a long time to break down in general, unless they are cut into little pieces. Before you toss something in, it is worth a quick online search to make sure you can. Before too long, you'll be a pro.

Compost should smell earthy and by keeping outdoor compost in the sun (only somewhat possible here in Washington) it will help to aid in the breakdown of the compost. You'll also want to make sure your compost is properly aerated and stays moist, but not wet.[55]

Another interesting thing I learned as I dove into composting (not literally) was the difference between things that are biodegradable and things that are compostable. I knew there was a difference, they are different words after all, but I wouldn't have been able to tell you what the difference was.

Something biodegradable will break down into smaller pieces but may take decades to disappear. To break down, the item requires heat, water, oxygen, and microorganisms, but it may never fully disappear. Some plastics biodegrade, but these only break into smaller and smaller pieces over time.

Compostable items fully break down into nontoxic components. This can't be said of plastics, as we learned earlier. The same components are necessary to aid in decomposition, but it can happen much more quickly, depending on the conditions. And instead of having the potential to harm the environment as they decompose, many compostable substances can nourish it instead.

Since I live in an apartment, my options for composting were limited. Luckily, I was able to find a countertop composter that works quickly and efficiently and is ideal for my home and lifestyle. It allows me to toss in scraps as necessary and although I wasn't initially a huge fan of having one more thing on my countertop, the ease with which it integrated into my routine, and the impact I knew it was having was definitely worth it.

There are comprehensive resources online for how to start a compost bin, so I won't list them here. The same goes for the things that you can (and cannot) put into your composter.

If you don't want to build or buy a composter, or don't have the space for it, the easiest way to start composting is simply to enroll in your local or county composting program. More and more areas offer them, and the ones that do are often working to expand. If this is available to you, and you don't want the effort of composting yourself, this is a great option.

Of course, if you are out of range of a local composting program, are on the lookout for a challenge, or want to keep and create compost for your yard or garden, you can start composting on your own. It is not hard, very green, and maybe even a little bit fun! There are lots of great composters available for purchase online. I ended up settling on the Lomi from Pela because it was small, efficient, and aesthetically pleasing!

If you have the skills, time, and interest, you can even build your own composter. Articles, plans, and YouTube videos abound.

Taking the time to care for the earth in one area, often leads to sustainable actions in many others. The EPA has estimated that households who compost send 28% less trash to the landfill than non-composting neighbors. I was also fascinated to learn that areas with municipal compost programs also tend to have much higher recycling rates.[56] Those are statistics I want to be a part of.

Every bit of food waste that isn't traveling hundreds of miles to a landfill is helping, rather than hurting, the planet. Even if composting isn't something you can do right now, consider what other sustainable actions you can take and let the effects ripple out from there.

FOOD WASTE + WORLD HUNGER

Let's return to the millions of people in the world who are undernourished or starving. Producing and killing animals for food consumption plays a part in this equation, but food waste is another piece.

With almost 1 in 7 people in the world suffering from hunger or starvation, and one-third of the food produced worldwide being thrown away, this issue should be relatively easy to resolve. Except that it's not.

I attended a conference in California with my father and a couple of my friends when we were in junior high school. The conference was about international orphan care and presented ways that each of us could help to create a world where every child has a family.

On the first day of the conference, we attended a lecture right before lunch. Now I have no recollection whatsoever of what it was about, but I remember being told that we could feed most of the hungry people in the world with just the food that we typically throw away. That thought has stayed with me ever since. I remember the feeling that if I didn't eat everything on my plate, I was contributing to the suffering of children around the world.

When we sat down to lunch after the session, that message was still fresh in our minds. But halfway through the lunch of double-decker hamburgers provided by the conference organizers, we all knew there was little hope of actually finishing our food. It was just too much. But we were determined, so we managed to finish it all — and were left feeling unbelievably sick for the rest of the trip. Looking back, it wasn't clear how the uneaten half of a hamburger we couldn't finish could somehow kill an orphan if we threw it out. As far as I know, there isn't an organization that takes leftovers across the world to help solve the hunger crisis. And I don't think there should be. There are much more productive and efficient ways to help solve the hunger crisis, and we can do it without creating unhealthy ideas about food, guilting people when they take too much, or stuffing ourselves in the process.

And, yes, I know that was the double whammy — eating a burger and almost throwing half of it away. Thankfully, I can say that I think my knowledge and consumption habits have come a long way since then.

Between 30% and 40% of the food produced in the United States is thrown away. That adds up to about 133 billion pounds of food going uneaten, or about 1,249 calories per person, per day. The average family in the United States discards about $2,275 worth of food every year. That's a waste in more ways than one and reducing that number will benefit your wallet and the environment simultaneously. The United States isn't alone in this. Europe and Industrialized Asia also have a high percentage of food that ends up as waste.

Consumers aren't the only ones who throw out food. Restaurants and fast-food chains do, too. Grocery stores throw out food that doesn't meet their appearance standards, that has had packaging changes, isn't in demand, or is left over. A total of approximately $161.6 billion in food waste comes from retailers, restaurants, and individual homes.

The real cost isn't just the hunger crisis and the impact on our wallets. This also has a significant negative impact on the environment. If we stopped wasting food (I know, an almost impossible goal, but hear me out), we would have an impact on carbon emissions equivalent to taking 1 in 4 cars off the road (another goal that seems almost impossible).

Fortunately, there are several things we can do to benefit our wallets, the environment, and the hunger crisis.

The first is to make sure we are buying food consciously. We start by asking ourselves a few questions: 1) Do we need to bring home all this food at once? 2) Can we eat it in a way so that the perishable items can be consumed first? 3) Can we freeze or preserve some of it to maximize its useful life? I believe that all of us go into the market with these thoughts in mind, but the sad fact is that at least a third of our food will still end up in the trash. Reducing food waste is something that will look different for every one of us, but we can all be conscious of what we are throwing away, why we are throwing it away, and whether there is something we can do in the future to ensure we'll throw less away next time.

One way that we can cut back on the amount of food we toss out is to take small servings and go back for seconds if we're still hungry. This will help keep unwanted food out of the trashcan. Other ideas include waiting longer between meals, buying foods that last longer, or taking steps to buy food with a few extra days of peak freshness. It can be helpful to prep the food as soon as you bring it home to preserve it longer. We should also avoid shopping when we are hungry so we avoid overbuying. And let's remember to use what might otherwise be thrown out to make broth or soup stocks, to turn into coloring dye, or feed to animals. We probably don't need to do all of these things, but we can all do something.

Making sure to store food properly and use it in the order that it is likely to spoil can extend the useful life of our food and will help to reduce the number of items that go bad before we can use them.

I might also suggest that cleaning out the refrigerator frequently is more than just a good idea to keep it clean, but it will also remind you of what you have and will help to answer the age-old question — "What's for dinner?"

Try experimenting with food scraps to make broth or using leaves and stems in new or unique dishes. The more food you use, the more food you use.

Another thing to keep in mind as we attempt to cut back on food waste is to understand the truth about food expiration dates. I'll admit, I'm a stickler when it comes to checking the expiration dates on my food. I have nightmares about pouring separated almond milk into my tea or eating a rancid nut. Even when things are sure to be edible, my imagination will turn food past the expiration date into bites of death straight from hell.

There are several terms to know when contemplating an item before you on your kitchen counter. The first is the "use by" date, also known as the expiration date. This is generally the day after which the quality of the product will begin to go downhill, some more rapidly than others. The safety of the food could be a concern, depending on what it is. Use your own best judgment.

The "best by" or "best if used before" date also tends to mark a decline in the quality of the item, but this date tends to be used for canned goods and other items that are not likely to deteriorate rapidly. The food is safe to eat, within a reasonable timeframe.

Finally, the "sell by" date is used to let the store know when it should remove the item from its shelves. Often this has to do with the appearance of the product and not whether it is expired or unsafe to eat. In fact, this date is typically only about two-thirds of the way through the expected lifespan of the product. You can feel confident that the item is still safe to eat, within a reasonable timeframe.

We are unlikely to eliminate food waste entirely, but we can reduce the impact by composting and we can encourage individuals and even businesses to buy imperfect produce that might otherwise be thrown out.

Before we move on, however, I'd like to give a little more consideration to helping end the hunger crisis. If we could divert just 15% of the food that goes to waste in the United States, we could cut the number of hungry Americans in half. Unfortunately, there is no clear or easy way to do that.

Vermont is breaking new ground by encouraging composting and banning the tossing of food scraps. They are also working on developing programs that will divert food to those in need. California, too, has mandated the composting of food scraps and has opened composting facilities. The new law further requires grocery stores, restaurants, and other food distribution companies to give the expiring foods to soup kitchens to feed the hungry. Hopefully, all US states will follow the example of Vermont and California.

In the meantime, there are more steps we can all take. The money we save by not overbuying food items can be donated to organizations that help feed the hungry. If we know that we aren't going to eat something in our pantry, it can be donated. We can even choose to purchase extra food items during our regular shopping trips to give to those in need. We can each make a difference through hundreds of small, intentional actions, whether by choosing to avoid meat, cleaning out our fridge, or donating money to organizations that provide food to those in need.

Sustainability and world hunger are deeply interconnected. Although the answers and actions necessary to pursue one and eliminate the other are rarely easy or obvious, it's up to each one of us to make changes. The world and those who inhabit it in the future will be the beneficiaries.

CHAPTER 8
AUGUST: SHOPPING

By August, I realized just how far I still had to travel on my journey to sustainable living, and, fortunately, or unfortunately, I knew that I still had a lot of purchases to make. Just as someone who wants to eat healthy will have to purchase fresh and often more expensive foods and cooking tools, I realized that I needed to change the figurative bread and butter of my life to avoid covering my body in toxic chemicals and filling the trash can more often than the recycling can.

I don't want to send the message that to live sustainably, you have to buy lots of new things. As I've said before, one of the best ways to live a more sustainable life is simply to use and use up what you already have!

But, the fact is, when you do finally run out of plastic bags, or an item you have can't be reused or repaired, then it's time to consider making a move to something that may be truly sustainable for the long haul.

In earlier chapters, I discussed items or brands I have purchased in the interest of making my life, home, and habits sustainable after lots of research. I mentioned those things to save you time and, hopefully, money, in the long run. There is no paid advertising or marketing behind any of the products that I have discussed, but my hope in naming specific brands I loved (or didn't) is merely to help you on your journey toward sustainability. During my research, I looked for someone, anyone, to tell me what to do, where to go, and what to buy to help the planet and make my lifestyle more sustainable.

This book is what I needed, but if I don't share something specific that you are looking for, I'm confident that you will find a product that will work well for you. The truth is, there isn't a perfect product, but there is a right product — and it is whichever one you decide works best for you. I just hope that my experiences will help you in your search for sustainability, and maybe save you some research time along the way.

The good news is that there are many good options — more and more every day. I do not doubt that by the time this book is published, there will be more new and innovative tips, tools, and products to make our lives even more sustainable.

Sustainability is a continuum. Reusable silicone bags are better than plastic baggies for food storage. But it's okay to use plastic bags if that's what you have in your house right now. If the alternative for you is eating out for every meal, that's probably not sustainable financially or environmentally in the long run.

A major aspect of sustainable living is becoming more conscious of what we consume. And if you've picked up anything thus far, it's probably the awareness that the human population consumes a lot. And, sadly, very little of it is done mindfully. Consider it from this perspective: the less we bring into our homes, the less we'll have to organize, store, maintain, and, ultimately, dispose of properly. Too often, disposal comes before the end of a product's natural life, but rather when it no longer fits, is out of style, or doesn't "spark joy."

I have been in the category of "mindless" consumer, too. I remember a time when I enjoyed meeting friends at the mall, dining at our favorite restaurant, and spending the rest of the day wandering through our favorite shops. We did this probably once a week, and sometimes three or four times. There were days when I walked back to the car with a full stomach but without shopping bags. But there were also many times when I picked up one or two new things — generally some fast-fashion pieces, or something for my apartment. Rarely were these things that I needed, and sometimes they weren't even things that I particularly wanted.

Thankfully, as I got older, I learned to pass on items I didn't need or want. I would occasionally return to the store a few days later if an item was still on my mind. That became a somewhat helpful litmus test for me. If the item was still there, great! And if it wasn't, then I clearly didn't need it in the first place.

Times have continued to change. My favorite restaurant has closed, and that alone significantly reduced the number of trips I made to the mall. Then I moved. The mall is miles away now and trying to go for any reason always feels like a hassle. I've also shifted friends and activities. Some of the people that I would often find myself casually shopping with, I don't spend much time with anymore. And I have found new activities to do with the others.

INTENTIONAL DECISION MAKING

Even as I write this, it's fascinating to me to look back over the patterns in my life that I was unaware of at the time. I was spending money eating at my favorite restaurant — that was something I planned for. But, at the end of each month, when I would review my spending, I found many entries for items from stores that I could not even recall with certainty.

The monthly reviews didn't trigger changes, however. It was the change in location and activities that ultimately brought lifestyle shifts and which eventually led me to my sustainability project.

Along the way, I noticed other shopping ruts that I had fallen into, some of which I will share in this chapter. And I would encourage you to consider if there are any shopping triggers in your own life.

Some of these triggers can be good. We need to know when there is just enough (non-dairy) milk left in the carton for one more bowl of cereal so we can add it to the shopping list.

Other triggers, such as certain friendships or emotional crises, are less helpful. There wasn't much intentionality at work when you suddenly realize that you've spent the last four nights at the mall and the trunk of your car looks like you've been Black Friday shopping.

When fresh groceries are delivered every Wednesday, a box of laundry detergent is automatically shipped every two months, and we spend many evenings mindlessly scrolling through online stores while half-watching Seinfeld reruns, much of our shopping is on autopilot. Although this is an easy way to live, I have to remind myself to stay in charge of my spending, my shopping habits, and my life.

As a professional organizer, this could be where I provide you with a flow chart or a list of questions to ask yourself before making a purchase. But I'm not going to do that.

Although these are tools that I have used in the past, and I know many other organizing experts alike recommend them, I don't think it's necessary. If you want to use these tools, a quick Google search can help.

I understand the appeal these tools have, and I have used them in the past with my clients. But the truth is, they aren't really necessary. If you are reading this book, it's more than likely that you are an adult. I trust you to make your own decisions, ones that will be good for both you and the planet. You are competent to decide whether to buy, or get rid of, something, and at what point in the future that thing you decided to buy should become something that you get rid of. Building the confidence to make decisions for yourself and knowing that you have your own back is much more important and beautiful than a flow chart.

I also want to remind you that things, in and of themselves, aren't innately bad — overconsumption is. Shopping isn't bad — overconsumption is. There are ways to shop and consume sustainably. And that amount is different for everyone! The amount for me is different now that I live on my own than it was when I was growing up with four younger siblings, or even when I had a roommate. The amount that you can sustainably consume is likely very different from mine. It just requires that you and I do the hard work of figuring out what that is for each of us.

This chapter will be a little different than the previous ones. I'm not going to share about brands or companies that I love. Although I have done that in just about every other chapter when talking about specific products or issues, I also want to give you the foundation to figure out for yourself what companies you want to support going forward and why.

Many industries have little to no regulations. Many companies exploit, underpay, and even abuse their employees. Some dispose of their waste improperly. Some place employees in unsafe working conditions. Some leave toxins and chemicals in the water, air, and ground for other people to deal with. Some abuse, maim, and kill animals. Some employ children.

Sadly, this list doesn't even begin to describe some of the atrocities committed by companies in the United States and abroad. And we probably don't even know the worst. While there are companies to avoid, there are ones that look very promising, both in terms of their mission and practices. But often even these sustainably produced items must be shipped halfway around the world before they can make it into our shopping carts or on our front porches. So, ultimately, we each have a responsibility to make the best decision for us about what to buy with the information we now have available.

Companies, products, and regulations change frequently, so this will require a lasting commitment and an ever-evolving skill for every one of us.

There are companies that I included in this book but later had to remove when new information came out about them. Just like everything else, there are no easy answers. We have to do the research ourselves or turn to other people and organizations that we trust who have done the research.

We need to know who is making our products, how they are made, how they get to us, how we will maintain them, and, finally, how we will dispose of them.

We must also accept it when we make mistakes as part of our learning. We can't afford to let the fear of failure overwhelm us or stop us from taking action. We can't stick our heads in the sand and ignore the issue entirely. We're not ostriches. We're much cuter, much smarter, and making the best choices we know how might just help preserve ostriches for generations to come.

THINK OF THE SUPPLY CHAIN

I know it's common for people to consider all of the things that had to happen for them to be born — both good and bad. This is even more common when you meet someone you love and then you consider all of the things that had to happen for them to not only exist *but* for you to meet them.

Along those lines, have you ever thought of the circumstances that got that cute summer dress, ugly Christmas sweater, or the sweatpants that you never let anyone see you wear, into your closet? I'm not implying that true love or destiny is at work here, but there is certainly an element of awe.

In the not-too-distant past, cotton was likely growing in Uzbekistan. When the cotton reached maturity, it was picked and sent to China for processing into thread. From there, it may have gone to Bangladesh to be made into that lovely daisy-patterned sundress that you always get complimented on. Once it was fully assembled, it was likely packed onto a container ship, traveled across the Pacific Ocean, and finally to a large port on the west coast of America. From there, it was loaded onto a truck, driven to your nearest shopping center, unloaded, processed, and put on a rack. You just happened to visit that shopping center, paused as you walked past the rack of dresses, picked it up, tried it on, checked out, and took it home with you.

That cotton came a long way to end up in your closet.

Now multiply that by the number of items of clothing in your closet.

Extrapolate that out based on an estimated number of items in your home. When you stop to think about it, that is a vast amount of time, effort, energy, production, and transportation, isn't it?

This is something we can keep in mind the next time we prepare to donate a box of household or personal items to Goodwill. Better yet, we should keep it in mind before our next shopping trip.

Being aware of the length of the supply chain helps to put the things we buy into proper perspective. And keeping this perspective will help us to make decisions about whether we really need the things that we want to buy.

Of course, the journey of the sundress doesn't end in your closet. It will continue until that day that you decide it's time for it to go. If you donate it to a thrift shop and the sundress is sold (only about 10% of clothing given to thrift stores is), it will have another owner before the process is repeated. If it isn't sold, your sundress will likely be shipped overseas for a chance at a second life. The US ships over 1 billion pounds of used clothes every year to other countries. Africa is a major recipient, receiving about 70% of the world's secondhand clothes. By shipping these unwanted items overseas, the hope is that these items won't end up in a landfill but will serve some additional use or purpose. But the reality is that this does have an impact on the local industries and economy and may not ultimately keep them out of the trash.

BUY NOTHING (OR LESS)

This isn't just the name of a local Facebook community where you can get free items from your neighbors, it is also a positive step toward living a more sustainable life. And although buying nothing may be something we can all manage in some ways and for some items, buying less may certainly suffice in others.

The first and most sustainable choice we can make is to not buy something or to use what we already have. The second-best choice is simply to buy less. And the third best choice is to buy better. When it comes to shopping, there really is little else to say. And the little else that needs to be said, is what I'll cover in the rest of this chapter.

Using what you have, buying less, and buying better is my version of "reduce, reuse, recycle." Either way, if we agree to follow all these principles, we are well on the path toward sustainable living.

SHOPPING SECOND HAND

We talked a lot about thrifting and shopping second hand in Chapter 3. But this option extends well beyond clothing. If you can buy something firsthand, the chances are good that you can also buy it secondhand, albeit with a few more scratches and a bit more wear than the new one.

But buying something second-hand means that you haven't required additional resources to be expended to produce a new product, and you are giving new life and purpose to an existing one.

Whether you enjoy browsing the local thrift store, searching online for something specific, clicking through Craigslist, or making known what you want on Facebook, there are many ways to shop second-hand, no matter what you are looking for.

BEG OR BORROW (BUT DON'T STEAL)

Just as you can gift or loan items to friends, you can borrow or even buy items from friends and family, too. I've always loved the idea of community sheds and workshops where tools are communal and you don't have to buy, own, or store the items you need just a few weekends a year.

There are even places, like libraries, where you can often borrow cake pans, many times in fun or interesting shapes, so you don't have to purchase pans just to use once.

I never stop being amazed at the many ideas and resources that are available to us which enable us to pursue our goal of increased sustainability. And I promise, the more you look for them, the more you will find!

LOOK LOCAL

As with food, it helps to shop within your community. Not only are you likely supporting a small business, but the items likely won't have been shipped around the world or produced with child labor or other inhumane practices. And no, the store owner's son or daughter working the cash register doesn't count as child labor.

If you find particular items or stores that you like, spread the word to friends and family! If you are looking for a particular recommendation, look within your community first, or search online! The local stores may not have a big online presence, but if they do, support them that way as well. A "like," "follow," or "share" can go a long way, especially if followed by monetary support as well.

Supporting your local community doesn't have to be limited to purchasing new items, you can also support the local seamstress, cobbler, or repairman while maintaining the items you already own!

When I was little, my mother took me to the local cobbler to have my favorite brown heels resoled. Although I didn't get to watch, I was excited when I got them back and they looked brand new! I wore those shoes as long as I could (I was a kid with especially fast-growing feet), but eventually, those shoes went to a new home and, I like to think, got another new sole for their new life.

ONLINE SHOPPING

When you can't find what you are looking for second-hand or locally, it is time to turn to the behemoth of the internet — although technically, you can use the internet to shop second-hand and locally, too.

Luckily, there is an ever-increasing number of businesses in the online space that care about sustainability and share about their mission and products with equal fervor. And since research on the internet is quite easy, it isn't hard to find out whether companies care about or mention sustainability at all and are backing up their talk with actual action.

If I'm looking for a particular product, I will poke around a website with "sustainability" in the search bar. If the website search yields 0 results, I move on to the next site. If a company doesn't care about my values, and there isn't a reason I really need one specific product, then I'm going to move on to find a product from a company that does.

Having information you need to make an informed decision is the first step and is often the biggest one.

I'm not going to tell you which factors you should consider when you're shopping online, although the ones we've discussed in this chapter and throughout this book are a good starting place. The choices that you make will largely be informed by the factors that matter to you the most and that have priority in your personal value system. When we are truly acting out of our deeply held beliefs, the impact can be seen everywhere, even in those items we add to our virtual shopping carts and the websites those shopping carts are on.

But please remember — buy less, buy better.

SUBSCRIPTION BOXES

I have strong opinions about subscription boxes of all kinds, but especially those that are distributing unsustainable products. Unfortunately, acquiring products this way is the exact opposite of intentional curation, one of the best ways to fight the throwaway culture.

When you sign up for a box, you are also opening yourself up to receive additional items that you don't want or need. These items will typically either get tossed out or pushed into the cycle. Makeup subscription boxes, particularly, generate a lot of waste (think small plastic bottles and tubes). These items will frequently expire, only to be tossed, and are not likely to be cleaned and recycled properly.

These products are often not financially sustainable either, at least in the long run. The subscription fees are low enough that they often fly under the radar, $8 here, $15 there. In the short term, it doesn't appear to add up to much. But if you get several of these subscriptions every month, reducing your bank balance while increasing the clutter inside your home, it might be worthwhile to reconsider.

If you are thinking about giving someone a subscription, make sure it's one that they will use. A box of hot sauce every month may seem like a good gift, but if the receiver can't handle the heat, most of it will go to waste. It may be better to gift a subscription that doesn't result in tangible clutter or potential waste, such as a Netflix membership or access to Spotify Premium.

Of course, not all subscriptions fall into this category. Having some groceries or other products that you use regularly shipped to you on a schedule can save you time and mental space. Just make sure that you evaluate this situation every so often so that you aren't ending up with too much at any one time. And keep in mind that it is most efficient to order in bulk and as few times a month as possible.

Sustainability is all about making mindful and purposeful decisions for yourself and the earth.

SHIPPING

Amazon Prime and the advent of two-day shipping is another indication that convenience and consumption have led us away from sustainability.

Unlike air travel that we can take into account in our carbon reduction calculation at the end of the year, most calculators don't ask, "how many packages did you order online in the last year and, on average, how quickly were they delivered?"

I confess that I enjoy fast shipping as much as the next person, but I need to remember that it comes at a high cost.

An easy change that we can all make is to ask for "plastic-free" or "no plastic" shipping in the "notes" or "comments" section as we check out. This request may not always be honored, but hopefully the majority of the time it will be. And hopefully, the day when we no longer have to request it is not too far around the corner.

Cardboard, brown paper, and paper tape are recyclable, and they are the best option whether you are buying something online or are sending a package to someone else. And if you have a use for the brown paper, boxes, or packing peanuts that you may end up with, that's best of all! If not, we need to dispose of them properly, or try to hand them off to someone else who could use them. Packing peanuts, bubble wrap, or other packing materials can sometimes be returned to a local shipping location for reuse. If plastic ends up in your package, you know what to do.

Consolidating purchases to a single retailer or asking them to combine multiple items into a single shipment, will also help. Fewer packages, fewer emissions. It's a small sacrifice to make for such large benefits.

Another simple swap is to cut back on the number of items you are having shipped. If you can pick up new bedsheets at the local TJ Maxx, maybe you could swing by there the next time you're in the area instead of having them shipped across the country (or the world). While there is always a cost attached because those sheets were shipped to your town and you had to drive to the store to buy them, at least you will be able to choose the cost mindfully.

PACKAGING

Although I could have included this information in Chapter 5 or 6, I decided to include it here because packaging plays a major role in so much more than just personal care products. The common denominator is that we acquire packaging through the shopping process.

The major news is that nearly 30% of municipal solid waste comes from packaging and containers.

It would be easier if we could just look for recyclable packaging, but that, unfortunately, isn't the only consideration. Even if we did that, we would still have to take the necessary steps to make sure the items are cleaned and recycled properly.

We also know that we should look beyond the labels to ensure we aren't falling victim to greenwashing.

As with everything else, reducing the amount of packaging you are consuming (or the items in packaging you are consuming) is always the first step. Then, the next step is to try to reuse the packaging if you can, whether it be cardboard boxes or tissue paper.

Whenever packaging material is involved, it's wise to remember that the lighter the weight of the packaging, the lower the CO_2 that was emitted by transporting it, and maybe also in producing it to begin with. Similarly, the less shiny the material is, the better, because waxed or coated cardboard and paper often cannot be properly recycled but must end up in the landfill. In the long run, paper, cardboard, or something biodegradable (like packing peanuts made from corn starch) are more sustainable than the plastic (or Styrofoam) alternatives.

Look for items packaged in clear glass (which can be recycled) as opposed to colored glass (which cannot), items produced in aluminum or steel packaging (which can be recycled), items with refillable containers, and items with minimal packaging. If there is an option to get your item "naked" (sans packaging), or if a similar, alternate product is available "naked," it's worth it to make the switch.

If you are looking to purchase something that comes in packaging material, look for businesses that package items with recycled materials which you can then recycle. If the item you are looking to purchase is zero-waste, or there is a zero-waste alternative, or it can be shipped to you using a zero-waste method, this is worth considering.

When placing orders, avoid items that come in packaging composed of mixed materials (if you receive an item in paper and plastic — you're going to have to take steps to recycle both). Remember, paper is only a better alternative to plastic if it can be recycled (no coatings, and so on), and if we take the necessary steps to make sure that it is. I also try not to purchase items that come with excess packaging (like cardboard dividers or plastic ties), items with extra seals (one is good, but too many is just too many), as well as ones with pumps, droppers, and aerosol cans which can be difficult, if not impossible, to dispose of sustainably.[57]

The best packaging is zero packaging. From there, the next best is less packaging, then reusable packaging, and then recyclable packaging. And I can't bring myself to list the straight-to-the-landfill kind as an option.

IN-PERSON VS. ONLINE

The answer to the age-old question about which is better, in-person vs. online shopping, can vary widely depending on a multitude of different factors, and it is no different when you are trying to determine the best way to shop sustainably.

As I said earlier, I am a fan (okay, well maybe not a fan, but a consumer) of Amazon. One of the big perks is being able to know that what I'm ordering will be on my front porch in 48 hours. Oftentimes, less. Sometimes the delivery happens so fast I don't know how it is possible.

I don't even live in the city. I can't imagine what it would be like to have something delivered in two hours, or practically before I could even walk to my front door.

You might think that driving to the local Target to buy a stick of (sustainable) deodorant would be more sustainable than purchasing that stick online and having it shipped to you from who knows where. And you'd be right, but also wrong.

Whatever item you may have run into Target to purchase got there in the same way it will get to your house, by truck. And if you need deodorant, dog food, or something else within two hours, or two days, it is probably faster and more sustainable for you to run to the store than to place an order with an international conglomerate, even if it can be shipped to you within two days, free of charge.

The more we buy and the faster we want it delivered, the more trains, planes, and automobiles will be required to get it here. This means a lot of packages delivered and a lot of emissions released into the atmosphere. While ever more stores, including the local retailers, offer delivery services, and while some may utilize smaller passenger vehicles for delivery, the majority will still use delivery trucks, which have a much larger ecological footprint. More trucks mean more pollution.

If you do need to order online, and I know you're not going to want to hear this, it is better to opt for fewer, more consolidated, orders that arrive at a slower pace. When I place an order on Amazon, I always check the option that tells them to combine the items into a single delivery. This may mean an extra day or two, but unless I'm ordering a gift for a birthday party I completely forgot about until two days before (which, I can assure you has never, ever happened, wink, wink), it is generally okay with me to wait a few more days.

To urge more consumers to receive fewer, slower shipments, companies could consider incentivizing that option, or at least point out the environmental benefits. Amazon often gives the option of receiving credit in a certain category if you decide to combine your packages and delay shipment for a slightly longer period, normally just 5 to 7 days where I live. Although this wouldn't be feasible for all businesses, it is an interesting idea that will hopefully continue to spread.

Delivery companies, too, have been working to increase efficiency, which on the flip side, often also results in fewer emissions. Emerging technologies enable delivery trucks to drive closer together to reduce drag and save fuel, traffic lights that communicate with delivery vehicles, and other advances are helping to increase these efficiencies even further. In the 1970s, UPS began encouraging drivers to take fewer left turns. By doing so they have been able to reduce emissions by about 100,000 metric tons of CO_2 each year.[58] Fewer minutes waiting in left-turn lanes and fewer emissions? This could be good for all of us.

A recent study reported in Environmental Science & Technology found that shopping at brick-and-mortar stores for the items we buy regularly, like toilet paper and toothpaste, often results in fewer emissions than ordering these same items from an online-only company. Of course, this assumes that we would be placing an order online for the same product we would buy in the store, as opposed to a more eco-conscious or sustainable alternative.

The reasoning behind the study does make sense. When we purchase items online, we normally don't buy very many at a time, as opposed to getting more items in bulk when we purchase in-store. Purchasing fewer items at a time often results in more packaging waste, particularly if items, even those purchased in the same order, come from different warehouses or distribution facilities.

The study calculated overall greenhouse gas emissions and greenhouse gas emissions per product purchased and included emissions estimates from the number of products bought, to the packing, transporting, storing, and delivering activities. They found that in both categories, the emissions overall are lowest for stores with online and brick-and-mortar locations (also known as "bricks-and-clicks"), and highest from stores that are solely online, with stores that only have brick-and-mortar locations somewhere in the middle.

Although that appears somewhat depressing, I find it hopeful. When we are given the option to buy the same items online or in-store, somehow, we end up making the right choice enough of the time that it can be efficient either way.[59]

One of the best ways to evaluate our contribution to overall emissions is to look at the emissions which result in last mile of delivery. The earlier study estimated that the emissions for placing an order with a bricks-and-clicks are half of those from going to the store yourself, and less than one-fifth if you placed your order with an online-only retailer. But once again, production, quantity, distance, and transportation mechanisms all play a role.

An important tool we can use to further reduce our emissions is trip-chaining, where we combine errands and shopping with our regular commute or other necessary outings, whenever possible. About 5% of our car use is typically attributed to obtaining food and other household items, and in the U.S. about 95% of our shopping trips are made by car, as opposed to other countries like the Netherlands, where biking or walking to the store is much more common.[60]

It may sound like the most sustainable choice for us is to take the car and head to the store, but, unfortunately, the research isn't quite that clear.

Recent research done by the University of Exeter in the UK found that on average, ordering delivery of a box of vegetables, rather than making a trip to a local farm shop, results in lower carbon emissions. Although a lot of the information that went into the research is highly specific to that scenario, a lot of the conclusions apply, whether you're purchasing vegetables or vitamins.

The research also considered the additional emissions produced by the requirement to keep the vegetables cold, in addition to the packing and the transportation of goods to a regional 'hub'. They found that if the drive to the farm shop (or grocery store, I imagine) was longer than 6.7 km (or just a little over 4 miles, for my US compatriots), then having the same items delivered to your home was a more sustainable option. Apparently, this statistic was still true even if the "farm shop" didn't require light, heat, or a means to keep the vegetables cool.[61]

This makes sense when you consider that the produce is already close to you and can just be delivered en masse to local consumers, as was suggested in the bricks-and-clicks research. One truck might be able to drive a couple of hundred miles around a county and deliver food to dozens of families, whereas those dozens of families would all have to drive their cars a similar distance to obtain the same results. And so, with the delivery option, the emissions per household can stay, overall, quite low.

This is another reason to use services like Imperfect Foods (which iron-ically, delivers a lot of vegetables). I was concerned about the emissions of food delivery until I came across this study. Long before I ever placed an order, I had seen an Imperfect Foods delivery truck near my house, and it is comforting to know that I am just one more stop on their route, rather than the grocery store just being another stop on mine.

The study further encourages us to view the carbon emissions behind each piece of food, rather than merely "food miles," the number of miles each piece has traveled to you. There are a lot of factors that go into the calculation of carbon emissions for a given product, from packaging, to transportation, to energy consumption. Since this, as with everything else, is so nuanced, and other factors like local economics and the impact of differ-ent production methods also play a role, it is a fair point.

But, unfortunately, the question of whether to shop in-store or online isn't answered by merely looking at carbon emissions and is further compli-cated by whether people gather information, purchase, and potentially return an object to the store, or whether they complete these steps online, or do a hybrid of both. While you likely wouldn't perform the gathering information phase for a t-shirt, maybe you would if you saw it online and went to a store to try it on. You might also be more likely to visit the store to do a return than to ship it back, although, hopefully, you wouldn't have to return it if you'd tried it on first! It is statistically more likely you will return something bought online. Although with something like a computer, you are much more likely to go test out the keyboard in person.

If you perform all three steps of the process online, as opposed to solely in person, your carbon footprint may be half the size of your store-shopping counterpart.

The factors that contribute to this are as varied as the things you are likely to find at your local store. The size and weight of the product ordered play a role. How close you live to the store and the means of transportation you take play a role. The distance of the warehouse you order from online plays a role, and as we already know, so does the speed at which you select to have the item delivered. The number of items purchased together, either online or in-person, also plays a role. As does the fact that it takes less energy to power a website than a retail store, although if you are also powering a warehouse, the benefits are likely more equal.[62]

Viewed together, online shopping, particularly when certain sugges-tions are followed, seems to be a more environmentally friendly approach to acquiring new things, but of course, this is dependent on a lot of factors. Now that you are more aware of what those factors are, hopefully, you can make a more informed decision about whether you hop in the car or onto the web to buy that cute t-shirt or your next laptop.

I tend to follow the principle that if I am in, by, or near a store, I should get everything I need. If I am not, or will not be any time soon, or if the things I need will not be available at the store I will be in or close to, then I order online — particularly if I am not in a rush or can order multiple items together. And if I am purchasing a sustainable item that I can only get from a certain retailer that is only online, then online it is.

GIFTS

Gift-giving is a very big part of shopping, so I decided that it deserved a chapter of its own. If you need a gift for an upcoming event, or are already thinking about Christmas, which is (pretty much always) just around the corner — feel free to jump ahead to Chapter 11. I won't tell.

REUSABLE GROCERY BAGS

I want to end this chapter talking about something that exemplifies the sustainability of shopping, or lack thereof, and perfectly encapsulates many of the recurring issues I faced during my research.

Over 500 million single-use plastic grocery bags are used each year. This is clearly an area where we can see significant improvement.

At the beginning of the year and my sustainability project, the county I live in started charging 8 cents per plastic bag. This was just the nudge I needed to remember to *consistently* bring my reusable bags into the store and put them to use. Although I had been carrying them around for months, I wasn't always perfect at remembering to grab them when I got out of the car.

You'd think that conventional wisdom and public policy would make the issue of reusable grocery bags a no-brainer, right? But again and again, I hear people discussing the environmental cost of reusable grocery bags. While some of these arguments did make sense, I didn't feel that they were proving the point. I wanted to ensure that I was making the right choice so I knew I needed to investigate further.

The major argument against reusable grocery bags is that they require more energy and emissions to produce. So, even though they may reduce overall waste, they are still an unsustainable choice upfront. Taking into account the number of resources required to produce them and the resultant levels of pollution, some people argue that we shouldn't opt for reusables, such as organic cotton totes.

In Denmark, the Ministry of Health and Food determined that a reusable organic cotton tote has to be used over 20,000 times, which depending on how much you shop, could take between 55 and 200 years, to equalize the environmental impact with that of a single-use plastic bag.[63] I don't own or shop with organic cotton totes, but this made me decide that I probably never will. Although the production of organic cotton may be more beneficial for the environment, using a regular cotton tote to shop with only has to be reused 7,100 times to outweigh the production costs.[64]

These statistics are largely the result of the cotton production process, which, as we've seen, is water and chemical-intensive. And when you are producing organic cotton, you can't use the same conventional pesticides. Thus, it requires more organic cotton plants to make enough organic cotton to make anything — from a t-shirt to a tote bag.

I don't debate that reusable grocery bags do take more energy and resources to produce. Similarly, it takes a lot more energy and resources to make a reusable high-quality thermos than a disposable paper Starbucks cup, but there aren't many people saying that's a reason we should stick to the disposable options. And since I've never heard of turtles eating that hipster organic tote or fish getting caught in masses of insulated grocery bags in the ocean, to me, steering clear of disposable, plastic bags is still the best option.

This point was proven again when I found that the reusable polyurethane bags, which are what you most likely bought at the grocery store (like the ones I have), only need to be reused 14 times to be considered more sustainable than conventional plastic bags. I'm glad to say that mine have definitely passed that threshold.

One purchase I made in this area that came in handy and reduced my stress was purchasing small, foldable bags that I can keep in my purse at all times. I carry a small purse but these bags fit well inside. These reusable bags come in handy when I need to grab a few things, or on the occasions when I forget to grab the larger bags from the car. I use Reisenthel foldable, reusable shopping totes. I would highly recommend these to anyone who has room in their purse, and of course, it always helps to keep larger ones in the car.

If you opt for reusable bags, be sure to clean them on a semi-regular basis. That way any leftover moisture, germs, or residue gets wiped away instead of ending up in the back of the car or the inside of your purse.

The bags that you already have are the most sustainable option for you. Keep using them instead of buying new ones. If you don't own one, find one to two that you will reuse as much as possible. Finally, I guess we should also steer away from organic cotton totes, if possible.

Shopping used to be mindless and easy. Our biggest worry may once have been whether that top we wanted was in stock. But it's not simple at all, really. Sustainability isn't simple and life isn't either. Fortunately, we can still have fun adding the things that we truly need and which are good for the planet to our cart, online and in-person.

CHAPTER 9
SEPTEMBER: WORKPLACE

The changes we make that will have the biggest impact on the planet don't just take place in the closet, the refrigerator, or under the sink. Sustainability extends to the changes that take place in our minds and to the behaviors we take both inside and outside the walls of our homes.

We can have just as great an impact through the changes we make at work, and as you will see, these changes are intricately related to many of the changes we have already discussed, as well as those that we will look at in coming chapters.

The reality is that when we leave our homes, we have the opportunity to inspire change in both the individuals and institutions that surround us.

THE CLOUD

Did you know that your digital life has a carbon footprint? And it is not an insignificant one, at that. I was shocked to learn that an inbox overflowing with random promotions also has an impact on the environment. This was something I had never taken the time to consider, but it makes a lot of sense.

It is easy to think that our emails, photos, and everything else live up in "the cloud" somewhere, but they also reside on a physical machine somewhere in the world. The electricity, energy, and air conditioning required to keep these huge servers operational and cool is enormous. Storage, therefore, for a typical email will emit 4 grams of CO_2 equivalent, so the emails you receive in an average year will have the same carbon footprint as driving approximately 200 miles.

This may not seem major, but every single email contributes to that carbon footprint. Take a minute to think about that the next time you hesitate to take the 5 seconds necessary to unsubscribe.

Unsubscribing is actually a great way to cut down on the number of emails you receive and will reduce your digital clutter, while benefiting the earth. It's also helpful if you delete old emails, documents, and photos that aren't of importance to you. Deleting old accounts, profiles, and email addresses will also help.

This year I've found that sustainability and my organizing background aren't always in alignment, but this is one of the areas where they are, which makes me very happy. Besides, who doesn't benefit from a little more organization, less digital clutter, and a smaller carbon footprint?

INTERNET

A similar, but broader, topic is the internet. Studies have found that the internet utilizes about 10% of all electricity worldwide. That electricity (as well as the other 90%) is generated through coal, natural gas, nuclear, wind, water, and solar power. All of these means pose individual and unique threats to the environment and ecosystem. I cannot address all of that here, but it is definitely something to be aware of.

APPS

Utilizing technology to help build a sustainable life seems like a no-brainer in the modern-day, and numerous apps can help on our sustainability journey. My Little Plastic Footprint is an app that helps users track their progress on the journey. Through the app, you can track your reduced usage and also research the products to avoid. Klima will help you reduce your footprint, fund sustainable climate projects, and see the impact of your offsets. Olio is an app that helps us reduce food waste. Using the app, you can share a photo of food items you no longer use or want and other local users (or even local retailers) will be alerted. Then you can coordinate a pickup with interested parties with the end result being that food otherwise destined for the landfill will be used. The EWG and Think Dirty apps help users avoid products that contain potentially toxic ingredients and find clean alternatives.

It has been said that there is an app for everything today, and apps that work with us to promote our values are a welcome addition.

MAIL

We've learned that electronic and digital forms of mail have an environmental impact, so we can only imagine the size of the impact that physical mail has on the planet. And although we tend to use email for quick and instantaneous communication, a whole lot of people still use snail mail. On top of that, we have dreaded junk mail, and even worse, bills.

I know the pleasure of receiving a handwritten card or letter in the mail, so I'm not in any way advocating that we get rid of mail altogether. Just as with everything else in life, that is not the practical or sustainable option in and of itself. However, we can take actions that will reduce certain kinds of mail — and the resulting environmental cost as well.

Bills are definitely the worst thing to get in the mail. Fortunately, I have arranged for most of my statements and bills to be sent to me online, via email. From paperless statements, to online payment processing, to autopay, there's simply no reason to have to get a physical letter from the cable or utility company. If you aren't using these online programs, I highly recommend them, both from an organizational and a sustainability perspective. But remember to delete old emails, attachments, and statements when you no longer need them!

Remember, too, that it takes a bucket of water to produce a single sheet of paper (not to mention the wood and the energy required), so every sheet of paper that you can keep out of your mailbox is a win for the planet.

The second most-hated type of mail is junk mail. In America alone, over 100 million trees are cut down each year to produce 100 billion pieces of junk mail. That is a horror! The average household receives 848 individual pieces of junk mail, and the production and delivery of this mail generates 51 million tons of greenhouse gasses. That's more than what is generated by all the registered cars in Los Angeles and New York City combined. And that is a statistic that I do not want to be any part of.

To combat this, we can do several things. We can start by posting a "no junk mail" sign on the mailbox, although, sadly, in the US this isn't a guarantee that we won't receive junk mail. Other countries have had greater success. Germany, for example, allows individuals to sue companies that distribute junk mail (if you have posted a refusal) and, in Canada, citizens have reduced junk mail by 80% by utilizing this method.

We can also use services like DMAchoice.org and CatalogueChoice.org. To stop receiving credit card or insurance offers, use OptOutPrescreen.com. Apps like PaperKarma can also help to reduce junk mail.

Unfortunately, despite all of these efforts, some junk mail is likely to get through. If it does, we need to toss them in the recycling can, not the trash. Today, 44% of unwanted mail goes to a landfill unopened, and while I'm not asking you to open junk mail, I am asking you to recycle it.

Generally, newspapers, magazines, and catalogs are items that people have had to request, so these items don't fall into the category of junk mail. When I was little, I loved receiving a fresh American Girl doll catalog each year. Today, I receive the Magnolia magazine every quarter. I love the anticipation of receiving it, pouring over it, and then letting it occupy a place of honor on my bookshelf. This is the only magazine I get, and the only one I want.

Whether you have dozens of magazine subscriptions, or just one, you deserve to know the impact they have on the environment, so you can make an educated decision about what you want to do about them in the future. About 24 billion newspapers, 12.5 billion catalogs, and 350 million magazines are printed each year. This requires the equivalent of approximately 169 million trees; enough to fill over 56,000 baseball stadiums. And this doesn't even consider the environmental cost of the production and distribution of these magazines and catalogs, which is huge.

USE THE REUSABLES

Our physical activity at work, and not just our digital life, can negatively impact the environment, too.

If your company is providing actual cups, mugs, plates, and silverware for your use, they are doing the most sustainable thing. If the company is only providing paper and plastic goods, it will be best for you to bring these items from home. The items you bring can be washed daily and stored in your desk or work bag for daily use. Ditch the plastic straws and stirrers for sustainable alternatives, too, while you're at it.

The same goes for using salt and pepper shakers over packets, cartons of creamer over plastic pods, or a bottle of ketchup over the peel top packets, whatever makes sense for your life, habits, and work situation.

OFFICE INITIATIVES

You may want to consider starting an initiative within your organization to promote sustainable practices. Of course, the overall impact would be largely dependent on the size of your company or individual office, but as we have discussed, no impact that helps the environment is too small. Some companies may be large enough to have a team or department that deals with sustainability-related issues, but even if yours doesn't, you can elect yourself CSO — Chief Sustainability Officer.

The key with initiatives is to make sure they are practical, actionable, and publicized. Initiatives that no one knows about won't be very effective, but they are also unlikely to be effective if they are too difficult or seem unimportant.

One place to start could be an initiative to reduce the use of plastic straws or paper cups in your organization; maybe even to the point where these items are no longer purchased in the first place. Company-wide recycling is probably expected and promoted for waste paper, but by expanding recycling to include metal and plastic, the company would be taking a major step in the right direction. Another important step could be posting signs that provide education to employees about what is recyclable and what isn't. Providing receptacles to encourage proper recycling may be what many people need to begin to make different choices. A more ambitious step could be to set up a composting system at work, or volunteer to collect food scraps for your home compost.

The steps we can take towards a more sustainable workplace are limited only by our imaginations and our willingness to step out.

PACKING LUNCH

I know that nothing sounds more dismal than a sad desk lunch, trust me, I've had plenty of those in my days of office work. But the truth is that packing your lunch will not only save you money and help you eat healthier, but it is also much better for the planet than having to travel to the local sandwich shop to purchase a lunch consisting of a sandwich wrapped in plastic, a plastic bag of chips, and (God forbid) a plastic water bottle.

And don't forget that those pre-packaged snacks you keep in your desk for that 2:00 p.m. energy dip probably contribute quite a bit of trash to your wastebasket each week.

Packing breakfast, lunch, and snacks each day will significantly reduce your environmental impact. If time is a concern, there are apps, tips, and products available to assist with meal prep and planning for the week (or even the month) — everything from making multiple batches to using Mason jars for everything.

If you aren't ready to go all-in on the idea of packing lunch perhaps you could try to bring lunch from home just one or two days per week, or bring all your snacks from home without extra packaging. Or consider bringing a cloth napkin and silverware from home to wash and reuse. At a minimum, when you find yourself at the deli around the corner, see if there are any sustainable swaps you can make for yourself and the planet.

DRINKING TEA

I've always been an avid tea drinker, and I drink a lot of tea while I'm at work. It helps me focus. One of my earliest memories of drinking tea is sitting at the kitchen table in my childhood home drinking Constant Comment tea (with lots of milk and sugar) out of a little Peter Rabbit mug. I have many friends who associate me with tea, and many friends have become avid tea drinkers as a result of my influence. I've also received many, many boxes of tea as gifts for birthdays and other celebrations.

When I started this research, I was shocked to learn that there is a lot of plastic in teabags, and as a result, in the tea that I drink!

Pressed tea bags (the ones with the crimped edges that often look like little ravioli) tend to be made up of 20-30% polypropylene plastic which is woven through the bag with the paper and melted along the edge to keep the tea bag sealed shut. Silken tea bags are actually made from plastic, not silk (granted, teabags made from silk don't sound particularly appetizing either.) Teabags on a string also contain plastic. Although the bag is normally secured with a staple or stitching to ensure it stays closed, the bag itself may have polypropylene plastic woven throughout to make it stronger. Teabag manufacturers tend to use fossil-fuel-based plastics, such as PET or nylon, or plant-based plastic.

Loose leaf and compostable tea bags are the most sustainable options, but there are plastic-free alternatives if you prefer teabags.

Yogi, Republic of Tea, Stash, Numi, Qi Tea, Higher Living Teas, and Pukka all are 100% plastic-free (although the packaging on the box may not be). Other brands may have some lines or products that contain some plastic. Unfortunately, some of the major tea players still use plastic, including Tazo, Teavana, Celestial Seasonings, Mighty Leaf Teas, and Twinings.

Another easy way I discovered to make the drinking of tea (more specifically the brewing of water) more sustainable is to boil only the amount of water that you need to use. Boiling a full pot when you only intend to drink one cup, wastes energy and generates unnecessary CO_2.

The same principle applies to drinking a cup of tea (or coffee for that matter). I have been known to make myself a cup but then forget to drink it while it's hot, which means it has to be heated up over and over again. Each time I reheat my cup, I use more energy. I finally invested in a Yeti mug with a lid and have found that the Yeti keeps my tea warm for much longer than a normal mug. I was also gifted an Ember mug, which not only keeps my drink warm but actually warms it to my preferred temperature! The Ember mug requires a little extra energy expenditure to stay warm, and you have to charge the mug periodically, so I don't use it all of the time, but it is nice to have the option! And while I love my novelty mugs just like everyone else, I try to only drink from them when I am sitting down to drink a cup of tea — not to tote one around the house with me all day.

Interestingly, although tea is brought to us from all over the world because it is generally small and light, it is relatively efficient to transport. The real environmental impact of drinking tea (or coffee) is from boiling the water. And, if milk is added, you have that additional environmental cost.

Unfortunately, these issues represent just the tip of the environmental iceberg. While the boiling and reheating issues apply to coffee drinkers too, the following will pertain specifically to people who drink tea, primarily those who love the convenience of a good tea bag.

I'll admit it. I am one of those people. For years, I have enjoyed the convenience of tossing a tea bag into my mug and tossing it out when I finished it. As an organizer, I love the aesthetic of a nice tea drawer, with all the bags arranged in the order of the rainbow.

I eventually migrated to brands that offer a biodegradable tea bag, like the British brand PG Tips. I also like that their tea bags don't have individual paper packaging they come loosely in a box.

But as much as I love tea bags, I realized that the most sustainable option going forward would be loose leaf tea. As the renowned tea drinker that I am, I was fortunate to have a variety of loose leaf tea already on hand. The only negative that I can think of is that the process of making loose leaf tea is a bit messier and requires a little more time and effort to clean out the steeper.

Another impact of drinking tea (and coffee) extends to the environment in which the plants are grown. Often wildlife is displaced and the habitat is upended as land and forests are cleared for plantations. When looking at tea (or coffee) to buy, I recommend that you purchase the ones that have a single point of origin, instead of being sourced from multiple locations Thankfully, there are brands like Yogi, which you can find at your local supermarket, and which strive to do good through reforestation and support of the local communities where plants are grown.

The issue of pesticides must be considered, too. As with other produce, it's best to look for organic products from smaller-scale farms, which affords the best way to avoid coming into contact with these harmful substances.

The unethical treatment of workers also applies here, unfortunately. Forced labor and low wages often help to reduce the cost of business for many tea brands.

Thankfully, there are organizations like Fairtrade and the Rainforest Alliance, which, while not perfect, were created to protect workers and the environment. It is worthwhile, then, to keep an eye out for these logos on tea (and coffee) that you buy.[65]

With so much to keep in mind, I was glad to find a few of my favorite brands, as well as some new ones, meeting the sustainability standards I was looking for. I also try to stick to brands that I can pick up from my regular grocery store. A quick visit to the website of your favorite brand, or a quick Google search to discover some new sustainable options can take you far when it comes to finding the right tea for your taste and habits. There are a lot of great options out there.

Today, I only drink tea when I need to. I use my loose-leaf steeper or plastic-free tea bag, and compost the used tea bag or leaves. And thanks to my glass hot water pot for boiling just the right amount of water, and my Yeti mug for keeping my drink warm for as long as necessary, I have become more sustainable and more conscientious about the tea that fuels my work.

DRINKING COFFEE

It seems to me that since most people prefer coffee, we should probably discuss the sustainability of drinking coffee. I drink coffee sometimes, too, although it's usually when I'm on the go, and we discussed how to get those drinks more sustainably in Chapter 4. For this chapter, we'll be looking at coffee at work, even the work-from-home kind.

More and more, people are making their morning cup of joe with a Keurig or other pod-dispensing machine. I love the ease and simplicity of dropping a pod into the Keurig and pressing a button. It's enjoyable to hear the machine whirr to life and watch the substance that on some days seems truly life-giving drip into an adorable mug.

When I decided to pursue a sustainable life, I knew my affair with pods would have to come to an end. While Nespresso technically offers recyclable pods, they can only be recycled through a store take-back program; they can't be tossed into the regular recycling can. Although this is technically better than tossing the used pod into the trash, many people probably do toss them anyway, and as we have learned, just recycling more isn't the sustainable solution in the long term.

I have heard people argue that K-pods can be recycled, but for that to be true, the pods have to be thoroughly cleaned first. And, unfortunately, even then, they may be too small to be recognized and processed at the recycling center. Plus, many pods have been made out of number 7 plastics, which are not recyclable and may contain endocrine disruptors.

This is an area where we probably can't afford to let convenience win. And let's be honest, making a cup of coffee the old-fashioned way using coffee grounds and a filter is not that hard.

If you have a pod machine that you love, you can purchase a reusable pod that you can fill with coffee grounds (or tea, or anything else!). And fortunately, buying coffee in a can is always less expensive than coffee in pods.

If you make drip coffee using a coffee maker, there are washable filters and reusable cloth filters available so you don't have to use the paper ones. If you prefer to stick with paper filters, after the coffee is made you can compost them with the coffee grounds inside (provided they were made from unbleached paper).

If you use a pour-over coffee maker, which is generally glass or ceramic, you can use a stainless-steel filter or a cloth coffee filter. If you are using a French press to make your coffee, congratulate yourself because you've arrived at the sustainable and low-waste goal. And you can use your French press to make loose leaf tea as well!

The goal is to make sure that whatever coffee tools you use, whether a drip coffee maker or an espresso machine, has been built to last, and can be repaired, if necessary. Sadly, most pod machines can't be repaired, but if yours is still going strong, be sure to use it as long as you can, with reusable pods, of course.

When it comes to choosing the coffee itself, look for brands with eco-friendly certifications like Fair Trade, USDA Organic, or Bird Friendly. Also, opt for shade-grown coffee, which sustains the rainforest, and is grown without chemical fertilizers, pesticides, or herbicides. When possible, look for transparency in the farms and farmers, too, to ensure fair and safe treatment of workers.

COMMUTING

In a world that is made up of more and more people working from home, commuting has become less of an issue. But it remains a daily reality for many people.

I can't tell you what a reasonable commute time and distance is, but I would encourage you to consider your daily commute, if any, because whether it's 5 minutes or 50, 5 miles or 50, all of it has an impact on the environment.

It's helpful to become aware of the ride-sharing and public access options available to you. You could also consider working from home, even just some of the time, if your position or company allows it. Relocating closer to work, while certainly having an environmental cost, might enable you to reduce emissions and energy usage in the long run, if that's important to you. In some cases, that might mean moving into the city, in others, it might mean moving further from the city. As with everything else, there is no inherently wrong house, job, or commute. It's the "unexamined" one, though, that may be taking a potentially unnecessary toll on both the environment and on you.

ELECTRONICS RECYCLING

I know it can feel risky to recycle an old smartphone. It's worrying that someone might somehow get access to your personal information, even if you've reset it. And I, for one, have never been able to figure out iCloud or other kinds of backups, so I'm always worried that something important will get lost in the shuffle.

This is a common problem because, as an organizer, I have worked with clients who have piles of old laptops and phones. We don't need them, but we're afraid to let them go.

Keeping them, however, won't do you or the environment any good. Giving up and tossing them into the trash may relieve you of the burden, but it definitely harms the environment.

A quick Google search will likely reveal the local stores or programs in your area that accept electronics for recycling. They may have particular requirements, but the important thing is that there is somewhere nearby you can take these items when they stop working or you no longer need them. New laws are constantly in the works that require companies to either accept old electronics back or sell the necessary pieces that would allow them to be updated for continued use. Although these laws have yet to pass on a national scale, it may be worth a quick search in your state.

PUT YOUR MONEY WHERE YOUR MOUTH IS

If you have a job that you love (like I do), congratulations! The reality is, though, whether you love or hate your job, a large reason you do what you do is to make sure you have enough money to pay your bills, and after reading this book, to also live more sustainably and purchase sustainable products.

If sustainability is a priority for you, it is important to make sure your finances are in line with that. And where and how you invest, where and how you save, and where and how you spend money can play a role.

There are a few companies, banks, and investment firms that prioritize the environment. Most others don't. I'm not recommending that you upend your portfolio or switch banks, but it is worthwhile to familiarize yourself with the companies you use and where they stand on the issues that matter to you.

I wasn't too far along in my sustainability journey when I realized that if caring for the planet was something that really mattered to me and would play an ever-increasing role in our culture, then I needed to invest in people, companies, and funds that felt the same way. This isn't investment advice (I'm not qualified for that), but it is life advice (as a life coach, I am somewhat qualified for that).

PAPERLESS

Many of the same sustainability issues that plague us at home also plague us in the workplace.

Since I have the advantage of running a largely online business, I have to deal with very little paper. But I have also spent many years working in an office, so I know the ins and outs of that, too. Of course, everyone hates to waste paper. And anyone who has ever had to buy a ream of paper knows that paper is not only environmentally costly, but it's also financially costly.

I was shocked to learn that in many offices 30% of print jobs are never picked up from the printer. I noticed this reality in my office work. Unclaimed things piled up on the counter nearby, and when the stack got too high, or an appropriate amount of time had passed, the entire pile was tossed in the shred bucket. The bad news doesn't end there, though. Of the print jobs that are picked up at the printer, 45% of them end up in the trash by the end of the day. There are a few situations in which this makes sense, but overall it suggests that things are being printed unnecessarily.[66]

In total, paper products account for approximately 70% of office waste. This number should continue to decline as offices become more and more paperless. But a completely paperless world is not one that we will likely ever see (which on one hand is good, because I love to wander through TJ Maxx and look at the pretty journals and planners).

In my business, I attempt to print as little as possible. I utilize online programs to send proposals and invoices. I print very little promotional material, and I don't give out business cards lightly. Every piece of paper makes a difference.

One small, but ingeniously sustainable idea I came across during this project was to use a stamp instead of a business card. When someone asks for your card, you can stamp a napkin, the back of a receipt, even a piece of cardboard, whatever is readily available. What a statement this makes! Instead of putting one more piece of paper into the cycle, you're reusing something that is already part of the cycle that has likely already fulfilled its original purpose. The only negative part of this idea is the stamp and the ink themselves, and the possible problem with carrying a stamp full of ink. That may not end well. But the idea is brilliant. So, we'll keep working on this one.

I'm sure that you're already aware of the impact our heavy dependence on paper has on the environment, so every small reduction will be beneficial. Isn't it worth 10 minutes of our time to consider additional ways that we can reduce paper consumption at work and at home?

Once the paper we use has served its purpose, we must recycle, recycle, recycle! It's wise to keep a recycling can in our workspace, if at all possible. I have watched many people toss mail, newspapers, and other non-sensitive work-related documents into the trash. Please don't do this. Take a few minutes and a few dollars and buy a recycling can for your office.

The overall impact of not recycling in the office, when multiplied by the population of the United States, is huge. Businesses in the United States throw out 21 million tons of paper every year. That's approximately 175 pounds per office worker. To put that in perspective, each year, office workers in the US throw away enough paper to build a wall 12 feet high, stretching from LA to NYC!

Although paper isn't infinitely recyclable, producing new paper from recycled paper requires less water, creates less air pollution, and can use up to 60% less energy than making new paper from trees. This means that it is infinitely worthwhile to recycle paper.[67]

So even if paper continues to play a part in our lives, we should remain conscientious about the things we choose to print and copy, as well as how they are disposed of.

PAPER + PRINTING

Whether buying paper for personal use, your home office, or if you are the purchasing agent for your company, buying paper that is 100% recycled is the most sustainable option.

When purchasing notebooks, look for those made from recycled paper, especially ones from FSC certified sources, or consider taking notes digitally! I use a combination of handwritten notes in a notebook, typing notes directly into my smartphone, or using my iPad. Perhaps a combination of tools will work well for you, too. It's wise to choose a system that will make it easiest to save, find, and use your notes in the future, and that you will be committed to using.

If you have a printer that allows you to print on both sides of a sheet of paper, and it makes sense for what you are printing, the double-sided option will end up saving half the amount of paper! This will reduce your expenses, delivery/shipping costs, and emissions, and will, of course, save trees.

INK

Ink, commonly referred to as printer toner, is closely related to the topic of paper, printing, and copying in the workplace. Unfortunately, as with paper, cartridges generated by most businesses in the United States don't get a happy ending. Of the approximately 16 million laser toner cartridges used every year, only an estimated 1.5 million of them will be recycled.

Fortunately, there is a readily available solution to the problem. Staples, Costco, OfficeMax, and Office Depot offer toner cartridge recycling programs. [68] You can even earn rewards for using these services. Many toner brands also will take back the used cartridges. In many cases, you can return a used cartridge to the company in its original packaging. If you want to make an intentional impact through your recycling, there may be a charity near you that accepts donations of empty cartridges to be recycled.

Laser printer cartridges represent, for the most part, the opposite of sustainability, at least on some level since they are made of metal and plastic and coloring. When a cartridge is tossed into a landfill, these 3.5 pounds of waste can take anywhere between 450 and 1,000 years to fully break down. But fortunately, 97% of the laser printer cartridge can be reused or recycled![69]

There is research that suggests that some fonts utilize less ink in printing, so if you print a lot, or are interested in saving ink, you may want to look at changing fonts. In general, sans serif fonts use less ink (since they don't have the little serifs on every letter), but even Times New Roman is a fairly low-ink font. You may also want to try Ryman Eco, Ecofont Sans, Courier, Century Gothic, Calibri, and Brush Script. Another eco-friendly idea is to shrink the font size and limit using bold text.

OFFICE SUPPLIES

This chapter would not be complete without a reminder that using what you already have (whether in the corporate office or your home office) is always better for the environment in the long run than purchasing something new, no matter how sustainable. Approximately 820,000 trees are cut down every year to make pencils. While I know that there's nothing quite like opening a fresh new box, I have several pencils at home that have some life left in them.

There have been times when I've been reluctant to actually use one of the pristine notebooks I couldn't resist buying at TJMaxx. I didn't want to disturb them, much less write in them, but rather than buying another one, I had to remind myself that the best option for me, my wallet, and the planet, was to use the one I already had on the shelf. This truth applies to everything; furniture, boxes, folders, binders, dividers, and anything else that I own.

When it comes time to buy something new or stock up within your organization, remember to apply the principles we've discussed and always look for plastic-free options, if possible. Then, take the time to properly recycle or dispose of these supplies when they reach the end of their useful lives.

FOUNTAIN PENS

Although I don't know that I will ever make the switch to putting ink in a fountain pen, I know people who swear by it! Since you can replace the ink cartridge in a fountain pen, that ups the sustainability factor over a normal pen. Using a converter to refill the pen can also be cheaper and generates less waste. Ink refills come in glass bottles, too, which as we know, is easily and infinitely recyclable. You may even channel a business titan from the 1800s. My work is so virtual that I don't use actual writing implements enough to justify using and refilling a fountain pen, but I think that if you do, you should automatically earn a badge of antiquated honor. It also means that you no longer have to save or try to recycle old pens, which is what the rest of us should be doing.

TRASH CANS

Although this technically goes for trash cans anywhere in your life, I think that this issue is worth considering here. I understand that the last thing you want to do when you finish a Diet Coke at your desk is walk back to the breakroom to toss the can in the recycling container, but if you're striving for a more sustainable life (or even just a bit of exercise), please do it.

I know a few individuals (who will remain nameless) that toss their used soda cans in the trash, trusting that they will remember to remove them later. Trust me. This rarely or never happens. Please don't do this.

Consider keeping a small recycling or shredding container near your desk, too, even if you are the one who will be responsible for emptying it at the end of the week. If it ensures that these cans will see a second life, it is most definitely worth it. Most of us have separate trash and recycling cans in our kitchens, so it just makes sense to also have them where we spend even more time, at our desks.

BLUE LIGHT GLASSES

Another tip that I find really useful (considering all of the time I spend at my computer) is wearing blue light glasses. Between coaching sessions, maintaining my blog, posting regularly on social media, writing this book, and of course, relaxing often with a good television show or an ebook, I spend a lot of time in front of a screen. I won't go into the science of why blue light glasses are helpful, but they have been proven to make a difference, and my personal experience agrees.

I purchased a pair from Amazon before I started my sustainability project. They were cute and pink and so matched my aesthetic (and therefore most of my outfits) pretty well. I wore them for several months, and while I didn't necessarily notice a difference when I wore them, I certainly did when I didn't.

After a few months, I noticed a small crack in the plastic on one of the eyepieces. A couple of days later, they broke entirely. After attempting some quick fixes, none of which lasted more than a few hours, I ordered another pair. But fast forward to today, well into my sustainability project, when I noticed another small crack forming. I knew where this was going to end up.

Sure enough, within the week, I put on the glasses and one of the lenses fell out onto my desk. I knew that gluing or taping them would be to no avail. But this time, I knew I couldn't simply order another pair from Amazon. This was a bad cycle. I couldn't justify purchasing a new pair, only to know it would have a limited lifespan. At this rate, I would be adding one or two glasses to the landfill every year, something I definitely did not want to do.

For those of you who wear glasses every day, the solution is fairly simple. You can have blue light protection added to the glasses you wear every day. Since I don't wear glasses, I needed to find a different alternative.

I attempted to work without glasses because not buying another pair would be ideal and I wouldn't be adding anything to the cycle.

After a couple of days without the glasses, though, I found that I had a low-grade headache by early afternoon. My eyes felt sore, and my sleep was thrown off. I don't know for sure that this was caused by not wearing blue light glasses, but it seemed to be the only thing that had changed. It could be a case of subconscious placebo effect, but even if that's the case, I was willing to get new glasses to get rid of self-imposed daily headaches.

The issue now became which glasses to buy. I refused to get another of the same kind through Amazon, so it was back to the drawing board.

At first, I decided to look for a metal pair, because I figured they wouldn't break as easily. I started my search on Amazon (I know, I know), just to see what was available. It turned out that all of the options were a "no-go" for me (I had no desire to look like an 80 year old librarian).

After finding nothing suitable on Amazon, I turned to Google. A quick search for "sustainable blue light glasses" revealed some great alternatives. I was once again reminded that it generally takes very little time and effort to make a sustainable choice! A little research (and perhaps a bit more money in the short term) will yield significant sustainable results.

I settled on blue light glasses from Blue Planet Eco-Eyewear. Each pair of glasses they sell is made with 70% to 100% recycled material and they have saved thousands of pounds of material from a landfill.

In addition, the company has been built on a foundation of giving back to the community and the world. The company donates one pair of glasses to someone in need for every pair sold. Thus far, the company has donated over 1,000,000 pairs to communities worldwide. Blue Planet Eco-Eyewear also plants a tree for each pair of glasses sold through a partnership with Trees For The Future, whose mission is to restore forests and reduce emissions, hunger, and poverty. The Forest Gardens that they create not only benefit the earth, but also the local communities, by providing sustainable food sources for people and animals. They also benefit the communities by providing wood to use as fuel, and ultimately result in an increase in the communities' annual income by close to 400% in just four years.

In addition to these global goals and outreaches, each month, the company's employees volunteer in their local communities. As we've learned previously, companies that believe in protecting and preserving the planet and supporting the people on it take additional actions to go above and beyond. Blue Planet Eco-Eyewear is a perfect example of a considerate company promoting its values on every level.

My new glasses have a similar style to the ones I had purchased on Amazon, but are gray, instead of pink. Although these glasses cost $40 instead of the $15, I had been spending on Amazon, they should prove their enduring value within a year or two. The company also offered me a 25% off coupon on my first order, and free shipping, as well as 20% off my next purchase, if I refer a friend, who will also receive the discount.

When I placed my order, the confirmation email confirmed that the company "will plant a tree for every pair [of glasses] sold [and work to] help restore the forests, sequester carbon, reduce hunger and poverty!" It also informed me that they "have been able to donate over 1,000,000+ pairs of corrective glasses to people in need via [their] Visualize Change Program." I'd never received such a gratifying email from any purchase I'd ever made before, and I was reminded that supporting businesses that support the world in all kinds of ways is a large part of what sustainability is all about.

Pela has also recently released blue light glasses and sunglasses that are 100% biodegradable. Pela Vision is certified BCorp, Climate Neutral and One Percent For the Planet certified. They are working to reduce emissions and donate 1% of gross sales each year to approved nonprofit partners to give back to environmental causes.

You may have blue light glasses that you love, or you may decide that you do not need them. Either way, if you find yourself in need of tools for work or home, the chances are good that there is a sustainable version waiting for you to discover.

PHONE CASES

I'm not really sure what made me decide that my phone case should be considered part of workplace sustainability. Perhaps it is because I spend a lot of time on my phone for work.

The small cases we put around our phones to protect them, which are necessary because phones aren't built to survive on their own, have the unfortunate commonality that the vast majority of them are made from plastic. Over 1 billion plastic phone cases are sold every year!

That isn't surprising, especially when you learn that cell phones outnumber people on the planet.

I admit to owning two plastic phone cases which still live in my electronics bin. One came with the phone; the other was a gift. Neither is perfect, but they do their job and keep my phone safe. I also know people who have dozens of cases and switch them out as mood (or outfit) demands. While each of us has the right to decide if this is how we want to live, we also need to make sure that the decision is intentional. Even something as small as a smartphone case will have an impact.

For a few years, I had seen biodegradable phone cases advertised and I thought that was unique, if a bit odd, and didn't give it another thought. That is, until my sustainability project.

Then I decided that I needed a biodegradable case, too, since my plastic ones were beginning to break down. Now I could walk my talk, phone in hand.

Since I had seen so many ads, I knew exactly what to do and got a case from Pela (yes, the same company that manufactured my composter!). Like Blue Planet Eco-Eyewear, Pela demonstrates its belief in their values through their products and profits. They give to grassroots environmental groups, to clean water projects, to preserving and conserving coastline, to providing plant-based meals, and more.

The 1 million people who have purchased Pela cases have been able to save 560,000 kg of CO_2 equivalent, which is equal to 72 million phone charges, 1.4 million miles driven, or 17 million plastic bags.

I love the pink Pela case that I have. It has been very durable so far and the color is very "on brand" for me. The only downside is that it gets dirty somewhat easily. From what I have read in other reviews on the Pela website, this is a common issue. The company offers tips for keeping the cases clean, but some cases, like mine, get visibly dirtier more often than others.

But I'm not giving up my pink case, and the way I figure it, we probably all should wash our phone cases a bit more often anyway.

I recently saw that Pela has come out with compostable Apple Watch bands and AirPods cases, more amazing developments. I'll be looking into purchasing these or similar products in the future, if needed. But since I already have non-compostable versions of both, purchased long before my sustainability project began, I'll be content to follow the ultimate sustainability principle for now, and use what I have.

I walked past someone in a parking lot a couple of weeks ago, and in passing, I noticed that they had a Pela case, too. I've never felt as bonded with someone I've never spoken to. It was exciting to know that someone else cares about the planet like I do. That moment gave me such a jolt of joy. I hope to have more and more moments like that as I connect with more people around the world who share my passion for sustainability, even if we never actually meet.

I was even more excited recently to see a friend with a Pela case on her phone. I thought it was a Pela case, but I didn't want to ask outright. I commented on the pretty blue color, which prompted her to tell me that it was a compostable Pela case! She had seen mine and had gotten one, too. She told me that she loves it and purchased a case for her AirPods, too. This interaction reminded me that even though our actions might be small, they can inspire others to make small changes, too, and the small changes, whether at home, on the go, or in the workplace, can quickly add up.

CHAPTER 10
OCTOBER: HOME

I have always been somewhat of a homebody. I can be home for days and be totally happy — cleaning, and reading, and writing, and baking, and going for walks, and watching TV. My home is my own little bubble and I am truly blessed to love where I live.

During the past ten months, I have been able to transform my life, primarily in ways that I can enjoy within the comfort of my own home, while still having an impact, however small, on the world at large.

As the weather turns colder and the leaves change color, all I want to do is stay inside at home, warm and safe. In that spirit, I wanted to take some time to focus fully on how we can make the most of the homes that we live in and make sure that the actions we take within will have the greatest benefit on the world without.

Also, as I entered October, I wanted to take some time to acknowledge how far I'd come. There are so many ways in which my home, and the way I live in it, are already more sustainable! The changes I've made include the cleaning products I use, how often I wash my clothes, the food in my fridge, where the food scraps end up, the makeup I use, the absence of Amazon packages landing on my doorstep, and the amount of water I boil when I make a cup of tea.

All of the changes have not been fun, in fact, some I have hated, and many have been so small that I've hardly even noticed them. Sometimes it is hard to identify all the ways that my habits have changed and I question if I really have been able to make any real shifts towards sustainability. But as I survey my home, I know that I have. I may not have achieved total zero waste or become a perfect vegan, but I have come a long way, and I know that even the smallest changes have made a difference.

But, there's no time to rest on our laurels when there is still much to be accomplished. So, I decided to start by looking into something that directly or indirectly is related to many of the habits and changes I've made — electricity.

ELECTRICITY

I think most children grew up, like I did, with a fairly constant berating about leaving lights on around the house. There is a common stereotype, too, of dads having the responsibility for switching off the lights with the trademark raised eyebrow. In my house, however, both of my parents took that responsibility very seriously.

Growing up, I recognized that this was something that they wanted me to do, and I complied (when I remembered), although more out of a sense of obedience than a recognition that I was doing anything for the environment or our electricity bill.

When I moved out, I definitely began to be more conscious of my electricity usage and overall energy consumption, since I was now the one footing the bill. As I shared in Chapter 6, I used to take 20, 30, or even 40-minute showers, but when I moved out, I didn't leave myself the luxury of lingering.

After I started my sustainability project, the conservation of energy and electricity took on a whole new meaning. Now, I was not only trying to keep my energy bill relatively low, but I also wanted to be a better steward of the environment and reduce the amount of energy I used as much as possible.

I soon began flitting around my house (and sometimes the houses of my friends, I'm only somewhat ashamed to admit), flicking off the lights that weren't in use, and even occasionally unplugging something that wasn't being used (I only do that at my house, I promise). Like Monica at the end of the *Friends* theme song, I would switch off a lamp while everyone else was sitting around. I didn't care. It makes so much sense and fits my personality, too. I'm such a Monica.

The number of calories I've burned walking around to flick off light switches and the time I've spent rescuing a recyclable item from the trash is significantly greater than the number of items I've saved from the landfill or the kilowatts of energy saved, but what's most important is that I am acting in line with my values.

My values haven't always been focused on sustainability, however. When I first moved into my apartment and had to establish electrical service with the local power company, I felt overwhelmed. I was overwhelmed with the whole process of moving. I was overwhelmed by the idea of living totally on my own. And I was overwhelmed by the numerous energy-saving and environmentally friendly options offered by the power company when I activated my service.

The conversation proved circular and the exact way these options would help the environment was confusing. Overwhelmed and indecisive, I hastily clicked through the options and finished signing up. I had other things I needed to get to, and I figured that I could always return to learn and research later. Once I really understood it, then I would make a decision.

You have probably guessed that I never did get back to doing that research. And now here I was in October facing an entire month solely focused on making my home more sustainable. Well, I figured, there's no better time than the present.

Imagine my surprise and enthusiasm, then, when I received an email from my energy company that brought the task to the forefront. Although the email was on a different topic, I was easily able to click on the "renewables" button and end up exactly where I needed to be.

A few weeks earlier (since I knew this was something I would need to be tackling soon), I talked to my dad about the renewable energy options, how they worked, and the impact they had. Much of my confusion centered around the idea that the renewable energy I could purchase wouldn't necessarily be used by me in my home. I eventually learned that a nearby dam or wind turbine generates energy that is added to all of the other energy available in the power grid. The power grid provides energy to my home and to everyone else's (sounds like something from Monsters, Inc.). Some of the renewable energy may end up in my house, heating my shower and powering my appliances, but it may not. There is no real way to ensure or even track that the power generated by green energy sources (that I'm paying for) is directed to my house. However, by paying for it, I am making sure that renewable energy will end up on the power grid as opposed to all of it coming from less efficient or nonrenewable energy sources.

With that understanding as the foundation, the energy provider's website made much more sense. After just a few clicks I found myself faced with the option to calculate the impact that utilizing the renewable energy options they offered would have. I entered a number that I thought was close to my average monthly usage and braced myself for what I expected would be a very high additional fee to get the equivalent energy from renewable sources.

The additional cost turned out to be a whopping $2.73.

By selecting the 100% green power option, 100% of my usage would be covered by the purchase of renewable energy, and my bill would increase by less than $3.

Not only that, but the reduction in my carbon footprint would be 3,836 pounds of CO_2, equivalent to 39 new trees planted and over 5,800 miles not driven. Since I live near Seattle, a diagram showed me that this would be equivalent to approximately 32 trips between Seattle and Portland.

By making this simple change, the three extra dollars I would spend each month would go towards supporting suppliers of wind, solar, and geothermal energy and establishing more of them. Some of the money would also support suppliers of energy from landfill gas, a byproduct from the decomposition of organic material in landfills, and biogas, a fuel that is produced as a byproduct of the decomposition of organic waste. Since these items will likely never be depleted or destroyed, and the pollution rate of these more natural alternatives is much lower, this is far better than solely supporting the use of coal and natural gas, as I was before.

The energy company offered two options for renewable energy. The first was "solar choice," which includes 100% solar electricity generated in Washington and Idaho. This option could be purchased in 150-kilowatt-hour blocks for a fixed cost per block, per month. Since my usage hovers around half of that, and because I wanted to support a more diverse range of renewable energy suppliers, I went with the second option. "Green power" is a blend of wind, solar, low-impact hydro, landfill gas, and livestock methane from Washington and surrounding states. This option could be purchased in 200-kilowatt-hour blocks, but there was another option that based what you pay on your average usage each month. Since I wanted to make sure I was always 100% covered, I went with that option.

I could technically have enrolled in both options, but I decided to stick with the "green power" option for now.

There is quite a bit of fluctuation in my energy bill as the seasons change (typically tripling as we move from late summer to crisp fall here in the PNW), but I still want to take the steps that I can to reduce my usage, whenever possible, through every season, and offset it all with green energy.

Thankfully, investing in renewables isn't the only sustainable solution. To reduce your bill and your energy usage, you can install a smart thermostat that automatically lowers your home temperature at night or when you are away. For every degree you reduce the thermostat, you can save between 1% and 3% on your energy bill — as well as saving the corresponding energy. Replacing the filter on your furnace or heat pump regularly will also help to ensure that it operates efficiently. By using your countertop appliances, such as a Crock or Instant Pot, you can further reduce your power bill since these appliances are more efficient than an electric or gas oven. If you use an electric cooktop, make sure the burner you select matches the size of your cookpot. Using a small pot on a large burner will waste 40% of the generated heat. My energy provider offers rebates and other incentives to encourage their customers to make energy-efficient upgrades to their homes. If you check, your power company might, too.

Today, I can relax knowing that clean water, rustling wind, and, I guess, cow manure, are powering my apartment, even if they're actually powering the home next door. And you can, too.

SOLAR POWER

Although it would be nice (or at least interesting) to live in a completely solar-powered home off the grid, it isn't realistic for most of us. Installing solar panels at home may be out of reach, too, for financial or logistical reasons.

If you can't, or don't want to, go totally solar, there are ways you can bring solar power into your home, instead of simply paying for it to be added to the power grid. There are companies developing solar windows which create energy to power many of the small devices in our homes. They are fully rechargeable, too. Some companies, like Grouphug, have designed their windows to be repairable, too — which we know is the trademark of a sustainable item.

If you decide to invest in solar panels, the local energy company or utility provider will have all of the information you'll need to capture your local rays of sunshine.

LIGHTING

It's a no-brainer that we should switch off lights when we aren't using them, but there are other things we can do to increase the sustainability of the light sources in our homes.

The fact is that 25% of the energy we use in our homes is for lighting. That is a significant chunk, indeed.

Most people are aware that LED lights are the most energy-efficient, but I don't think they understand why. If you simply want to know what kind of bulbs to buy, get LEDs. You can skip the rest of this section. If you are interested in knowing why LED bulbs are the best, read on.

LEDs, short for light-emitting diodes, share the hardware store shelves with two general alternatives, incandescent light bulbs and compact fluorescent bulbs (CFLs). Beyond the equally intriguing names, the positive similarities end.

Although both incandescent and CFL bulbs can be purchased at a cheaper price than LEDs, they have a much shorter lifespan. This means that they will end up costing you more in the financial sense and in terms of electricity usage in the long run. A single LED bulb can last up to 50,000 hours. That means the bulb will last 5.7 years if left on 24 hours a day. A CFL bulb will last for just 10,000 hours or so. An incandescent bulb should last for approximately 1,200 hours. If you were to compare the cost of all three bulbs over 50,000 hours, an incandescent bulb will end up costing you about $300, a CFL bulb about $70, and an LED bulb about $50.

The cost differences are comparable to the carbon dioxide emissions of these different bulbs. Incandescent bulbs emit 4,500 pounds of CO_2 a year, whereas CFL bulbs emit about 1,050, and LED bulbs about 450.

Although it may seem that a CFL bulb and the LED alternative are closely ranked in most areas, some CFL bulbs contain mercury, and mercury is something that we all want to avoid, for our sake as well as the planet's.

To summarize, LED light bulbs will last 25 times longer, use 75% to 80% less energy, and offer the best light quality. So what are you waiting for? "LEDs" go!

LEDs also let us choose the right type of light to serve our purposes. No matter what kind of light you are looking for, brightness is determined by lumens, and light color is designated using the Kelvin scale (K).

This is also another area where smart technology comes in handy. Smart light bulbs allow you to dim the lights, set timers, or even change colors. You can set up motion sensors that will turn the lights off automatically when you leave a room. Smart lights, and entire lighting systems, can be controlled remotely. In that way, you can turn on (or off) all the lights with the touch of a remote. This is especially handy when you are watching TV and the motion detector thinks you've left the room.

WATER USAGE

The average family in the United States uses approximately 127,000 gallons of water per year. One of the biggest ways we can reduce this number is by installing low-flow fixtures. Even appliances like washing machines, dishwashers, and toilets can be made to operate on less water.

A toilet may use up to 33,000 gallons of water per year compared to a newer model which may use just 9,000 gallons per year, a savings of 24,000 gallons. This makes me wonder what it would be like if I had to collect and carry that much water to my house every year. Although I'd be fit and strong, I probably wouldn't have time to do anything else. Saving 24,000 gallons of water is significant savings for the planet and it could also save us up to 18% on our water bill.

If every family in the US would make the switch to low-flow appliances and fixtures, we could save millions of gallons of water every day. Just consider if a metropolitan area, like Los Angeles, where water shortages frequently occur, could save the usage of millions of gallons through this one simple change. If 100,000 families got a low-flow toilet, at least a million gallons could be saved every day. This number would only increase as additional individuals, families, and businesses followed suit.

Ultimately, though, even if you want to make the switch to high-efficiency fixtures, disposing of the old fixtures will create waste. You can consider donating the old ones to Habitat for Humanity but realize that this means that (assuming they are used again), they will still be using the same amount of water as before. I believe that this outcome is still better overall than replacing an old fixture with an inefficient model that will use the same amount of water or energy and having the old one end up in a landfill. Please take this into consideration as you make your plans. There is no right or easy answer, but I hope you will make a decision that represents what is best for you, your home, and the environment.

Another aspect of sustainable water usage is to consider the energy required to heat it. This applies to washing machines, dishwashers, showers, and even the sink. As I was researching, I took a few minutes to take a survey so the power company could perform an analysis of my energy usage (I had fun with it; it felt like I was back in middle school and obsessed with Buzzfeed).

When the results came in, I was shocked; about 49% of my energy bill goes to heating water. And I am careful to wash dishes and clothes at the coldest settings possible! I take short(ish) showers, albeit warm ones! It was hard to believe that much energy could go to just heating water.

The questionnaire didn't ask questions about the water temperature I use, so I'm hopeful that the analysis isn't completely accurate. And since I am just one person, in a small apartment, running the dishwasher once or twice per week, and using the washing machine once or twice per month, my energy bill is generally small. Perhaps half of the energy I use does involve heating water, in spite of my Herculean efforts to cut back. In the final analysis, I am glad I've implemented as many changes as I have, and I am even more convinced than ever of the importance.

Since "water heating" was my largest energy use category, I was offered a few "water heating tips," most of which are things I've written about here. These suggestions included using a low-flow showerhead, shortening showers, and lowering the temperature of your water heater, which is something I hadn't thought of on my own, but I'm sure would be a good idea. The power company stated that by making any one of these changes, I would save about $10 per year. I'm not on a mission to save $10 a year, but I am on a mission to become more sustainable, so those recommended changes are done and done.

KILLER COSTS

When I first moved into my apartment, I was terrified of my energy bill. Even though how high it would be was directly related to how much energy I used, I felt like I had a tenuous grasp on just how much that was going to be. Sure the cost might be $ 0.092 per kWh, but how much is that really? And what does that look like in actuality?

I quickly got into the habit of taking shorter showers, keeping only one or two lights on at a time, and wearing my robe when I was at home so I could keep the thermostat as low as I could while staying comfortable. These steps had a beneficial impact on my total energy bill each month and on the environment, although I wasn't even aware of it at the time.

I felt like I was doing a number of things to reduce my energy usage and I was curious about how that related to others in my local area, and around the world. Was I still using too much energy? Should I be doing better?

I learned that the average annual energy bill for a single-family home in the United States is $2,200.

I live alone, and my energy bill runs between $20 and $80 a month, depending on the time of year. When I sat down and calculated my total average energy costs, it was about $480 a year. I estimated that if I lived with an average single-family in an average single-family home, and we have similar energy habits to my current usage, the annual energy bill could be expected to be a little less than $2,000. I was both intrigued and surprised by this.

On the one hand, it means that I am doing a bit better than the average person at keeping my energy bill down. But, on the other hand, the difference seems hardly worth mentioning. And I'd spent the better part of a year striving to live more sustainably for the long term. Either the US population as a whole is doing a really good job, or I need to step up my game (or maybe it's a little of both).

With this in mind, I decided to dive in and see what other changes I could make.

I still don't understand the whole cost per kWh thing. And I still have no idea how much that is in actuality. If that interests you, there are books out there on the topic, but they haven't made their way onto my reading list.

I decided that it would be much more sustainable in the long run to reduce my energy usage in other ways. I had no intention of setting the house thermostat to 50 degrees, giving up showering altogether, or washing my clothes in nearby Puget Sound. There had to be more things that I could reasonably do that would be sustainable, in every sense of the word.

I discovered a simple tip that applies to almost everything electrical: turn it off and unplug it. A laptop left plugged in while on "sleep" mode can cost up to $15 a year; a desktop can cost up to $75 a year. A laser printer can cost up to $130 a year. While these costs will show up in your energy bill, I was even more concerned about the wasted energy. Lamps, phone chargers, and curling irons, if left plugged in, will continue to draw energy. These products have been referred to as "energy vampires," and I think it's safe to say we want to keep all vampires out of the house.

I found it ironic that these items are also commonly referred to as "phantom energy users." Apparently, we needed to make it clear that what these devices do is stealthy and serious! And a little scary besides.

I have always been in the habit of unplugging appliances and devices when they aren't in use: my laptop, KitchenAid mixer, and hot water pot, for example. But things like the TV or the microwave felt almost glued to the wall and convincing myself that I could or should unplug them felt like a major hurdle. I'm still not great at unplugging these things, but the realization that sustainability is a practice is a constant reminder.

If you also don't like the idea of continually unplugging appliances and devices, you may want to invest in smart power strips. These power strips set computers and other devices to automatically go into "sleep" mode when they are not in use in case you forget to turn them off. An added benefit is that they help to monitor and maintain your power usage.

I found this subject to be particularly interesting because devices that are always plugged in can generate lots of unnecessary expense in electricity, energy, and water bills. And this equates to unnecessary environmental costs as well. Making these simple changes can be powerful. It's my hope that each of us will begin to care more and more about sustainability as we also care about our wallets. There isn't always such a clear link between sustainability and our pocketbook, and sometimes living sustainably actually means spending more money. But in this case, what's best for our wallets is also what's best for the planet, too; even if it takes a bit more effort on our part, by remembering to unplug the printer.

HOME BUILDING

I have never built a home, although I hope to one day. And when I do, I'm excited to make it beautiful, functional, and a beacon of sustainability. I have read a number of books and articles about what makes a home structurally sustainable, including things like solar panels, proper kinds of insulation, nontoxic building materials, and low VOC paint. If you are interested in learning more about this topic, want to make the physical structure of your home more green, or are looking into building a sustainable home from scratch, I encourage you to dive into the research. And if you are going to be building, I hope you will look for, and support, builders and designers who are as environmentally minded as you are. The rest of us will be at the mercy of the builder as to the kind of insulation and building materials we have to live with, at least for now.

DISASTER PREPAREDNESS

I tend to think of the Pacific Northwest as the ideal place to live. We have no poisonous spiders or snakes, very few truly dangerous animals, no hurricanes, tornadoes, or flash floods, very few forest fires, and only an occasional earthquake. But since the threat of an earthquake is always on the horizon, I understand the need to keep things on hand at home and in the car in case the worst happens. If you aren't fortunate enough to live in the Pacific Northwest, then I'm assuming that you are even more prepared, since you likely have to deal with some or all of the terrifying things I mentioned above.

Those items you keep on hand for an emergency are varied but very necessary. Living a sustainable life should not get in the way of your personal safety, so it's important to keep extra water on hand (yes, in plastic jugs), or foil packages of dried food. There are other resources available to help you prepare an emergency kit and I encourage you to get them.

Staying safe will allow you to stay sustainable.

YOUR FOREVER HOME

When safety is no longer a concern (because you are dead), it is still possible to be sustainable. And I need to state that I hope that a lack of disaster preparedness, or a disaster itself, was not your downfall.

I've never understood the desire to be buried in one's finest clothes alongside your favorite possessions in an expensive coffin with all the bells and whistles (not literally, although that reminds me of a funny story). Not only does that cost a load of money, but it's also detrimental to the earth, which I hope you've spent much of your life caring for. The chemicals placed in your body, the coffin itself, the stone, the vaults… very little of this is done with the earth in mind.

Cremation is a slightly more environmentally friendly option than straight-out burial, but even that requires chemicals along with a massive outlay of resources and results in a residue of chemical byproducts. Liquid cremation is a better option. It creates fewer emissions and has a smaller environmental impact. Liquid cremation is only legal in a few states at the present time, however, but will hopefully become more available in the future. Fortunately for me, Washington is one of the states that allows this option, so should I decide to go this route, it is available to me.

Although it generates more emissions, I have let my family know that if I die in the near future, after my usable organs have been donated, I would like my remains to be cremated and the ashes used to directly nourish the growth of a tree through The Living Urn or a similar program. Of course, I want to live and continue to help people reach their goals and work to preserve the planet as long as possible, but I'm also pleased with the prospect of helping a Magnolia tree (my favorite kind) to become all that it can be, when I am no longer here.

Other options for green burial include being buried in a wooden box without embalming or having remains placed in a cement vault. These are more sustainable options than full-on mummy-type burials.

Remains can even be used to preserve and protect ocean creatures. Cremated remains can help to create ocean habitats as the ashes can be mixed with concrete and placed in the ocean as a reef 'ball.' These reef balls provide a habitat for sea creatures of all sizes both inside the hollow ball or along its textured surface.

Another green(ish) option for cremated remains is to have the ashes compressed and turned into a precious stone, such as a diamond. Through heat and pressure, the carbon is separated out and is then turned into graphene and finally, a diamond, or other stone.

If becoming a gem isn't quite your speed, you can go the opposite direction (at least in my mind) and utilize a mushroom suit. Instead of being buried in a coffin or wooden box, you could be dressed in a cotton "suit" that has been integrated with microorganisms, including mushrooms, that will aid in the decomposition process. I thought mushrooms were gross when I learned about them in middle school life science class, but this takes it to a whole new level. Not only does the mushroom suit not harm the environment, but it also actually aids in the transfer of nutrients from our body to the soil, plants, and the environment.

Or you can consider joining me by having your remains placed inside a tree urn.

This is an area where you get to choose the best option for you, and then communicate your wishes to your loved ones. None of us knows when we will go, and hopefully, we won't go for a very long time, but when we do, we can make sure that we leave the earth as sustainably as possible.

FURNITURE

In the US, 9,680,000 tons of furniture waste end up in landfills each year. I've seen some pretty nasty couches that were more than ready to find a final resting place, but I have a hard time believing that over 9 million tons of furniture fall into that category every year.

If you have furniture to dispose of that doesn't fall into that category either, it probably doesn't need to end up in a landfill, at least not yet. You can sell it online, list it for free, give it to a friend, or donate it to someone in need. The landfill doesn't need to be the first option, and it isn't even necessarily the fastest or easiest option. And it certainly isn't the best option for the planet.

When looking for new furniture, you can always consider buying second-hand, vintage, or refurbished. Another possibility is to freshen up what you already have with a slipcover or through reupholstering. If you are looking for something brand new, I'd suggest that you shop online or in-store for brands that strive to care for their employees and the planet.

RENT OR REFURBISH

Although we probably don't want to rent everything (at least I don't), through at least considering the option in certain cases, and taking advantage of it when it makes sense, we can reduce the amount of 'stuff' entering the cycle.

You can rent homes, cars, clothes, and everything in between. You can even rent furniture from companies like IKEA, Feather, and Muji.

If renting doesn't make sense for you, you can also look for refurbished options on phones, furniture, and many other things. Once again, this reduces the number of items that will need to be produced in the first place.

DECOR

Decor is a pretty broad category, and I'm dumping into it everything we use to decorate our homes — from the throw pillow on the couch that is older than I am, to the star-shaped ice cube trays that come out early in July, to all of the things that will turn our homes into a winter wonderland at the end of the year.

There isn't anything new to present here, but these ideas, once again, bear repeating.

First, the things that you already have are by far the most sustainable. If I came to your house to do an organizing session with you, chances are good that boxes of surplus decor would probably follow me out of the house. For most of the people I know, the need for more decor of any type is not an issue.

Although if you, like me, are a fledgling adult who has recently moved into your own 'first' home away from home, there are probably a few things that you'll need; and we'll get to that soon.

But, if you find that you have too much decor, the first thing to try to lighten your load is gifting or donating it. Conversely, if you find yourself in need of a particular item of decor, first try finding it at a thrift store, donation center, secondhand, or online. It goes both ways.

Can you beg, borrow, or steal? Okay, not really, but you get the idea. If you need new strands of Christmas lights, you likely know someone who needs to get rid of a few strands of Christmas lights. By looking around before buying new, you will probably save a few dollars, possibly divert something from a landfill, and definitely take sustainable action.

PILLOWS, BLANKETS, AND COVERS

I know the tug that comes when I'm walking through Target to buy that one grocery item and I see the most beautiful throw pillow ever! While it's easy enough to add the pillow to my cart (and, ultimately, my couch), it is worth taking an extra minute to see if it was made with natural fibers, rather than synthetic ones, since the synthetic fabrics will shed microplastics when washed or cleaned.

And I need to remember that pillows just like this are also likely to be found secondhand and won't require me to add something new to the cycle.

CANDLES

Once you've used all of the candles you probably have on hand, or if you are looking to purchase candles as a gift (one of my favorite things to give or receive!), look for the ones with a soy base instead of paraffin candles which have a petroleum base. If they come in a glass jar, too, they can be cleaned and recycled; or even reused if that is more your speed (or if it is just a particularly beautiful jar).

Another great gift idea and something that we should all have on hand is a rechargeable lighter. These lighters are much more sustainable than plastic single-use (or even thirty-use) disposable lighters and are definitely safer than having a box of matches lying around.

READING MATERIALS

I love that you bought, borrowed, or stole a copy of my book (well, hopefully, you didn't actually steal one).

Books, themselves, require a lot of resources, so I did my utmost to ensure this book used as little as possible. If you like to read, too, I encourage you to use the local library as much as possible. I get most of my reading material there, and I only purchase the books that I've read and loved (this is the organizer in me). This habit keeps new things from entering the cycle and maximizes the use of the things that already are. I also take advantage of the library's extensive collection of digital books and audiobooks.

Similarly, you can subscribe to programs like Audible, Kindle, and Scribd to access electronic books and audiobooks at home or on the go. This is one area that Amazon is actually playing a role in benefiting the environment!

SENTIMENTAL ITEMS

Although this book wasn't intended as a book on 'organizing,' I did want to take a moment to share something that most of us have to deal with and that does, ultimately, affect our environmental impact.

If you want to get rid of something, do it. If it is something you think a friend would like, gift it. If you think it would benefit someone else, donate it. If you need a little extra cash, sell it.

If it was a gift from someone special and you're struggling to let it go, I get it. But the fact is, if it is not serving your life, the gift is likely draining your energy and taking up mental space while you decide whether or not to get rid of it! If it has served a purpose as a thoughtful gift to you, and now it can serve another purpose for someone else, let it go.

If you have memory items, as I do, you probably know that you'll hang onto them forever. One way to keep a handle on this is to just determine how much space you want to give these things. I have made the personal determination that I am willing to keep one tub for each decade of my life. This will keep such items in check while still allowing me to feel like I can keep the things that truly matter to me. Of course, there are plenty of things that I am satisfied to just snap a picture of, or scan, before letting them go.

If you have a plethora of family heirlooms that you no longer want or use, you can offer them to other family members before taking the actions mentioned above. If no one in the family wants them, proceed as you see fit. And if you do gift them, remember to let them go emotionally as well so you won't feel any pain if the new owners ultimately let them go, too.

ORGANIZING

If you'll allow me a few minutes more to stay in organizer-mode, I'd like to discuss why decluttering and organizing can play foundational roles in a sustainable life.

First, when you know where to find something, you'll save lots of time that you would otherwise spend looking for it, and you are much less likely to end up with duplicates, which cost you time, money, and space. And even with a duplicate, without organization, there is no guarantee you'll be able to find the new one, either, when you need it.

Although decluttering and getting rid of things may seem a bit counterintuitive, it actually will benefit you in many ways moving forward. By letting go of those things you no longer enjoy or that don't fit (you or your home), or that no longer serve you, you can free up energy and space in both your home and mind which can be dedicated to other things, such as living a more sustainable life.

I now own a countertop composter. That means I've had to get rid of (or move) things that would otherwise take up space on my countertop. Sustainability sometimes requires more things in some areas of life (like reusables) and fewer things in others (fewer, better personal care products). Just as no definition of sustainability will work for everyone, no single way to organize will either.

But as you are striving for greater sustainability in your home, you can ask yourself some of the following questions to determine what should stay, what should go, and what is sustainable for you.

Three core questions to ask yourself when you are in the process of decluttering are — Do I use it? Do I need it? Do I love it? If the answer is no to all of these, then out it goes. But since our focus here goes beyond file-folding or organizing your bookcase into a ROYGBIV rainbow, some additional questions to consider are: Is this item helping me live a more sustainable life? Am I caring for this item properly? Does this item make it easier or harder for me to live out my values? And so on.

And remember, any item you donate or pass along, provided it is in good condition, will likely find a new home and renewed purpose, and thus, will be keeping a new item from being added into the consumption cycle. Unfortunately, many thrift stores receive too many donations, and so many of these items end up being shipped overseas to countries that may or may not be able to manage the quantities, or they may end up in landfills. But don't worry, there are many solutions to the excess problem.

Gifting items to friends or family (provided that they actually will use and love them) is by far the clearest and most sustainable option. Second, selling items, whether online or through other channels, will provide you with a little money and, hopefully, a new owner who will care for the item. As an organizer, I typically don't recommend selling items unless they are high-end or large (a couch as opposed to a t-shirt), although you are free to do whatever you are comfortable with! I consider listing items on Craigslist for free, or gifting them through the Buy Nothing community, to be almost equivalent to selling them. Even if you don't make any money, you'll have the satisfaction of knowing that the items are likely to end up with new owners who truly want them if they are willing to reach out to you, and then travel to pick them up.

If you have a product that merely needs to be used up, I encourage you to do that or see if there is someone in your life who will.

There are, of course, things you will end up donating; potentially, a lot of things. But when it comes to a carload of items, there are alternative things you can do as opposed to dropping all of it off at the local thrift store. Many homeless or women's shelters are looking for personal care items and gently used clothing. Bedding and blankets can be donated to humane societies and animal shelters. Some schools and teachers will take arts and crafts supplies. Books and movies may be accepted at local libraries. Building materials and household goods can be donated to Habitat for Humanity.

Many of these stops can be made on the way to your local thrift store.

Tracking down all of the options can be a pain, I know. But if it guarantees that these items are used again, and maybe even loved again, rather than landfilled, isn't it worth the extra effort? And doing the research now may establish donation avenues for you for the rest of your life! You can also share the resources you discover with others to divert even more stuff from ending up in a trash heap. In a society built on convenience, it makes sense that it will take extra effort to undo the damage and slow the roll.

Whether you start with a drawer or your whole garage, any progress is better than none at all, and when you are truly acting from a desire for increased sustainability, the impact will be greater than just having everything in its place, although, you'll certainly end up with that benefit, too.

MOVING

As an organizer, I know that a physical move is the perfect time to cut the clutter, minimize, simplify, and hopefully end up on the other side with only the things that matter most to you (instead of "Oh my word, how did we end up with three vegetable spiralizers?").

Ideally, wherever we live and however long we live there, we want to be surrounded by the things we care about, with our consumerism well under control, and our lives simple and sustainable.

But sadly, that is very rarely the reality.

So in addition to a general recommendation to declutter, buy less, say "no" as much as possible, and maintain what you own, when it comes time to move, we want to do that sustainably, too. The fewer things we bring into our new home, the fewer things will have to be moved (or removed) next time.

If you haven't figured it out by now, I'm pretty frugal. I hate buying things that are moving-specific, i.e. boxes, paper, tape, etc. That means I avoid bubble wrap and anything else that I don't absolutely need. Thus far, this has served me well. Hopefully, fingers crossed, I will continue to maintain my 'no-broken-items' streak.

As with everything else, it's best to start by packing in things that you already have. Bins, tubs, suitcases, bags, even the produce boxes they use to send home all of your groceries from Costco, can all be used for moving purposes. To protect items, I prefer to use packing paper (which can be composted!), or towels, clothes, tablecloths, blankets, robes, and anything else I have on hand.

To find previously used moving boxes or other packing supplies, I suggest you check Craigslist or your local Buy Nothing group. There is always someone moving to, or away from, your town. Once you are unpacked and settled, you can in turn offer those same moving materials to another person.

PETS

Approximately 67% of the US population owns at least one pet. I have an adorable cat, Shakespeare.

If you, like me, are in the majority of people who have a pet, here are some things you might want to consider toward the goal of reducing your pet's environmental footprint, or should I say "paw" print.

When purchasing food, snacks, or treats, you may want to see what options might be available to buy in bulk in your local area. If that isn't possible, or even in some cases if it is, look for packaging that can be recycled.

General and conventional wisdom seems to recommend that you not try to DIY your pet's food regularly, because of the variety of nutrients that they need. A variation on this argument is the reason that I don't make most of my personal care products at home either. It's probably no surprise that I decided to stick with store bought over homemade in this area, too.

When purchasing pet toys, look for those that will be long-lasting and that come in recyclable packaging. As with everything else, resist the temptation to go overboard, or depending on your pet, you can always try to DIY.

Dog waste can't be put in the public compost system, but you can toss it into your personal backyard compost if that is something you are comfortable with, or you can use a special animal-waste composting program. These options will vary based on your location. As I'm sure you know by now, scooping waste into a plastic bag and then tossing it into the trashcan to ultimately languish in a landfill is not a sustainable option. Bio Bags or

Flushpuppies are plastic-free options. Some people have chosen to use toilet paper, but I will admit, that is not an option I think I would try.

Cat waste is more challenging. Since most cats use a litter box, it's important to choose a litter that is biodegradable. The bigger question is what to do with the old litter when it is time to clean the box. One option is to flush the waste down the toilet. However, some cats carry a parasite, Toxoplasma gondii, that will kill marine life if it ends up in the ocean. If you have an indoor cat, the chances of getting this parasite are low, however, it is still technically possible. You can get your cat tested if you want to know. In any case, if you choose not to flush, you can consider the same options discussed for dog waste above. I have heard that people can train their cats to use the toilet, but once again, this isn't an option I would ever try.

TOILET PAPER

If you looked into UNPaper Towels after reading Chapter 2, you may have noticed that the company, Marley's Monsters, also makes Toilet UNPaper. This is something else that I have been unwilling to try. If you want to, good for you, but I have nothing further to say on the matter. Other than that regular toilet paper seems to decompose just fine.

Despite my immediate and thorough revulsion to toilet paper alternatives, I decided to make a deeper exploration into whether or not there are other, more sustainable, toilet paper options available. Statistics show that approximately 27,000 trees are consumed every day through our use of toilet paper. Each roll requires about 1.5 pounds of tree pulp and 37 gallons of water. Nearly 15% of global deforestation is attributed to toilet paper production alone. That means that every man, woman, and child on the planet will require approximately 150 pounds of tree pulp each year. That equates to about 380 trees in a single lifetime. That's a lot of trees going down a lot of toilets.

One alternative, of course, is to use or install a bidet attachment to the toilet. If that's your speed, go you. Bidets use about one-eighth of a gallon of water per use, so compared to the water that goes into toilet paper production, that is probably a fair trade. Bidets can also reduce (or maybe even eliminate) toilet paper use altogether.

I feel that overall it's most important for each of us to be aware of how much toilet paper we use. There's typically no need to use half the roll.

For sustainability, bamboo-based, tree-free, plastic-less toilet paper is the best way to go. The Natural Resources Defense Council reports that if every US home would replace just one roll of toilet paper with a tree-free roll, about 423,900 trees could be saved.

If you want to contribute to that accomplishment (hopefully buying more than one roll), look for toilet paper made from 100% recycled paper (no virgin trees), or an altogether tree-free option made from bamboo or sugarcane. You can also look for rolls that come unwrapped or are wrapped in paper, as opposed to plastic. Cardboard rolls, boxes, and even the paper around the rolls can be composted or recycled, too.

You may find an option for you that fits these qualifications locally, but if not, they can be ordered online through companies like Bippy or Who Gives a Crap. Bippy uses zero trees to produce toilet paper, opting instead for bamboo. Who Gives a Crap makes toilet paper from 100% recycled paper; has no plastic packaging; is made without inks, dyes, or scents; and donates 50% of its profits to ensure everyone has access to clean water and a toilet.

Many of these are subscription-based products, but since toilet paper is one of those things that we always need and don't want to run out of, they may be worth considering.

CLOTH NAPKINS

Prior to my sustainability project, I thought that cloth napkins were odd. They felt awkward, large, and thick. Unless I was folding them into a holiday tree shape for the Christmas table place settings, I had absolutely no interest.

But as I started the project, I knew that it was time to reassess napkins. I noticed that as the year progressed, I'd begun to use my UNpaper Towels as napkins. Because I live alone, I never went through all of them before laundry day, so I never ran out.

In the future, I might consider investing in something specifically designed to be a "napkin," but for now, I'm happy with my substitutes. This was also a perfect way for me to embrace using what I have, not needing to purchase something new or different. Sustainability will look different for all of us. For you, it might mean buying a set of nice secondhand cloth napkins or using the ones that have been in the family for years, or it could be (like me) finding something similar and calling it good enough.

THE TISSUE ISSUE

Another household staple with a conventional swap is facial tissues. My dad has used handkerchiefs for years and I always thought that was strange and even a bit gross. Enter my sustainability project.

When I decided that my UNpaper Towels could work as napkins, too, I also decided that sustainable toilet paper could work just as well as tissues. I wasn't really in the habit of buying tissues anyway (opting for toilet paper when I was home instead), and I'd already managed to up the sustainability factor of that habit. I haven't experienced a period of serious illness to this point, but this certainly works for me right now.

Choosing handkerchiefs instead, carrying a few of them on the go, and keeping some in the car or purse, seems to work well for many people. For home use, you can consider placing a few handkerchiefs inside a refillable tissue box holder, making them just like the disposable ones! And after use, they can go straight to the washing machine, laundry hamper, or wash bag to await the next load along with your reusable napkins, cloth paper towels, and other sustainable swaps.

If you aren't weirded out by the idea, some nice handkerchiefs can probably be found at secondhand and thrift stores. You might even find some in your family with historical significance. Of course, you can also invest in some new ones, although that means that something new is entering the cycle. Or, like me, you can (at least for now) forgo them altogether.

DISPOSABLE TABLEWARE

As an organizer, I have walked alongside families coming out the other side of a long renovation. I understand that during periods of transition, using real plates and real silverware for every meal isn't feasible. Although there are those people who will try to wash and reuse whenever they can, there are often lots that will get thrown away. And that's okay. When you don't have a dishwasher or oven and your refrigerator is in the middle of the living room, it's okay to use a few paper plates.

The same is true if you're going through a move, having a lot of company over, throwing a party, or anything else. It is okay to give yourself grace, especially when it comes to paper products. Of course, it's not something that you probably want to make a habit of every day, especially if sustainability is one of your major values.

The key takeaway here is to be aware of your consumption and mindful of its impact. For example, it takes 8 gallons of water to make a single paper plate. While this is a lot and not great, it still isn't worth guilting yourself over— especially if you're living through a stressful renovation.

So, whenever possible, purchase disposable items that are made of recycled material or bamboo, and/or are compostable. Although none of these are perfect, and they shouldn't become our primary dining implements, they exist for a reason, and living through a stressful renovation is a very good one.

It is ironic that often the people who opt for disposable items because they are looking for a convenient option, are also less likely to take the necessary steps to dispose of their disposables properly. Once most paper products have been used, they can be composted, since they are too dirty to be recycled. Sadly, many people just toss them into the trash. This doesn't have to be you. It is possible to support yourself and your values at the same time.

FOOD STORAGE

We've talked previously about the potential dangers of plastics, so it is not surprising that the prevailing advice on the health and sustainability front is to invest in glass containers whenever possible. These containers can be used in the oven or microwave, are infinitely recyclable, and won't stain or get discolored.

It's probable that you have plastic containers in your pantry, so the best option is to use them; don't just throw them away. If you don't want to use them for food storage any longer, they can be used to store other household items in your home or garage, to collect compost scraps at home or on the go, or as doggie bags for leftovers going home with dinner guests (with the assurance that the containers don't need to be returned).

If you want the plastics out of your house immediately, they can be donated. The professional organizer in me requires me to add that when purchasing containers, you want to buy only one or two sets that are the same or very similar. This will keep everything streamlined and the pieces can be interchanged in case something goes missing.

BAGGIES – PLASTIC OR OTHERWISE

Reportedly, the average American uses 540 plastic baggies each year. I'm honestly not entirely sure how that is possible, but it seems to me that this is another statistic we can reduce with a minimum of effort.

Silicone bags are an easy, reusable alternative to plastic. I purchased mine from Stasher and I haven't had to purchase a plastic baggie for years! I inadvertently ended up with a few when family came for a visit which I have dutifully reused and repurposed. I love that the reusable bags can go in the dishwasher, fridge, and freezer. They can even be placed directly in boiling water or into the oven! Disclaimer: I haven't tried either of these yet but am fascinated by the idea.

I'm excited to use my reusable bags forever. The only problem is that I might need a few more, but that problem is easily remedied.

Growing up I used to tell my mom that one day I hoped to be rich enough to never have to wash and reuse a plastic baggie. Washing out the sandwich bag was the worst end to the school day, especially when the sandwich was peanut butter. My mom teases me now because I always reuse a sandwich bag, but they aren't plastic and they can go in the dishwasher. So while 8-year-old-me might be unhappy with this development, grown-up-me is very pleased indeed.

BEESWAX COVERS

As I have said before, using what we already have, instead of buying, is the sustainable option in the long run. Food is no exception. When I started this journey, I made the decision that I would not buy items like plastic bags, plastic wrap, or tin foil anymore. This affected my ability to store food and forced me to find some creative solutions in the short term. I was really just holding out until October when I could focus on ways to preserve food sustainably.

Looking back, there were definitely some vegetables and bread that I had to toss because I wasn't able to preserve them adequately, even in the fridge. Maybe I should've tackled this category earlier in the year, but there was no point in second-guessing myself. Now, I want to maximize the food that I have (especially when it is farmer's market-fresh in some cases), so I knew I needed to do some research in this area.

Since I'd already invested in Stasher bags which made storing food easier and more sustainable, I was definitely on my way. However, there were some things I couldn't fit into a Stasher bag, such as an entire loaf of banana bread. I didn't want to have to cut the loaf into multiple parts to use the bags I have or buy more bags in the event I have a multi-course meal with lots of leftovers. I needed an alternative.

I heard about beeswax wraps from people in the sustainability community, but I admit I was skeptical going in. However, they seemed to be my best potential option at that point. I decided to get a few beeswax wraps and overall I'm satisfied. They do the job, even if, like other sustainable swaps, they take getting used to.

You can make your own beeswax wraps if you are really into DIY, or if you just want to give it a shot. There are lots of resources online that can help but I am not your girl.

Another option to consider is cloth bowl covers. I may purchase some of those down the line if I determine that they would be a worthwhile (and sustainable) addition to my kitchen.

ROLLS OF UN-REUSABILITY

Aluminum foil has been a kitchen standard for decades. I know plenty of people who swear by it. This is evidenced by the fact that each Americans throws away approximately 3 pounds of aluminum foil each year which will take about 400 years to break down. Technically aluminum can be recycled, but in foil form, it can be difficult to do so, and producing the product is very energy intensive. Mining aluminum, which tends to be the opposite of eco-friendly, plays a part in this. Additionally, research has indicated potential health risks for humans and other creatures from some exposures to the material.

This was an easy one for me to give up, not the least because I was never able to figure out how to get it out of the box without cutting myself since I was a kid. I'm pretty sure I haven't purchased foil even once since I've lived on my own.

For baking, I use silicone baking mats instead. They actually work well for more than baking. They have replaced my need for wax and parchment paper entirely, too. However, I've also heard that a bamboo pot scraper is useful to clean up anything that sticks to your pots and pans and keeps you from needing to line them at all.

Storing food, as you might do with aluminum foil, or cooling food, as you might do with parchment paper, can also be done using other, more sustainable, kitchen products as well. It is probably worth your time to do a little experimentation to see what sustainable options you can find that will work for you. And chances are, there is someone else who is a sustainability or zero-waste guru who might have faced the exact situation and can offer some pointers.

If you decide to keep a roll or two of aluminum foil in your kitchen drawer for culinary emergencies, that is okay, but making a switch for everyday use is the sustainable choice, and you will no longer have to use those dangerous boxes.

While we're on the topic of silicone, I'd like to share another sustainable favorite of mine. If you like to bake or find yourself slaving over a hot stove even occasionally, it is probably worth investing in silicone baking cups. They are easy to find and they clean up easily; just toss them in the dishwasher.

I grew up using them, and although I often wished I had special ones for Halloween or Barbie-themed parties, I'm glad to know I was taking sustainable action, even if I was totally oblivious at the time.

FILTERED WATER

For many people around the globe, the only safe way to stay hydrated and healthy is to drink filtered water. If that's you, you know who you are. But if it's not you, and you're looking to reduce waste, you probably already know that filtered water sold in individual water bottles is not a sustainable or healthy option. If you filter your water at home through a pitcher or other filtration system, there is likely a lot of plastic involved there, too.

Activated charcoal is generally used as the sustainable filtration method and will eliminate lead, mercury, copper, aluminum, uranium, and molybdenum which can be found in tap water. Some companies produce charcoal filters that can be added to an existing filtration pitcher, sans plastic, or you can get charcoal sticks to place directly in your water bottle if you are on the go.

SALT + PEPPER

So much of what I have learned throughout my sustainability project came down to salt and pepper.

We all use them sometimes. During October, I found myself at the end of both shakers. They had lasted for several years, but the shakers were made of plastic, were not refillable, and not a kind I felt even the tiniest bit motivated to try and figure out how to recycle.

I was initially overwhelmed by these two tiny objects. How many people around the world had shakers just like these at home? How many of them will be thrown away in a single year? The possibilities started to spin around in my head.

Then I realized, it's not really about these two shakers I have to dispose of, it's about the ones I will purchase to replace them. The end result was that instead of buying another set for .99 cents, I took the time to obtain a secondhand, refillable set. I should be set for life, provided I don't drop them. And I will hopefully never consume another set of disposable plastic shakers.

This was a good reminder to me that it's not about the actions I've taken in the past. Although those choices may not have necessarily been good, it doesn't serve me in the present to dwell there. Guilt about the past won't necessarily drive me to productive action, at least not from a place of compassion or motivation. Let the past be the past. Learn from it. Move on. Do better next time. And let our sustainable action be as salt to the rest of our lives.

CHAPTER 11
NOVEMBER: GIFTS + PARTIES

With Christmas (and my birthday!) right around the corner, I decided to spend November looking at how to do the holidays more sustainably; specifically what gift-giving and partying look like while trying to live out your values and protect the planet.

A few of you may want to take issue with the fact that I am looking ahead to Christmas in November, but please bear with me. I don't listen to Christmas music until after Thanksgiving, I promise, but I want you to enter the month of December armed with all of the information necessary for you to enjoy a festive and sustainable holiday season.

I could have waited until December to address the topic of gifts, but I didn't wait that long to begin my shopping list for friends and relatives. And since that was where my mind was for much of this month, I decided I wanted to spend this month focused on gift-giving. I'm pretty type A, so for me, this process usually begins around September, so please appreciate that I have put this off as long as I could.

I also want to ensure that the information in this chapter doesn't just apply to the holidays. Whether we like it or not, we give gifts and throw parties all year round. Weddings, birthdays, baby showers, wedding showers, Easter, and Valentine's Day — the list goes on and on. It is my sincere hope that the principles I share here will be applicable no matter which event is coming up next.

Thankfully, since we've already discussed shopping and brands in Chapter 8, I felt more than ready to tackle this subject.

GIFTS FOR ME

Let's start with what it looks like to receive gifts while trying to live a truly sustainable lifestyle.

Since there are many things I have determined never to buy again or need never buy again, you might think that buying gifts for me would be somewhat difficult. And you would probably be right.

Sometimes people actually ask you what you want or what they could give you. In those situations, I used to draw a complete blank. So, in order to combat my inevitable inability to think of a single thing in the moment, I now try to keep a short list of ideas for things or experiences I would enjoy in the back of my mind (or in the notes app of my phone). Now, when people ask, I'm ready and I've learned that I'm much more likely to end up with gifts that I want and will use. My list includes items I need or want, things where sustainability may not come into play, or things I can never have too many of and that I use all the time, like candles. Even if people don't ask the question, we can still share our list (or an item or two from it) with close friends and family.

Having a list helps to ensure that I don't end up with an eighth throw blanket (although, confession, I do love throw blankets!). If I want something in particular, it also helps to be specific, so the more specific the item that you want, the more specific your list should be. If you say you want a black t-shirt and forget to mention that you want a particular brand or one with sustainable values, you will almost certainly get one from Amazon delivered in several layers of plastic.

"I would like socks from X brand," is a reasonable request, but a note of warning: Don't ask for $80 socks from a broke college friend. It is okay, however, to ask for quality things that have been made sustainably. The more you share about your journey toward sustainability and what you're learning, those around you will want to support you, and you may inspire them to do the same in the process.

The more I share about my own journey and what I learned, the more I see the people around me give me gifts that are aligned with my new life and values.

Remember, everyone giving you a gift wants to get you something that you will use and appreciate. And the best way to make sure that they do is to express your desires and values beforehand. There isn't much you can do after a gift is given, except express gratitude, and maybe at some later time, when appropriate, begin to share your desires and values.

What you do with a gift after it is received is, of course, up to you. But as an organizer and someone who cares about sustainability, if it's not something you love or will use, you should give or donate it to someone who does and will.

GIFTS FOR OTHERS

Whenever possible, we want to give gifts that are wanted by the receiver. The surest way to do this is to ask that individual what they want. A sad fact is that an average of $15 billion is spent each year in the US on unwanted gifts. Research indicates that each one of us will receive at least 1 unwanted gift each holiday season worth approximately $50. And about 6 million people in the US will throw away that unwanted item. Clothing accounts for 43% of unwanted items. Household items account for 20%, cosmetics or fragrances are at 12%, books/literature are a close 8% and technology, food, music, and other miscellaneous items account for about 4%.

If there is any way to get your hands on a list of what the gift recipient might like, both of you will be glad you did. Of course, when you ask directly, more often than not, you will hear "Oh, I don't really want anything in particular" in response. If that happens, you can turn to some of my suggestions below. Also, feel free to use these ideas in the event that your friend asks for something completely unsustainable, like a case of plastic water bottles.

Naturally, I love the idea of no gifts, at least intellectually. That is the most sustainable option of all; not adding another thing to our homes, lives, and, ultimately, landfills. At the same time, I know that Christmas probably won't feel quite the same without presents under the tree. And you can forget about showing up at a child's birthday party without a gift!

If you, or your loved ones, feel that no gifts are most in line with the way you want to live and express your values (and assuming that you're all adults), this is a great way to go. But I know there will be many of you, myself included, who will still want to give (and sometimes receive) gifts as a way to express the love we have for those in our lives. For those of you, I will discuss a few options to make gift giving more sustainable.

The first and most obvious answer is to give fewer, better gifts. There are some people in my circle who, when the holidays roll around, like to express their feelings by giving lots of small gifts. In the past, I have tried to do the same for them. But this year, I decided I would commit to giving each friend only one or two (and sometimes three) items. I tried to look for things of higher quality; especially things I know are made sustainably.

This opens another door. You can give people gifts that will help them on their sustainability journey and that will hopefully positively benefit both their life and the environment. However, gifts like this should be given only to those individuals that you know will love and use them. A metal straw, reusable tumbler, or produce bags, can be wasted objects, too, if they go unused. Also, consider whether or not your gift is likely to be taken the wrong way. You don't want your gift to be perceived to have a hidden agenda or strings attached, and with guilt served up on the side. But if you feel that the gift recipient will receive the gift in the spirit with which it is intended, then definitely give those things that are in line with your (and the recipient's) personal ethical and sustainable values.

If you can't find something you know the recipient will love and use, you could steer away from an actual, physical present and opt for a different kind of gift.

An option that I frequently hear mentioned in organizing circles (that helps to lead to less physical clutter) is the gift of an experience. Fortunately, this also tends to be a fairly sustainable option. A watercolor or ballet class, a dinner out, or a concert ticket can be great gifts for friends and family members. Some other ideas include taking the gift recipient bowling or golfing (mini or regular), ice skating or roller skating, to play laser tag, go rock climbing, visit a museum, escape from an escape room, to see a movie or show, skydiving or sailing, for massages or facials, skiing or snorkeling, to a theme park or water park, to a wine or coffee tasting, or even just on a picnic or walk! These gift experiences may require a bit more work on your part than simply buying and wrapping a gift. You will need to ensure that what you are giving is something that they will actually enjoy. And, if you are buying them an experience that occurs at a certain place on a certain day, you'll need to make sure they are able and willing to make it to the venue.

You could also gift something like a zoo membership to a family with young kids or a photo session for a friend who just had a baby. These things are a good middle ground because while they don't require physical space, they are also more flexible as to how and when they are used.

The biggest downside to giving experiential gifts is that they tend to be a little more expensive. But, while they may cost a little more than, say, a nice candle, depending on the person, occasion, and experience, they don't have to break the bank.

If your family sets a spending limit for gifts, i.e., $20, you're going to have a harder time finding an experience you can purchase for that amount. But if price is less of an issue, they are a great way to give something outside the box.

Another way you can bless a loved one with a gift, and also extend the benefit, is by making a charitable donation in their name. This season of the year is also an amazing time to donate to causes or organizations you care about, whether as a gift in honor of someone else or not. You can also support specific companies by purchasing their products, whether for yourself or to give away as gifts. Oftentimes, as we have seen, these companies are also supporting initiatives that work to help protect the planet. There are also many organizations doing amazing work but that don't have a product to sell. If you end the holiday season with a little extra left over, perhaps from giving fewer gifts or none at all, there is no better time than now to donate to the causes that matter to you.

Just make sure that if you are donating on behalf of someone else that you give to a cause or group they actually like and support! This can be a sweet way for you to give a "gift" to your friend that won't clutter their house, that supports a cause they care about, and is very sustainable. One further caution. Be sure that this person will appreciate a gift like this. While it's said that it's the thought that counts, there are some people for whom a physical gift matters a bit more.

Another way you can give an intangible gift is by giving your time. A friend with a new baby might love you to babysit for a night or two. Your mom might love help going through all of the old family photos. A sibling may need a car wash. The key to these gifts is to make sure that you actually *do* them. It's best not to offer to do something you aren't actually willing to do, or that you will dread. This will absolutely take away from the joy of the gift. Although sometimes giving these gifts can be a little anticlimactic (nothing to unwrap), there are lots of ways you can make giving the gift more special than just announcing the promised act of service. I won't list specific ideas or examples here, but I trust your creativity. Of course, there's always the standby coupon book for kisses and hugs!

When giving a physical gift, it can help to stick to perishable items. Instead of adding permanent physical clutter to someone's home, give a lovely candle, a box of chocolates, flowers, coffee beans, spice mix, hot cocoa mix, baking mix, hot sauce, beauty or body products, wine, specialty food items (ones local to you are extra special!) or a box of tea — whatever they will enjoy. Once the item has been used up, the remnants (if any) can be disposed of properly and the receiver will be left happy and clutter-free (at least, as far as you are concerned).

There have been times in my life when I have received a perishable gift that wasn't really in line with my taste. So, be sure that you don't give a candle to someone who is sensitive to smells, chocolate to someone trying to lose weight, or tea to someone who prefers coffee. Aside from that, though, this can be a unique way to show someone just how well you know them by getting them something they will really enjoy using. It is also a great time for you to exercise your sustainability skills by choosing something low or zero-waste!

As we've discussed previously in this book, supporting your local economy can do lots of good for your community. Shopping locally also opens up many new avenues. You may not make jam, but chances are someone in your local area does and would love you to support their business (especially around the holidays). An author from your town might autograph a copy of their book to your friend. You could bring locally grown flowers or ice cream from a local creamery to a dinner party. The ideas are only as limited as the place where you live (and if you live in Antarctica, that just might mean bringing penguins or ice).

You can also consider giving homemade gifts! It's not just the postman who would love to receive a platter of Christmas cookies. And if you're a great baker, I'm sure you have friends who would love cake or loaves of bread as well. If you sew, giving reusable bags out of scraps of fabric would be a great gift. If you are into canning, homemade peach preserves will be very appreciated. If you make candles, you're already there. If you have any talent at all, consider using it to bless others this holiday season (and any time throughout the year).

And of course, there are always gift cards! Gift cards can seem somewhat impersonal and distant, but they can also be great and meaningful gifts. If you are unsure of what someone would like, this is a perfect way for them to find something intentionally they will truly love and enjoy that (hopefully) won't become added clutter. You can give a gift card to a store or restaurant you know they love, or maybe one that you have discovered during your sustainability journey.

A downside to gift cards is the fact that they are, for the most part, plastic. This is unfortunate. Most gift cards are made from polyvinyl chloride (PVC) which is not accepted by most curbside recycling programs. You can, of course, save them and then send them to a special recycling center to be recycled, but I would be surprised if many consumers actually did that. It is also likely the retail stores don't recycle them, either. I have seen Best Buy locations accept gift cards as part of their recycling program, so that's an option for you, perhaps. If a store offers cardboard or paper gift certificates, as many local businesses do, this would be a great alternative.

There are a few large stores, such as H&M that will offer cardboard gift cards as well. During the Christmas season prior to the start of my sustainability project, I received an H&M gift card from a friend. I knew I was just days away from the start of the project and, although at the time I didn't realize all that it would entail, I was a bit hesitant to use the gift card. I had heard bad things about H&M and definitely considered it to be a fast-fashion brand.

I was impressed, however, that instead of the usual plastic rectangle, the H&M gift card was made of pretty sturdy cardboard, while still being the same size and shape I was used to. And, on the back of the card, was the little recycling symbol. I immediately wondered why every retailer has not made the switch to this kind of gift card! As it turned out, the card held up just as well as a plastic one but could be properly disposed of with much less effort and environmental harm.

Although I am still unhappy with H&M for other reasons, I remain impressed with their gift card alternative, especially since it is something I haven't seen in many other places. I hope to see much more of this in the future.

There are people who will find this next idea unappealing, even unacceptable, but if you have friends who are dedicated to living a more sustainable life, you could consider going the secondhand route for gifts. There are actually some great items you can find secondhand. Not only will this approach likely save you money, but you (and your gift recipient) will have the satisfaction of knowing you didn't add anything new to the cycle. Once, my parents found a platter that a friend had painted several years earlier and later donated to the local thrift store. They purchased the platter and gifted it back to the same friend as a joke. I can't think of anything else that could have produced the same reaction and created such a unique memory!

Finally, if none of these ideas appeal to you, know that there really is no wrong choice. You can take someone out to dinner. Get them a tree for the yard or a plant for the house. Buy them a star. The gift ideas can extend as far as you are willing to take them, and in the case of a star that is several lightyears from here.

WRAPPING

I've always been awed by beautifully wrapped gifts under the tree at Christmas or at a birthday party. I'm more of a cover-it-in-wrapping-paper-and-stick-a-bow-on-top kind of person. Now, while I still appreciate the impact of a well-wrapped gift, I'm also much more aware of the impact all of that paper, plastic, and trim will have later.

Opting for recycled and recyclable wrapping paper is ideal. The American Forest & Paper Association reports that recyclable wrapping paper can be used at least seven times to make new and innovative paper-based products. There is a difference, however, between paper that is *recycled* and *recyclable*. If just 1% of people in the US used recycled paper to wrap one gift each year, over 2,000 trees and 900,000 gallons of water could be saved. True recycled paper is made from 100% post-consumer waste recycled materials and has been made by diverting paper scraps that otherwise would have ended up in a landfill. Thus, by using recycled paper, you are also eliminating the methane that would have been released if that wastepaper had ended up in the trash.[70]

Some gift wrap that has a glossy sheen has been coated in polyethylene, polypropylene, and laminates. This undermines the ability of the wrapping paper to be recycled and used again. The same goes for wrapping paper with foil and glitter. The mylar that is used (yes, mylar, remember the balloon nightmare I shared at the beginning of the book?) can't be separated out from the paper to allow it to be recycled. This type of gift wrap may be recycled, but is not recyclable.

It's worth mentioning that thin wrapping papers, even those without the sheen or sparkle, might also not be recyclable. Like tissue paper (which can't be recycled, either), it doesn't have enough fibers. The good news, however, is this paper can be tossed into a compost bin!

To test whether or not wrapping paper can be recycled, scrunch it into a wad. If it doesn't bounce back to the original shape, it most likely can be recycled! But, if you aren't sure, unfortunately, you're better off tossing the paper in the trash rather than potentially contaminating any other recyclable material.

The American Forest & Paper Association has said that "wishcycling—the hope that putting something in the recycling bin will actually get recycled—can actually hamper the recycling process, because non-recyclables (plastic bows) and contaminants (glitter) can prevent otherwise recyclable paper items from resurrection."[71]

If you want to wrap gifts sustainably, you can also use newsprint, old calendars or maps, and even brown paper bags. Paper tape is preferable to the plastic alternative. The same applies to ribbon and twine, too. As a general rule, keep your eyes open for paper that is recycled *and* recyclable, and even compostable, because why not?! You can also opt for soy-based inks and those that have been produced using water-soluble dyes — as always, the fewer chemicals that are used in the production process, the better. If the paper comes folded (sans cardboard roll) and wrapped in something other than plastic, you have hit the sustainable jackpot! Once your package is tied up with string, add a twig or sprig of some kind and you are good to go!

A sustainable option (that will probably outlive you) is purchasing a roll of butcher or kraft paper. In most cases, butcher paper can't be recycled (since it is coated in wax), but it can be composted if it is shredded or torn into small pieces first. Kraft paper, on the other hand, is recyclable, compostable, and can be purchased in recycled varieties. A 100-foot roll costs about $25, so buying a roll of paper to use for gift-giving is a choice that is sustainable for both your wallet and the planet. You can go totally biodegradable if you wrap your gift in kraft paper, tie it up with twine, and decorate with natural elements like greenery or a cinnamon stick!

And once your gift is wrapped, the options for decorating are virtually unlimited. I use markers to write a personal message or even just who the gift is for (in my fanciest cursive, of course, which is getting better all the time!). You can add ribbons or string, have an available toddler cover it in artwork, or turn to the thousands of ideas on the internet to help you wrap in style.

In keeping with the general rule, if you need to use a box, the one you have on hand is always better than the one you have to buy. If you have to buy one, once again opt for recycled *and* recyclable. Similarly, if you're looking for a gift bag, try reusing one you already have, from your last birthday, or any of the preceding birthdays. I grew up seeing the same gift bags and boxes under the tree each Christmas. Although the collection changed slightly over the years, seeing those bags year after year was like seeing the familiar faces of your favorite people around the holiday table, but in this case, under the tree.

If all the bags you have are dotted with snowflakes or princesses and you're going to a housewarming party in the summer, those probably aren't appropriate, and it is understandable that you'll need to get a new one. If you have to purchase a gift bag, look for one that has the potential to be used again and again for various occasions. That way, if it ends up in the back of your closet, or under someone else's bed, the chances are good that it will see another use (or possibly twenty) before it reaches the end of its life.

Another alternative to consider is using cloth to wrap gifts, which is a tradition in some cultures. The Japanese are known for furoshiki, a wrapping cloth. You can find a cloth for this purpose or use silk scarves, cloth napkins, or even handkerchiefs. There are lots of beautiful options out there and numerous videos that demonstrate different ways to wrap! And the best news is, these cloth wrappings can be used again and again.

Your wrapping choices may depend on the type and size of the gift. I don't think I would wrap jewelry in butcher paper but would prefer cloth wrap instead. I also wouldn't wrap a child's toy, such as a Barbie doll or Lego set, in cloth, but would definitely use kraft paper (decorated with whimsical doodles, of course). It's wonderful that the options for wrapping gifts today are as varied as the gifts we need to wrap.

PARTY DECOR

While not strictly *gift*-related, parties, and the decor they require, are a closely related category.

As with everything else, the best and most sustainable decor is what you already own. The next best option is to utilize things you find outside, such as flowers or fresh branches, which can add a lot. Consider using pumpkins for fall or Thanksgiving, holly boughs or fir swatches around the holidays, tie-dyed eggs or fresh flowers in the spring, and sand, shells, or just a freshly cut watermelon in the summer. Any natural elements that you find to decorate with are likely to reflect the season and the location where you live, a bonus rather than a negative. And by opting to use these things, rather than the "natural-looking" decor from somewhere halfway around the world, you will have made a sustainable choice. And give yourself bonus points if your natural decor from outside is also compostable.

Since natural decor doesn't go with every theme, another option for party decor is using decor that can be borrowed or rented. At the bottom of the list is, of course, buying something new that will be used and discarded.

Regardless of the choice you ultimately make for the decor for your event, using less as opposed to more is not only recommended design advice, but it's also the sustainable choice. You can also consider using food, lighting, music, and a variety of other factors to decorate, dress-up/dress-down, and set the desired mood for your event, none of which will have a negative impact on your wallet or the planet and might have a very positive effect on your party.

And speaking of parties, there are a few other considerations, beyond the decor, that can contribute to overall waste.

REACH FOR REAL

Whether you are serving a sit-down meal (tablecloth and all) or are planning to let your guests graze on fan-favorite finger foods, one of the best sustainable choices you can make when party planning is to opt for real. I don't mean real food (although choosing that over processed food is also a positive choice), I'm talking about everything else: real plates, napkins, cutlery, cups, etc., as opposed to the disposable alternatives.

I personally don't enjoy doing dishes or laundry, but if I have started the party with an empty dishwasher and washing machine, I'm generally good to go when the last guest leaves. If you don't have these modern conveniences, you can try to enlist the help of friends who offer to help clean up. You always have the choice to get the cleanup done immediately, or (if you're willing to hate yourself in the morning) just leave it stacked up to tackle the following day.

If you don't own enough of something you need (i.e. chairs) for the number of guests you are expecting, you can borrow or rent reusables for the occasion. If you plan to throw large parties regularly, it is probably worth considering investing in an average number of sets that will have you covered in the future, provided you also have the storage space.

If you are throwing a huge bash and really don't want to use real for a given event, or for any other reason you feel the need to go with disposable items, please look for ones made of recycled material that can be composted (or in some cases, recycled).

And, if you do go with disposables that can be recycled or composted, make sure to put the appropriate bins around for your guests to use to dispose of their leftovers (food and implements). Of course, these should also be clearly labeled, or you could end up with more work and mess than you've bargained for!

If you are a guest at a party, you may not want to use a fork you brought with you, but if you do, feel free. Whenever you find yourself in a situation where you need to use disposables, be mindful of your usage, try to compost and recycle if possible, and remember that this doesn't mean you don't care about the planet!

"Reach for real" goes for food, too. Fresh is almost always best especially when purchased locally, in-season, and with minimal packaging. It probably isn't realistic to try to make 100% of the food for every party you throw, and there's no need to try, especially if it takes your time and attention away from the party itself. But by selecting foods with minimal packaging, making what you can (or want to), and shopping locally when possible, you will help reduce the party's total footprint! The cake you bake at home may not be quite as fancy as the one you could purchase under a plastic dome, but it will be a masterpiece of your own creation.

DRESSING UP

During your lifetime, you'll attend a variety of events, and some will require a more particular standard of dress than others. What you wear every day to school pickup is different from what you'd wear to a spring wedding, and also different (I assume) from what you'd wear to a party with a 70's theme.

I'll say it again. The first and most sustainable option for finding things to wear to any event is, unsurprisingly, to shop your closet. It is unlikely you will always find just the right piece for every event, and that is okay. When you need a Dolly Parton look-alike outfit, you need a Dolly Parton look-alike outfit!

This is the perfect opportunity to flex the muscles we developed in Chapter 3 and utilize our burgeoning skills at thrifting (either online or in-person), renting, borrowing, or swapping. If you do find the perfect piece (or 5) at your local thrift store, you can always donate it back again when you're finished with it (assuming you don't plan to make it a regular part of your wardrobe). In this way you won't be spending much money, you'll be keeping your closet lean, and you won't be adding anything new into the cycle.

If you can't find just the thing you're looking for, however, you can extend your search to consignment shops, shopping online, or buying new. Although these aren't the ideal, sustainability-speaking, they might be the only solution for some pieces, events, and outfits! You can always look at companies and brands striving to decrease their environmental footprint to see if they have what you are looking for. Remember, if you do end up with a new piece in your cart or closet, that doesn't mean you aren't still a sustainable shopper!

HOSTESS GIFTS

This is where parties meet gifts, at least in one sense. Whether you are a strict believer in bringing hostess gifts to every event, or you avoid the practice altogether, the choice is up to you. For sustainable ideas, options, and choices, however, I refer you back to the "Gifts for Others" section.

My rule of thumb in this area is if I'm going to someone's home and I feel comfortable asking for water or putting my feet on the coffee table, a hostess gift is not necessary, unless they are throwing a full-blown party, of course. But if it's a party, or if I am going to visit someone for the first time, I try to bring a small gift. I prefer fresh flowers (although, I know there is a natural controversy here), a nice bottle of something, a candle, or a special food of some kind.

PARTY FAVORS

The sustainable option is pretty clear in this area; avoid party favors whenever possible. Avoid buying them and avoid bringing them home. It is common for guests to forget the party favors upon departure; whether intentionally or not, I will leave you to decide. Generally, favors won't be missed if they aren't provided, and rarely are they something people are thrilled to receive.

I can't begin to count the number of beer koozies, seed packets, and mini jam jars I have managed to avoid bringing home, as a professional organizer and as a mindful human being.

If you have young children and feel that party favors are a necessity, I encourage you to look for favors in alignment with the rest of this chapter (and the book as a whole). Or if, as an adult, you really don't want to send your guests away empty-handed, you can always send them laden with party leftovers.

LEFTOVERS

When you want to manage leftovers sustainably, but you don't want to put trackers on the bottom of each of your glass food storage containers, life can get tricky.

By this time, you have learned the optimal and sustainable way to store leftovers (beeswax and glass, anyone?). But when the leftovers aren't going straight to the fridge, we have to think a bit outside of the box, or plastic bag.

Reusable, or at least recyclable, is the way to go. You can keep a stash of glass jars (i.e. pasta sauce jars) or other containers on hand for this purpose. As an organizer, I don't love the idea of storing these things, but I do keep a very small collection of items for an occasion like this. You can also use this as an opportunity to phase out of the plastic containers you have or you may want to consider purchasing a few extras, even the plastic type (I won't tell!), so you can send leftovers home with friends.

If your guests are particularly responsible, you could send the food home in a loaned container, or if your guest brought a dish that is now empty, you can use that. Luckily, we are limited only by our imaginations (and the type and amount of food we are trying to send out the door).

There are compostable or recyclable to-go containers you can purchase to have on hand if that is easier for you or if you regularly share leftovers. I always feel better about using these options when I trust the recipient will actually take the necessary extra step to compost or recycle them, but ultimately that isn't something we can control.

We just need to do our best, and trust they will do their best, and, hopefully, together we can reduce our overall use of disposables (and maybe get all of our glass containers back).

As I was wrapping up November and my focus on gifts and parties, I was left feeling more excited than I had felt for several months. I'm pretty sure the feeling was at least partly attributable to the natural joy of the season, but upon reflection, the month had also been a surprising reminder that sustainability isn't all about research and major life overhauls. The fact is, we can make a difference and spread sustainability at the same time we are enjoy the some of the most joyful parts of life. Give the gift of sustainability, or if that isn't the right fit, then at least, give sustainably.

CHAPTER 12
DECEMBER: BOOT CAMP SUSTAINABILITY

At the end of her happiness project, Gretchen Rubin spent December in "boot camp perfect," resolving to do everything that she had worked on over the year to the best of her ability. So in true Gretchen Rubin fashion, I wanted to spend the last month of the year reflecting on all that I've learned and the progress I've made in my attempt to live out sustainability in all that I am and all that I do.

Boot camp sustainability for me looked like recycling everything possible, taking shorter showers, washing fewer, fuller loads of laundry, carrying a refillable cup, eating ugly foods, consuming fewer animal products, purchasing responsibly, doing research, gifting in line with my values, buying less, buying better, and striving to take sustainable actions whenever possible.

As my official sustainability project came to a close, I decided to take time to consider how I would continue to live out my sustainable values in the future, by continuing to take action and deepening my knowledge.

I learned so much over the course of my project. While I'm sad to remember the version of me that used makeup tested on animals, tossed tea bags in the trash, and frequented the local H&M, I am not that person anymore. I can no longer claim the innocence and ignorance that I hid behind before, and for that I am grateful.

I also reviewed those new habits that I've established. I'm proud to say that most of them have been fully integrated. I turn off the lights. I eat less meat. I drink non-dairy milk. I shop secondhand. I take shorter showers (at least, most of the time). I compost and recycle.

Some of the new habits didn't stick because I hated them too much, like the navy showers. But many of them stuck even though I didn't like them, such as using reusable makeup wipes. Some of them are continuing to evolve. I'm still looking for makeup and body products that are right for my skin and the planet.

I was happy to be reminded of just how far I have come; all the changes I have made, and the impact that I have had, even in small ways. My life isn't perfect, it's never going to be. But that's not the goal, and it doesn't have to be.

Looking ahead to the coming year, I know that most of my new habits, behaviors, and purchasing patterns will continue. Although I may not be as actively engaged in research and study, I know I will continue to learn and live out my values. Not just in the coming days, but for the rest of my life.

REFLECTION

In order to honor the catalyst for this crazy journey I've taken over the last year, I decided that in the month of December, I should reread the book, *How to Give Up Plastic*. I've shared through my blog that I often use the month of December to reflect on the best books I've read over the previous year. I also enjoy re-reading personal favorites from years past.

How to Give Up Plastic was one of several memorable books I'd read and I'm glad that I took the time to read it once more. It reminded me again just how much I've discovered through my own research this year.

As I went through the book again, I came across the passage that began the transformation in my life. "Ever since a YouTube video emerged of a straw being slowly, painfully extracted from a turtle's nose, plastic straws have been in the spotlight."

When I read that for the second time, I was surprised that the passage that jarred me the first time hardly registered at all during the recent reading. Maybe my year of research and writing had desensitized me to these horrors. Had I become hardhearted or heartless? Perhaps the other distressing depictions I'd seen this year had made this one pale in comparison. Or perhaps it was the opposite. I may have been pushed initially into my sustainability project because of the pain and suffering I'd seen (and I plan to continue until that kind of suffering is eradicated), but now I will also continue because of something more.

Reading about the suffering of animals caused by humankind transformed my life. It was my lightning bolt moment, the catalyst for change. From that moment I knew I would live and act differently. It has not been easy to change. There were many times I tossed a dirty recyclable in the trash and started to walk away, only to sigh, turn around, clean it, and put it where it belonged, the recycling bin.

Whether I did that because of a suffering turtle, or because I now viewed myself as someone who lives a sustainable life, who can say? The answer is probably some of both. I didn't know when I read that book how it would transform the next year, and ultimately my life, but it did.

One of the things I never expected to discover on this sustainability journey was a love and compassion for the creatures we share the planet with. Perhaps I should have seen it coming since the journey was launched just by reading a sentence about a turtle. My shock only grew as I heard many more horrible stories about bunnies, beagles, sharks, alpacas, and all of the animals we exploit for food.

These horrible things are out there for you to discover if you feel led to. I'm hopeful that as time goes by, the stories (and pictures) that are now seared into my memory will no longer be seen — because they are no longer happening.

Maybe you love animals, too. Maybe, like me, you've been inspired to new affection by some of the shocking statistics I've shared. Possibly, animals are still just animals to you. But no matter which category you fall into, sustainability is of the utmost importance, for us and for them.

I have learned that being sustainable and taking action in alignment with it takes a little more time, and often a lot more effort and intentionality. But in many ways, that is exactly the point. We, as human beings, fully embraced "throwaway living" as it was advertised and utilized all the conveniences that came with it. We need to reverse that shift. Unfortunately, making the switch back will not be easy. It never is, but no one can argue that it won't be worth it.

The worst mistake we can make is to assume that other people will make the changes necessary to save the planet. The second worst mistake is to know we need to do something but then do nothing. I have made both mistakes. And I have written this book to help you avoid both, if possible. If you're like me, and you're stuck in one or both of these positions, I hope I will be able to help you move forward to join me on the side of sustainability.

Sustainability isn't about going out and replacing all of the things you have with newer, more environmentally friendly, versions. Start by fully using what you already have. Sure, Igloo may have just come out with a biodegradable cooler, and that may be something that you look into purchasing when you need one, but for now, use the one you have in the garage. It's clunky, possibly ugly, and a little too big or too small, but it is what you have now. Utilizing it fully is the most sustainable choice you can make. There are some things that we use up more quickly, such as foundation and countertop spray. These are things we can assess and make switches or substitutions for in the short term. But sustainability isn't just a short-term game. It's a long-term lifestyle, if not an infinite one. It can be tempting to replace things with sustainable items because they are new and exciting, but that pull towards consumerism is what got us here in the first place.

Instead, make small personal changes as you can, when you can. Until then, make the most of what you have. And make sustainable choices that will support you all along your journey.

IDENTITY

Throughout this project, in order to be able to reimagine my identity as someone who is "sustainable" and makes sustainable choices, I had to let go of other aspects of my identity that I'd held for a long time.

One self-imposed label was that I am a person who is rough on shoes. It was just a fact. I don't buy shoes frequently, but before I am done with them, they generally look like they've been run over five (or 500) times. Instead of using the evidence to tell myself that I am a horrible person and will never be able to effect positive change on the environment, I chose to view this characteristic as more evidence of my growing sustainable superpower. I hold onto shoes and wear them as long as possible, and when I replace them, I look for options that I believe will serve me well and last a long time. In other words, I buy less and I buy better.

But I also let go of the idea that I am hard on my shoes. I don't tell myself (or other people) that anymore. Instead, I remind myself that I take care of my shoes like I take care of the planet. With this identity firmly in place, I am much less likely to stand on the back of my sneakers, even just to quickly grab something from my car. I am also more likely to wipe off the mud at the end of a rainy day (plenty of those here in the Pacific Northwest).

The hardest part of living sustainably is that I can no longer not live sustainably. I can't close my eyes to trash on beaches, close my ears to the sound of cows being led to slaughterhouses, or harden my heart against people facing abuse to make an $8 t-shirt.

To live sustainably in big and small ways sometimes requires us to let go of identities we have assumed in the past and take on new ones instead. In some cases, we have to let go of facts and stories we have told ourselves much of our lives, or we may have to reinterpret those facts and stories to support our new identities. We get to assume our identities as people who care about the planet and the people and creatures on it. More importantly, we get to assume our identity as people who take action. Let's go easy on the earth, and with ourselves, too, while we're at it.

Today, I will opt for simple and sustainable or clean and green over toxic and throwaway, any day. I know and believe that I am a sustainable person, living my sustainable values. And you can be, too.

MY CARBON OFFSETTING

Since I had now reached the end of the year, I knew it was time to calculate my total carbon footprint. I visited carbonfootprint.com which I had checked out back in April and re-calculated my numbers for the whole year.

With a calendar and some bills in hand (well, on the computer), I sat down for what I felt was the moment of truth. I looked at everything from airline flights to food to electricity to that train trip. There were a few numbers I had to estimate and some that I felt I was guessing at, but for the sake of honest assessment, I always tried to overestimate the guesses.

When I pressed "calculate," the result was a total of 6.34 metric tons of CO_2 emissions. Initially, the number meant little to me (although it felt like a huge number) without context. The average footprint for people in the US is 16.49 metric tons. The European Union average is about 6.4 metric tons. And the worldwide average carbon footprint is about 4.8 metric tons. The calculator also points out that the target to combat climate change is a worldwide average of 0 metric tons.

At that point, I was given the opportunity to pay for my offset by supporting various programs from increased energy efficiency to reducing deforestation, reforestation, and other community projects around the world. Some of the programs offered in developing countries have important additional benefits beyond reducing carbon emissions. These range from installing efficient household cookstoves to clean drinking water projects. The offsets ranged from $9.97 to $18.83 per ton. I was happy to pick the program most in alignment with my sustainability (and other) values and offset my emissions for the year.

The website also gave me the opportunity to pledge how much I wanted to reduce my carbon footprint in the coming year and made me write the steps I intended to take to do so. I appreciated the (electronic) certificate I received, both for my offsetting and pledge to continue to make sustainable choices in the coming years.

I was more than happy to pay for these offsets, and I was pleased overall with my results. What felt initially like a Buzzfeed quiz I used to take growing up, had a significantly more important impact. Although I was reminded that I still have a way to go to further reduce emissions and that there are lots of opportunities to increase my positive impact, I was also glad to see that I have already come a long way and the calculation of my total emissions was just one proof of that.

GET INVOLVED IN GOVERNMENT

Although my personal sustainability project was all about the changes I wanted to make in my life to reduce my environmental impact, I wanted to take some additional time at the end of my journey to consider how this impact could be expanded beyond my life (and this book, of course), through the realm of government.

As I acknowledged at the beginning of this book, to truly create systemic sustainable change, organizations, companies, and governments need to step up. But that doesn't mean our actions as individuals aren't important, too. When we are living out our personal values, we are in a better position to take our advocacy and desire for change to the next level, if we feel so inspired.

Don't stop living a more sustainable life out of the fear that it won't make a difference, or because you feel you'll *have* to become involved in promoting governmental change. Of course, if you want to, then, by all means, do that, too!

Businesses and governments listen to their clients and constituents, but the communication channel goes the other way, too. Clients buy what businesses produce and constituents obey the laws that are passed.

Clients and constituents can lead businesses to implement positive changes. For example, by expressing a desire for a reduction in plastic waste in my state, the government passed a plastic bag ban. Customers must now bring reusable bags from home or pay a surcharge for plastic bags.

If you want to become involved, begin by increasing your awareness about the important issues in your community. Then work to increase the awareness of your fellow consumers and government leaders. Ask for the changes that need to be made. Learn about referendums, proposed policy changes, bills, and laws. Call your elected officials. Attend peaceful protests. Post signs in your community.

Do whatever you feel called to do and that is within your rights. Stand up for yourself, your values, your community, and your world.

COMMUNITY CONNECTION

While the change we are striving to make will ideally impact the world as a whole, another way to expand our impact is to connect with like-minded people. Don't hesitate to connect with those in your community. You will be encouraged.

Start with family members and friends who share your sustainable values. Then reach out to your online "friends" to broaden your community and find others with the same interests. There are countless apps to help you meet up and connect with others in your local area who are interested in the same things. There will be events and activities in your community that will attract like-minded people. Attend those, if you can, and bring along members of the community you know would enjoy them, too. Then, use a hybrid of connecting with new friends online and in your local area to continue to grow your green network.

It is encouraging to be surrounded by people who also choose to opt for non-dairy milk for the same reason you do, who carry a metal straw in their purse or backpack, or who rush around the house turning off lights moments after someone leaves a room.

You can also host or participate in the clean-up of a local park, woodland, or beach. You could give a presentation or teach a class or workshop (in-person or online) and share what you've learned about sustainability, demonstrate how to make a sustainable DIY product (and maybe let your audience make their own), or share about how sustainability interacts with your area of expertise, be it gardening, cooking, shopping, or anything else! Just make sure to leave your audience encouraged and empowered to continue moving toward sustainability long after your presentation is over!

Spread the word about the local farmer's market and encourage local restaurants to cut back on plastic waste and/or commit to giving out disposables only when customers specifically request them.

Invite people into your sustainable routine. Share how you compost in your apartment, shop for clothes second-hand, or purchase necessities at a local zero-waste or low-waste store. The knowledge you've gained on your sustainability journey is sure to help someone along theirs, and it's always better to have someone along for the ride.

You may be surprised by the people who join your sustainability community. When I first shared about my project with my friends, they were extremely excited for me, some cautiously so. I know that if they had been derogatory or negative about it, it might have dampened my excitement, although I know I wouldn't have given up on the idea altogether.

If you are struggling to get friends or family involved in your plan for a new, more sustainable life, that's okay. I encourage you to take the action that you feel called to. It can take other people some time to get on board. Especially if this idea comes out of the blue for you (as it originally did for me), those closest to you will probably be surprised and may need time to adjust.

It is important, though, to make sure you aren't changing with the expectation that others will follow your lead. All you can do is be an example, and respect whatever choices, decisions, and actions those around you may take. If you start to feel frustrated with what others are doing, remind yourself of the reasons why you want to live a sustainable life and why you are choosing to take the actions that you are, because it is all a choice.

When you live in alignment with your values, people will notice. And your values probably don't include coercing others into making the same choices (although sometimes that might be nice).

Who knows who you might influence to join your sustainability crusade. You'll be surprised by the people who begin to follow in your footsteps, from the actions they take, the things they no longer buy, even down to the case they have on the cellphone in their hand.

It wasn't long into my journey when I noticed several friends had purchased Pela phone cases or discussed nontoxic makeup. Whether they were inspired by me or by something else, I was inspired and excited by the impact that I knew they were having on the planet. And even if people you know will never get involved, since they know sustainability is something that matters to you, they may send you articles, research, and information to support you on your journey; and that is worth being inspired by, too.

As you strive to live more sustainably, you'll become aware of people all around you who are, too, and maybe you'll inspire more people to join the movement. Remember, it can be as easy as one glass of milk, one gallon of gas, and one phone case at a time.

THE EXPANDED IMPACT

As my year dedicated to sustainability drew to a close, I got a few emails from brands I had purchased from that shared the positive impact they (and their customers) had on the planet over the course of the year. It was wonderful to see how far my dollars went to support the causes I care about. I didn't just spend money on a new thing or product, I supported and invested in this planet we call home.

One of these emails I received came from the workout clothes manufacturer, Girlfriend Collective. They informed me that their products had diverted 9,773,326 water bottles from landfills, prevented 8,670,564 pounds of CO2 from entering the atmosphere, saved 21,135,125 gallons of water, conserved 426,571 kWh of energy, and removed 7,813 pounds of fishing nets from the ocean. But the positive impact didn't end there. They also donated over $100,000 to support racial justice issues, over $40,000 to climate action causes ($37,000 of which went to One Tree Planted, the equivalent of planting 37,000 trees), and over $30,000 to support other causes in the community such as Feeding America, When We All Vote, and Baby2Baby. They also introduced a recycling program for their clothing, called ReGirlfriend, to reuse and recycle as much as possible.

Blueland sent an email to share that 1,468,983,000 (that's almost 1 and a half *billion*) bottles were diverted from oceans and landfills. They saved 5,525,418 feet of plastic packaging because most of their products come in tablet form. And 691,543 pounds of CO2 were saved since tablets were shipped to customers rather than full bottles of soaps and cleaners.

I also received an email from the power company letting me know about the impact of being enrolled in their Green Power program: 1,040 kWh purchased, and my carbon footprint reduced by 1,218 lbs. CO2e, equivalent to 1,856 miles not driven, or over 3 months of my regular mileage! The email also let me know about new solar installations and donations made and encouraged me (and others involved in the program) to continue to look at how we could involve green energy more and more in our daily lives.

Emails like these were a great reminder that by investing in companies that share my values, I am investing in my values. And that feels so much better than most purchases ever will.

Just a few months later, I got another email from the power company. My kWh of electricity purchased had already jumped to 1,721. My electricity carbon footprint had been reduced by 2,015 pounds of CO2e. And they let me know that was equivalent to enough renewable energy to power 156,455 smartphones.

They also told me that along with over 60,500 other people involved in the Green Power program, and those enrolled in other environmentally conscious programs, 594,470,387 kWhs had been purchased. This is enough renewable energy to power 57,073 homes, and enough carbon reduction to offset the energy needs of 8,194 homes for a year.

This reminder, and the reminder that together we can make a difference, was exactly what I needed to go forward, beyond my sustainability project, to continue to live out my values in the new year.

CONCLUSION

I write this as I sit on the patio on a surprisingly beautiful Pacific Northwest evening. The mountains are tinged with a subtle pink from the setting of a sun I can no longer see. The birds are still twittering, happily. I would've thought it was well past their bedtime. My feet lie in the grass at the edge of the patio. A cool breeze rustles the trees. A mosquito buzzes by my ear.

There is no better time to sit and reflect on this journey — this project. I have learned and grown so much. I'm sitting here, with nature all around me. My phone is at my side, in its biodegradable case of course, along with my laptop, which I intend to keep for the foreseeable future. I am in harmony with nature (except perhaps that mosquito).

We are at peace, the environment and me. As I want it to be. As it should be. In some ways, that's what this was all about. I want to do my part to ensure that there will always be plenty of birds chirping, trees swaying in the wind, and grass growing to bury my feet in. These things are, on some level, my responsibility, our responsibility.

At times during this project, I wondered how any of this could matter. Would using tablet-based soap and a compostable phone case really have an impact on the world around me and the environmental future of this planet? I believe it does.

This is not to say that we don't need to lobby big corporations and fight for change in the legislature. We absolutely should. But we can't do it with a Starbucks paper cup in our hands and bunny-tested mascara on our lashes.

Like all great change, it starts with us.

I'm reminded of Smokey the Bear, protector of the forests of my childhood. By the time I became an adult, posters bearing images of Smokey were largely out of fashion. But I remember him and the message he urged, "only you can prevent forest fires," something my five-year-old self took very seriously but remained unsure of how to carry out such a mission.

Now as an adult, I've heard and believe the warning cry: "Only you can save the world." So here I am. Can I do it alone? Of course not. That's the reason I wrote this book. I need you. We need each other.

Only you can save the world. That's all any of us have ever wanted anyway, isn't it? In childhood impressionability, we were shown cartoons of Spider-Man, Kim Possible, and the strange crime-fighting group that was Scooby-Doo. The characters in these shows went to great lengths to preserve life as we know it.

Each of us is now faced with the same mission. But in this version, the consequences are real. And we don't have webs, naked mole-rat sidekicks, or a Mystery Machine to help us out.

But we do have each other, and vast stores of information available to us on the internet. So, with the internet's help, we can discover and make the changes that need to be made and then, save the world.

There are so many things to learn and be and do. And I'm just starting to learn about them all. Some days, I am discouraged by all the research not being done, the research misinterpreted, and the research ignored. While the world itself is constantly changing, so is what we're learning about it and how we are treating it.

But that is what makes this such a beautiful journey. We all have something to learn from each other. There will always be someone who knows more, who has considered this from another angle, and who is "doing it better" than you are.

But that's okay. Be inspired, rather than challenged. Share what you've learned and how you've grown. This is a journey of mutual support; of progress, rather than success, all at once.

Just as we can't do sustainability perfectly, we can't expect that companies will either. But we can push each other to greater and greater heights, choosing progress over perfection.

If I'd decided that I was done the first time I was overwhelmed or the first time I realized that I couldn't do this perfectly, I wouldn't have written this book, and you certainly wouldn't be reading it.

I knew I couldn't do it perfectly, but I couldn't accept not doing it at all.

I wrote this book because I was totally overwhelmed. And I figure you might be, too. On the other hand, you may already be a vegan, a minimalist, a person who lives off the grid, or even someone who generates a single mason jar of waste each year.

This book is far from comprehensive. There are many topics, perspectives, and nuances that weren't presented. But although my project may be at an end, this is really just where our journey begins. Feel free to use this book as a jumping off point or to start somewhere else entirely. At some point along the way, you may you find yourself on the floor surrounded by 500-page books with no idea how to reconcile it all. Take my advice, push the stacks aside and you will find me there, too.

There are companies doing amazing things in the sustainability space. Unfortunately, I could not share about all of them, as much as I would have liked to. And the good news is that more and more companies are starting to fill the gaps. When you come across a brand or a company that shares your values, do your research, and then support them as you can!

But bear in mind that even the brands making the largest efforts on the sustainability front aren't perfect. Patagonia, a brand known for fair-trade practices, close monitoring of its supply chain, and work to ensure safe working environments for employees at every level, won't be perfect. We must continue to hold these brands to a very high standard as we appreciate the work they are doing. But, for now, perfection is unattainable, and if that is our only goal, we will never make progress.

COMMITMENT

As a coach, I often tell my clients that the only thing standing between them and reaching their goals is commitment. Commitment is what will get you through the things you are scared to try, the hard things, and the mistakes you'll make even when you try your best. Commitment will help you plan for when things don't go the way you wanted them to. When you forget your reusable grocery bags, go to a friend's house and they are serving meat, or when you find yourself climbing in the car with a bag from Forever 21, commitment will help you devise a plan for what you'll do in that moment and it will help you follow through.

Commitment is a muscle: open, willing, and dedicated to growth. It will grow stronger as time goes on, the more you use and intentionally practice it. And sustainability is much the same way. Similar to working out and strengthening your actual muscles, you'll never regret building the muscles of commitment or sustainability.

Remember to treat yourself with compassion, admit your mistakes, honor how far you've come, and keep going. Keep living your sustainable life.

ENOUGH

Our society focuses so heavily on consumerism; it's always more; more stuff, more activities, and more output. Thanks to minimalism and similar movements, the focus has begun to shift to the idea that less is more. It urges us to have less stuff, participate in fewer activities, and produce less, but more meaningful work.

I want to buy less and I want to have less, but I don't want to do less or have less of an impact.

Perhaps the right mindset is one that combines "less" and "more." Or, put another way, perhaps our focus should just be on buying, having, and doing "enough."

And that has turned out to be the focus for me for much of this sustainability journey.

Having enough to live on. Having enough to thrive. Having enough to help further the causes I care about. Having enough of letting the world bear the brunt of my unconscious and irresponsible choices. Taking enough action. Not wanting more, not settling for less. Letting enough be enough.

WHERE DO WE GO NOW

If you're like me, you're hurting for people and the planet, for creatures and cultures, and for animals and ecosystems. In order to keep making the important changes and taking the important actions, we must balance sustainability for the earth and sustainability for ourselves.

If we burn out in our environment-saving work, we may not have the energy, passion, or motivation to continue on.

That is why I haven't filled this book with a prescription for the planet or given you a step-by-step guide. You must find the things that will work for you, and I hope that this book has given you information, guidance, and support in figuring out what that is.

Analysis paralysis can hold us back from making the decisions we need to make. Trust me, I know that this book has a lot of information. But I also know that it only holds a fraction of the information that I came across as I was writing it. And I know that all of it is only a fraction of the information out there.

Many books either covered every nuance or left some important nuances completely unaddressed. Some discussed the issues in detail, without giving actual practical action steps. Still others discussed issues and solutions, but the solutions could only result from seismic cultural shifts, or a complete change of heart by companies, corporations, or governments across the world.

My goal with this book was to offer you a starting place. This is not a comprehensive compendium, but hopefully will give you just enough to get started. If you don't know where to begin, pick one thing. There is no right or best thing. You can start big or start small.

If you still don't know where to start, let your mind zoom out and think of the book as a whole. Then ask yourself what stood out to you most. Or ask yourself what you want to try first. Or consider what excites you. Take the answer your brain gives you, and then do it. Even if it's hard (because it probably will be). If the first step isn't hard for you, the fifth, twelfth, or hundredth, may be. And that's okay.

Start based on what matters the most to you. It always helps to prioritize the things that you care about, in your closet, and in the actions you take. If activism is most important, start there (Chapter 12). If animal welfare stands out to you, start there (Chapters 4 and 6). If you care desperately for the people who are undermined in the cycle of stuff today, start there (Chapters 3 and 7). If you just want to decrease your personal impact on the planet or increase your personal sustainability, start anywhere, but be sure to start.

If you still can't think of anything, close the book, open it to a random page, and without looking, put your finger down. Try that. And if your finger lands on an area or topic where you're already striving for sustainability, give yourself a gold star, and try the exercise again.

Let the space between where you are and where you want to be inspire you, rather than discourage you. Instead of seeing this book as a long list of things you need to do better or areas you need to improve, just decide to view it as things you can learn, try, and utilize.

The goal isn't to get to 0 emissions, reduce your waste to what can fit in a Mason jar, never travel again, or never so much as look at a Big Mac. Those things are only a piece of a much larger puzzle, and it may or may not be a piece in the puzzle you are trying to put together. If it is not, feel free to toss it out, you don't want it to get in the way of all the pieces that combine to make the picture you want.

Sustainability is not a competition, because that is not inherently sustainable. Instead, use it as a way to connect with others and the planet in a new and deeper way. And who knows, you may end up more connected to yourself, too.

If you are stuck in the weeds, or can't see the forest for the trees, zoom out, remind yourself of the big picture, and why sustainability is something that you choose to engage with in the first place. Because it is a choice. And it is something you want to do.

PERSONAL SUSTAINABILITY

Another point I want to offer for your consideration as you finish this book and go out to make sustainable changes is to consider how to make these changes sustainable for yourself. Chances are, you didn't read this book over the course of a year and you probably didn't implement most of these changes as you read through the book, although if you did, I would be very impressed. Now you're nearing the end, and the list of things you could and should do, may feel endless. Trust me, I know. I wrote this book because I felt that way, too. And I felt that way through most of it. But since I undertook my sustainability project over the course of a year, I had the time and space to implement changes, to think them over, and to purposefully decide what to integrate into my life.

As you endeavor to live more sustainably, recognize that it likely isn't sustainable to make all these changes at once. Changing products, composting, keeping track of your carbon output, shopping second hand, shortening your showers, cutting back (or cutting out) meat and dairy, unplugging your appliances, and all the other things I've mentioned in this book would overwhelm you if begun all at once. You'll have much better luck in the long run if you intentionally integrate the changes that will work best for you, and fit most seamlessly into your life, over time. Sustainability is far from easy and convenient (in fact, those are the two things we must battle against) but throwing yourself into a slew of sustainable systems is probably not sustainable in the long run. Do whatever works best for you: start a year-long project, try something new each week, go through the steps with friends or a book club, jump around, or just take the tips one at a time.

I hope that you've been inspired by some of the stories and statistics I've shared. Maybe you've already begun an overhaul of your life. I love seeing people passionate about sustainability. Just make sure you give yourself the time, space, and grace to maintain your energy and momentum.

When you're evaluating your new, more sustainable life, be open to changing in more ways than just the products you use.

Switch to a reusable to-go cup instead of the paper alternative, and also cut back on how often you use it. Stop buying single-serving prepackaged snacks; whether you find a different snack, package your own, or stop snacking altogether is up to you. Choose the reusable razor or stop shaving altogether. Creating sustainable habits is as important as purchasing sustainable products.

Making your own soap and makeup may be right for you, but it isn't right for me. But I will do the research to make sure that the items I purchase are good for my body and the planet. If you want to do something and you are willing to choose it again and again you will be acting sustainably, otherwise, you never will be.

Sustainability is important, but don't let the sheer amount of tips, steps, and tools dull your spark.

FUTURE FOCUS

The hardest part about striving to educate myself and live more sustainably has been my inability to live, learn, and consume in the same way as before. I can never go back. I can't use a paper towel or walk past an H&M without thinking of the cost (the financial cost being the least of my concerns). And sustainability extends beyond my day-to-day life. As I look to the future, I know that it will influence so much of what I do and become. I'm excited to walk this path with you; learning and supporting each other. Each of us taking action and, together, making a difference. .

And there is a lot to look forward to. Awareness and information about sustainability is increasing. Companies, organizations, and individuals are continuing to innovate new products and ideas, while simultaneously reducing waste and emissions.

It is beautiful to see that many of the things that have the potential to harm our environment are becoming less and less important. A BBMG survey in 2019 found that 9 out of 10 respondents felt that "having meaningful relationships with others" and "living a healthy, balanced life" are important factors contributing to a good life, whereas "owning a home" and "owning a car" were seen as less important. In a society that is known for consumerism, this is good to hear. Although the change may not be widespread or clearly visible, if sentiments like these are true and continue to be lived out, they will be.[72]

LOOKING BACK + LOOKING AHEAD

Toward the end of my sustainability project, I remembered a trip my family took to Florida many years ago. My family was in a rented minivan, fresh from the airport, and headed to a fun weekend at Disney World with one of my best friends. I distinctly remember staring out the window and saying, out of that strange conviction that an 8-year-old sometimes has, that one day I was going to tear up freeways and plant trees instead. There should be more trees, I reasoned, since trees were good and helped the earth. This thought was likely triggered by the surprising lack of trees in Florida in contrast to what I was used to seeing in the Pacific Northwest.

We kept driving on, and I don't remember any response to my comment. But a few minutes later my dad sighed and said, "Oh dear, it looks like it's going to take us twice as long to get there! Someone put trees in the middle of the freeway, and we'll have to go around." Already having forgotten my earlier comment, I wiggled in my booster seat to get a clear view of these trees, ready to unleash my 8-year-old fury on whoever would dare do such a thing, delaying my vacation. In that moment I was more concerned with mouse ears, roller coasters, and potential time delays than I was about trees, but the conversation stuck with me.

I hadn't thought about it in a long time, but as I was reminded of the moment, I realized how much it reflected on the things I'd learned throughout my sustainability project. When we realize there is something wrong in the world (freeways instead of trees), we want to quickly solve the problems (plant trees instead of freeways). But unfortunately, fast and easy solutions don't often benefit us in the long run (in this case it would kind of ruin much of the convenient transportation for people and items). We don't want to regress as a society (give up roads altogether), but we can utilize our knowledge and technology to further our goals (transport sustainable products and goods and make sure that trees get planted). And thankfully, we can also have fun along the way (like going to Disney World).

By the time you are reading this, some of the information that I've shared may have become obvious or obsolete. But that would be a very good thing! Research is continually being done, products are being developed, and environmentally beneficial inroads are being made. We have a long journey ahead of us, but no one of us has to do it alone. We must all keep learning, growing, and working together. I hope you will implement some of the tools and advice that I have shared in this book, but that ultimately, it will only be a starting point to spur you on to have greater and greater impact.

It can feel as though sustainability is out of our hands. It can be tempting to think that if companies or institutions or governments changed, then all of this would be easier and the impact would be greater. While this is certainly true in some ways, it is also a lie. Changes can't be made on those levels without changing us, too. If you have influence in any of those areas, use it. But even as a consumer and citizen, our actions and beliefs and values can make a difference. We are completely responsible for all of our actions, and the impact they have on the world, both for good and for evil. While they'll never be perfect, they can be sustainable.

Be imperfectly vegetarian or vegan or zero-waste. Live off the grid, or ditch dairy, or switch to public transportation. Whatever you choose to do, don't be afraid to be imperfect. But take action, because conscious and intentional changes will make a difference.

Go, and be imperfectly sustainable.

ACKNOWLEDGMENTS

Mrs. Pope, thank you for teaching me the power of a RASIT paragraph, rekindling my love of reading, and always encouraging me to write.

Heidi, Kaitlyn, Kathleen, and Mariah, thank you so much for your feedback, inspiration, and support throughout this journey. From the first page, to the last, you listened to me drone on about statistics, complain about the editing process, and reminded me why I wanted to write this book in the first place.

My dearest siblings, your eye rolls were noted, but so was every time you disposed of something in the proper receptacle — which, was most of the time.

Mom and Dad, I couldn't have done this, or anything else, without your support. Thank you for the example you've always been — that I can do whatever I want and put in the work it takes to get there, this book clearly being no exception. From my first stories on lined notebook paper to the monstrosity of a first draft this book turned out to be, you've encouraged me to write every step of the way. And that is why we are here. I love you more.

And finally, dear planet and each turtle, tree, and human on it, this was for you; you are worth it all.

Here's to taking action now to make a better, safer, and healthier future world for all of us.

BLURB AND BIO

THE SUSTAINABILITY PROJECT: MY JOURNEY FROM TOXIC AND THROWAWAY TO CLEAN AND GREEN.

The journey of a thousand miles begins with a single step… or, in this case, with a single Instagram post. After stumbling across an image depicting the horrific impact on an innocent sea turtle of humanity's dependence on plastic in a throwaway culture, Carly Tizzano sets out on a year-long journey to understand the true cost of modern living on the environment. In the process, she discovers that her lifestyle and personal choices impact far more than just sea life. Her investigation makes her even more determined to redefine her values, personal habits, and her overall relationship with the planet.

In this honest treatise of the power and pitfalls of her year-long pursuit of sustainable living, Carly details the latest research and statistics, and shares the tools, tactics, and methods she employed in her attempt to protect the environment and live out her personal values. Come along with her on this journey as she experiments with new products and re-discovers old ones, establishes new habits, redirects her mindset, and discovers that while sustainability may look different for each of us, it's a goal and a direction that all of us can move towards.

BIO

Carly Tizzano has always been passionate about helping those in need, beginning with volunteer opportunities at the age of six and a trip to Africa at the age of eleven to help build a school for orphans in Uganda. In middle school, she organized a friends' club to raise thousands of dollars to support local and international communities. These projects included digging a well in India, supporting an orphanage in Haiti, and building a school in Columbia. Her natural drive led her to finish high school at the age of sixteen. She went on to get her undergraduate degree at nineteen. In keeping with her desire to help others, she launched her first business as a professional organizer and became a certified life coach a few years later to help others reach their personal goals.

An unexpected encounter with a sea turtle caught in a painful predicament inspired her year-long journey to discover ways of being more intentional in her relationship with the earth. She decided to share her research and experience to encourage others in their efforts to protect this planet we call home. Carly lives in the beautiful Pacific Northwest with her cat, Shakespeare.

ENDNOTES

1. Lola Mendez, "Greenwashing Is Real—Here's How to Avoid It," Architectural Digest, May 7, 2020, https://www.architecturaldigest.com/story/greenwashing-and-sustainable-brands.

2. Jacqueline Poh, Laura Millian Lomrana, and Eric Roston, "Here's How to Tell Green Good Deeda From Greenwashing," Bloomberg Quicktake (website), updated July 9, 2021, https://www.bloomberg.com/news/articles/2020-06-29/here-s-how-to-tell-green-good-deeds-from-greenwashing-quicktake.

3. Emily Laurence, "How To Avoid Greenwashing To Ensure the Food You Buy Is Truly Good for the Environment," Well and Good (website), August 17, 2020, https://www.wellandgood.com/what-is-greenwashing/.

4. Emma Seymour, "What Is Greenwashing?" Good Housekeeping Institute, March 9, 2021, https://www.goodhousekeeping.com/home/a32191077/what-is-greenwashing/.

5. Michael Bloch, "Recycling plastics – what the numbers mean + cheat sheet," Green Living Tips (website), August 1, 2009, https://www.greenlivingtips.com/articles/recycling-by-the-numbers.html.

6. Recycling Association of Minnesota, "What Do Plastics Recycling Symbols Mean?" accessed June 27, 2022, https://recycleminnesota.org/wp-content/uploads/2014/08/What-Do-Plastic-Recycling-Symbols-Mean-Fact-Sheet.pdf.

7. Alex Truelove, "It's 'America Recycles Day.' Is the United States Set Up for Recycling Success?" U.S. PIRG, November 15, 2018, https://uspirg.org/news/usp/it%E2%80%99s-%E2%80%9Camerica-recycles-day%E2%80%9D-united-states-set-recycling-success.

8. "Recycle Right in Kitsap County," Kitsap County (website), accessed June 27, 2022, https://www.kitsapgov.com/pw/Pages/recycleright.aspx.

9. "Recycle Right in Kitsap County," Kitsap County (website), accessed June 27, 2022, https://www.kitsapgov.com/pw/Pages/recycleright.aspx.

10. "Recycle Right in Kitsap County," Kitsap County (website), accessed June 27, 2022, https://www.kitsapgov.com/pw/Pages/recycleright.aspx.

11. Beatriz Marin-Aguilera, "The (discarded) material culture of the pandemic," Ceatriz Marin-Aguilera (blog), September 7, 2020, https://www.beatrizmarinaguilera.com/the-discarded-material-culture-of-the-pandemic/.

12. Michaela Barnett, "The Lie Behind Plastic Pollution Is That We're Responsible," Gizmodo, June 29, 2020, https://earther.gizmodo.com/the-lie-behind-plastic-pollution-is-that-we-re-responsi-1844181198.

13. "Ultimate Roundup of Marine Pollution Facts: The Causes and Impact on both Marine and Human Life," Condor Ferries, accessed June 27, 2022, https://www.condorferries.co.uk/marine-ocean-pollution-statistics-facts#:~:text=BY%20POLLUTION%20STATISTICS-,How%20many%20marine%20animals%20die%20each%20year%20from%20pollution%20and,just%20the%20creatures%20we%20find.

14. Sarah Gibbens, "You eat thousands of bits of plastic every year," National Geographic, June 5, 2029, https://www.nationalgeographic.com/environment/2019/06/you-eat-thousands-of-bits-of-plastic-every-year/#close.

15. Beth Daley, "What a sustainable circular economy would look like," The Conversation, May 6, 2020, https://theconversation.com/what-a-sustainable-circular-economy-would-look-like-133808.

16. Christopher Snow, "A Dishwasher Uses Less Water Than Washing Dishes by Hand—Here's Why," Reviewed (website), August 27, 2021, https://www.reviewed.com/dishwashers/features/please-stop-hand-washing-your-dishes.

17. "5 Tips to Use Your Dishwasher in a More Eco-Friendly Way," American Appliance Repair Blog, accessed June 28, 2022, https://www.americanappliancerepair.com/5-tips-to-use-your-dishwasher-in-a-more-eco-friendly-way/.

18. Oscar Holland and Edward Scott-Clarke, "How laundry is spilling plastics into the ocean," CNN Style, updated June 8, 2020, https://www.cnn.com/style/article/laundry-plastics-microfibers-world-oceans-day/index.html.

19. Caroline Delbert, "For Longer-Lasting Clothes, Science Says Use This Wash Cycle," Popular Mechanics (website), June 16, 2020, https://www.popularmechanics.com/science/a32870876/longer-lasting-clothes-wash-cycle/.

20. Marisa Crous, "Fashion waste: this is how long it takes your clothes to decompose," News24, January 18, 2018, https://www.w24.co.za/Style/Fashion/Trends/fashion-waste-this-is-how-long-it-takes-your-clothes-to-decompose-20180118.

21. Jasmine Fox-Sullivan, "The Beginner's Guide to Cutting Your Closet's Carbon Footprint," Who What Wear (website), April 20, 2022, https://www.whowhatwear.com/how-to-build-a-sustainable-wardrobe/slide35.

22. "The Fashion Transparency Index 2021," Fashion Revolution (website), accessed June 27, 2022, https://www.fashionrevolution.org/about/transparency/.

23. Elizabeth Segran, "A complete guide to buying ethical clothes on a budget," Fast Company (website), September 4, 2018, https://www.fastcompany.com/90217759/a-complete-guide-to-buying-ethical-clothes-on-a-budget.

24. "Children's Place Retail Stores, Inc. ESG Ranking," CSR Hub (website), accessed June 27, 2022, https://www.csrhub.com/CSR_and_sustainability_information/Childrens-Place-Retail-Stores-Inc.

25. "About Girlfriend," Girlfriend Collective (website), accessed June 27, 2022, https://girlfriend.com/pages/about-girlfriend?ke=eyJrbF9lbWFpbCI6ICJjYXJse S50aXp6YW5vQGdtYWlsLmNvbSIsICJrbF9jb21wYW55X2lkIjogIk5uQ0dzUiJ9&utm_ campaign=Order%20Confirmation%20Email&utm_medium=email&utm_source=Klaviyo

26. "Tights—How to make them last (pantyhose, too!)" Care to Keep (website), accessed June 28, 2022, http://caretokeep.com/tights-how-to-make-them-last-pantyhose-too/.

27. Petra Alexandra, "Honest Review: Swedish Stockings v.s. Sheertex," Petra Alexandra (blog), January 20, 2020, https://petraalexandra.ca/2020/01/20/honest-review-swedish-stockings-v-s-sheertex/.

28. Elizabeth Segran, "Adidas and Allbirds join forces to design the world's most sustainable shoe," Fast Company, May 28, 2020, https://www.fastcompany.com/90510038/adidas-and-allbirds-join-forces-to-design-the-worlds-most-sustainable-shoe.

29. Blake Morgan, "11 Fashion Companies Leading The Way In Sustainability," Forbes, February 24, 2020, https://www.forbes.com/sites/blakemorgan/2020/02/24/11-fashion-companies-leading-the-way-in-sustainability/?sh=5232f2536dba.

30. Dora Chi Xu, "Does Everlane Live Up to Its Green Halo?" Ecocult (website), June 16, 2020, https://ecocult.com/is-everlane-ethical-sustainable-eco-friendly/.

31. Ula Chrobak, "How to buy carbon offsets that actually make a difference," Popular Science (website), December 3, 2020, https://www.popsci.com/story/environment/carbon-emissions-offsets-buy/.

32. Adele Peters, "This app measures your carbon footprint in real-time as you shop (or change your habits)," Fast Company, December 14, 2020, https://www.fastcompany.com/90585117/this-app-measures-your-carbon-footprint-in-real-time-as-you-shop-or-change-your-habits.

33. Anna Funk, "9 Well-Intentioned Efforts That Actually Aren't Environmentally Friendly," Discover, April 18, 2020, https://www.discovermagazine.com/environment/9-well-intentioned-efforts-that-actually-arent-environmentally-friendly.

34. Angelika Pokovba, "These 8 'Sustainable' Habits Aren't as Green as You Might Think—Here's How to Fix Them," Real Simple (website), April 22, 2020, https://www.realsimple.com/home-organizing/green-living/sustainability-mistakes.

35. "The Power of Slow Travel (How To Experience More When You Travel Slow)," Travlinmad (website), accessed June 28, 2022, https://www.travlinmad.com/blog/slow-traveling-what-it-is-how-to-do-it.

36. Scott Faber, "80 Years Later, Cosmetics Chemicals Still Unregulated," EWG (website), June 25, 2018, https://www.ewg.org/news-and-analysis/2018/06/80-years-later-cosmetics-chemicals-still-unregulated.

37. Toni-Marie Ippolito, "The Dirty Dozen—Top 12 Ingredients to Avoid in Cosmetics," Viva Magazine Online, January 23, 2020, http://vivamagonline.com/the-dirty-dozen-top-12-ingredients-to-avoid-in-cosmetics/.

38. David Andrews and Carla Burns, "Is Teflon in Your Cosmetics?" EWG's Skin Deep (website), March 14, 2018, https://www.ewg.org/skindeep/contents/is-teflon-in-your-cosmetics/.

39. Katie McPherson, "Why Are Clean Beauty Products More Expensive?" HuffPost, updated January 8, 2021, https://www.huffpost.com/entry/why-clean-beauty-is-more-expensive_l_5fdb7307 c5b6f24ae35e39d8.

40. "Companies That Do Test on Animals," Beauty without Bunnies database, PETA, accessed June 29, 2022, https://crueltyfree.peta.org/companies-do-test/.

41. "9 Vegan Makeup Brushes for a Flawlessly Fur Free Face," Sustainable Jungle (website), accessed June 28, 2022, https://www.sustainablejungle.com/sustainable-beauty/vegan-makeup-brushes/.

42. Fermin Koop, "What's the most sustainable toothbrush? Study finds a surprising answer," ZME Science (website), September 17, 2020, https://www.zmescience.com/science/whats-the-most-sustainable-toothbrush-study-finds-a-surprising-answer/.

43. Chong-Jing Gao and Kurunthachalam Kannan, "Phthalates, bisphenols, parabens, and triclocarban in feminine hygiene products from the United States and their implications for human exposure," Environmental International, no. 136 (March 2020): 105465, https://doi.org/10.1016/j.envint.2020.105465.

44. Kim Heacox, "The Amazon rainforest is losing about 10,000 acres a day. Soon it will be too late," The Guardian, October 7, 2021, https://www.theguardian.com/commentisfree/2021/oct/07/the-amazon-rainforest-is-losing-200000-acres-a-day-soon-it-will-be-too-late.

45. Hannah Ritchie, "How much of the world's land would we need in order to feed the global population with the average diet of a given country?" Our World in Data (website), October 3, 2017, https://ourworldindata.org/agricultural-land-by-global-diets#:~:text=Livestock%20takes%20up%20nearly%2080,as%20shown%20in%20the%20visualization.

46. "Environment," Pew Commission on Industrial Farm Animal Production (website), accessed June 28, 2022, https://www.pcifapia. org/issues/environment/#:~:text=The%20United%20States %20 Department%20of,times%20greater%20than%20the%20amount.

47. Betty Hallock, "To make a burger, first you need 660 gallons of water . . ." Los Angeles Times, January 27, 2014, https://www.latimes.com/ food/dailydish/la-dd-gallons-of-water-to-make-a-burger-20140124-story.html.

48. Ezra Klein, "Cows R Us," The American Prospect, January 29, 2007, https://prospect.org/article/cows-r-us/.

49. Sarah Gibbens, "These 5 food show how coronavirus has disrupted supply chains," National Geographic, May 19, 2020, https://www. nationalgeographic.com/science/2020/05/covid-19-disrupts-complex-food-chains-beef-milk-eggs-produce/?cmpid=org=ngp::mc=crm-em ail::src=ngp::cmp=editorial::add=Science_20200520&rid=8D454-6A2D7B90FDE1E1A7E3ABFA2ECA8.

50. "Changes in the Size and Location of U.S. Dairy Farms," Economic Research Service/USDA, infographic, accessed June 28, 2022, https:// www.ers.usda.gov/webdocs/publications/45868 /17034_err47b_1_. pdf.

51. M. Shahbandeh, "Per capita consumption of beef in the U.S. 2000–2031," Statista.com, March 2, 2022, https://www.statista.com/ statistics/183539/per-capita-consumption-of-beef-in-the-us.

52. Laura Reiley, "If you want to save a cow, eat an Impossible Burger. Or stop eating cheese." The Washington Post, February 26, 2022, https:// www.washingtonpost.com/business /2020/02/26/cows-impossible-burger-meat-dairy.

53. Eliza Erskine, "Report Finds 13 Dairy Companies Produce More Emissions than the Entire State of Florida!" OneGreenPlanet.org, posted 2020, accessed June 29, 2022, https://www.onegreenplanet. org/environment/report-finds-13-dairy-companies-produce-more-emissions-than-the-entire-state-of-florida/.

54. "Campus Recycling," UCSF Office of Sustainability, accessed June 29, 2022, https://sustainability.ucsf.edu/Learn_to_Sort_Your_Waste/compost.

55. Marshall Shepherd, "Tips To Start Composting From A Climate Scientist's Personal Journey," Forbes, July 5, 2020, https://www.forbes.com/sites/marshallshepherd/2020/07/05/some-tips-to-start-composting-from-a-climate-scientists-personal-journey/?sh=df8f0e3c26e0.

56. Alex Truelove, "It's 'America Recycles Day.' Is the United States Set Up for Recycling Success?" U.S. PIRG, November 15, 2018, https://uspirg.org/news/usp/it%E2%80%99s-%E2%80%9Camerica-recycles-day%E2%80%9D-united-states-set-recycling-success.

57. Emma Seymour and Birnur Aral, "How to Spot and Use Eco-Friendly Packaging," Good Housekeeping, April 7, 2021, https://www.goodhousekeeping.com/home/a32222804/eco-friendly-packaging-alternatives/.

58. Andy Murdock, "The environmental cost of free 2-day shipping," Vox, November 17, 2017, https://www.vox.com/2017/11/17/16670080/environmental-cost-free-two-day-shipping.

59. Parija Kavilanz, "Online shopping can be worse for the environment than driving to a store," CNN Business, July 7, 2020, https://www.cnn.com/2020/02/26/tech/greenhouse-gas-emissions-retail/index.html.

60. Kyle Mandel, "Online vs. In-Store Shopping: The Eco-Friendly Choice Isn't Always Obvious," Huffington Post, February 26, 2020, https://www.huffpost.com/entry/online-in-store-shopping-eco-friendly-choice_n_5e558762c5b62e9dc7d8ec3f.

61. University of Exeter, "Buying Local Isn't Always Better For the Environment," ScienceDaily, February 5, 2009, https://www.sciencedaily.com/releases/2009/02/090202113553.htm.

62. Dimitri Weideli, "Environmental Analysis of US Online Shopping," (master's thesis executive summary, MIT Center for Transportation and Logistics), https://ctl.mit.edu/sites/ctl.mit.edu/files/ library/ public/Dimitri-Weideli-Environmental-Analysis-of-US-Online-Shopping_0.pdf.

63. Angelika Pokovba, "These 8 'Sustainable' Habits Aren't as Green as You Might Think—Here's How to Fix Them," Real Simple (website), April 22, 2020, https://www.realsimple.com/home-organizing/green-living/sustainability-mistakes.

64. Anna Funk, "9 Well-Intentioned Efforts That Actually Aren't Environmentally Friendly," Discover Magazine, April 18, 2020, https://www.discovermagazine.com/environment/9-well-intentioned-efforts-that-actually-arent-environmentally-friendly.

65. Sara Spary, "How Much Is Your Cup of Tea Costing The Environment?" Huffington Post, October 17, 2018, https://www.huffingtonpost.co.uk/entry/how-much-is-your-cup-of-tea-costing-the-environment_uk_5bbb343de4b01470d0531089?guccounter=1.

66. Ryan Deer, "The Facts: Office Workers & Their Waste Generation," Roadrunner (website), April 28, 2021, https://www.roadrunnerwm.com/blog/office-worker-waste-generation.

67. "How Recycling Saves Energy," Harmony (website), accessed June 29, 2022, https://harmony1.com/recycling-saves-energy/.

68. "How to Recycle Ink Cartridges," Earth911 (website), accessed June 29, 2022, https://earth911.com/recycling-guide/how-to-recycle-ink-cartridges/.

69. Elizabeth Mott, "Proper Procedure to Dispose of a Laser Printer Cartridge," Chron (website), accessed June 29, 2022, https://smallbusiness.chron.com/proper-procedure-dispose-laser-printer-cartridge-59963.html.

70. Yelena Moroz Alpert, "11 Eco-Friendly Gift Wrapping Options You Can Feel Good About," Real Simple (website), November 30, 2020, https://www.realsimple.com/holidays-entertaining/gifts/eco-friendly-wrapping-paper.

71. Yelena Moroz Alpert, "11 Eco-Friendly Gift Wrapping Options You Can Feel Good About," Real Simple (website), November 30, 2020, https://www.realsimple.com/holidays-entertaining/gifts/eco-friendly-wrapping-paper.

72. Giselle Defares, "4 ridiculously easy ways you can be more eco-friendly," The Next Web, August 11, 2020, https://thenextweb.com/world/2020/08/11/4-ridiculously-easy-ways-you-can-be-more-eco-friendly/.

www.ingramcontent.com/pod-product-compliance
Lightning Source LLC
Chambersburg PA
CBHW052122270326
41930CB00012B/2716